The Inventor's Guide to Trademarks and Patents

The Inventor's Guide to Trademarks and Patents

Craig Fellenstein

with Jaclyn Vassallo and Rachel Ralston

Upper Saddle River, NJ • New York • San Francisco
Toronto • London • Munich • Paris • Madrid
Capetown • Sydney • Tokyo • Singapore • Mexico City
www.phptr.com

The publisher offers excellent discounts on this book when ordered in quantity for bulk purchases or special sales, which may include electronic versions and/or custom covers and content particular to your business, training goals, marketing focus, and branding interests. For more information, please contact:

U. S. Corporate and Government Sales
(800) 382-3419
corpsales@pearsontechgroup.com

For sales outside the U. S., please contact:

International Sales
international@pearsoned.com

Library of Congress Catalog: 2004117189

Pearson Education, Inc.
Rights and Contracts Department
One Lake Street
Upper Saddle River, NJ 07458

ISBN 0131869124
Text printed in the United States on recycled paper at *R.R. Donnelley& Sons in Crawfordsville.*
First printing, December 2004

Pearson Education LTD.
Pearson Education Australia PTY, Limited.
Pearson Education Singapore, Pte. Ltd.
Pearson Education North Asia, Ltd.
Pearson Education Canada, Ltd.
Pearson Educatión de Mexico, S.A. de C.V.
Pearson Education—Japan
Pearson Education Malaysia, Pte. Ltd.

Dedication

I would like to thank my family, who is definitely more important to me than competing with Thomas Edison's 1000 (plus) inventions. It was my family who put up with my many late-night hours, allowing me to develop and deliver this book. These are my loved ones who look at me when I get bright, new ideas, shake their heads, and say "that might make a good invention."

One of my children discovered inventive ideas of bacon that cooks itself, and blenders that can cook while they blend—which frankly, causes me to wonder why I spend my time trying to figure out (and invent) how to best schedule a grid-computing job, with an attractive return on investment, and a prioritized network circuit. But, now that I think about this, I wonder: could these grids be utilized to manage the kitchen blenders (and other appliances) with recipe parameters about what they are cooking—and, do this as they are blending and preparing other foods? Would this, could this, should this be a "smart home" invention?

Craig Fellenstein

Acknowledgments

This book has been a real challenge to produce, yet an incredible joy to deliver. Three co-authors worked together on this text, to produce this unique book—a book that is intended to teach almost anyone how to think like an inventor. We have even attempted to "give away" valid new inventions, as we lead you through simple inventing exercises. Our hope is that you will utilize this book as a "guide book," while continuing to develop your own invention ideas. We hope that you will see these inventions, yet unclaimed, and file them as patents.

Jaclyn Vassallo and Rachel Ralston are two very bright young people, who worked in collaboration to deliver, as my co-authors, this book. Both of these young people were also recent participants of an innovative U.S. educational program, entitled "Information Technology Leadership Academy (ITLA)," which among several things, teaches young people how to develop businesses through the utilization of IT. The ITLA does this all, while at the same time teaches high school-age students how to think as business leaders and inventors. I commend Jaclyn and Rachel on a job well done, both as co-inventors and co-authors on this book.

I, along with my co-authors, would like to take this opportunity to collectively thank several working colleagues for their support, professional guidance, advice and counsel in bringing together some of the complex topics addressed in this book. We would like to thank Albert Schneider, CIO of the IBM T.J. Watson Research Center, for a very special support role he has served to more than 200 young inventors in the public high school system. Ed Kelley and Rick Hamilton, both Master Inventors for the IBM Corporation, we thank you for providing us with valuable insights in several topic areas. Michael Mino, the Founder of the ITLA, we thank you for your leadership and expertise in inspiring so many young people in the areas of business leadership, information technology, and inventions.

Thanks to attorney David Mims, whom for years has provided professional support and encouragement as we continue to serve as inventors in our professional careers. We would like to thank the reviewers of this book, Ashley Gillespie, Michael Mino, Edward Kelley, and Rick Hamilton, for their expert attention to details and content, as this book was being prepared.

We would like to especially thank Joshy Joseph, a co-author on *Grid Computing*,[1] a book released earlier in 2004. Mr. Joseph helps in many invention areas related to our professional responsibilities, and he is also an Assistant Editor-in-Chief for the IBM On Demand Business, Industry Book Series. Ashley Gillespie is another student of the ITLA, and she spent many long hours reading this content, helping us to deliver the content. Thank you, Ashley, for all of your hard work on this book.

A very special thank you is due to my Pearson Acquisitions Editor, Jeffrey Pepper and Senior Project Editor, Kristy Hart—a great team to work with on a book development effort. This team provided excellent support and endless patience in the many activities encountered throughout the entire development and production of this book. Without all these individuals, this book would not have been produced in its timeframe, depth, breadth, and quality. We would also like to extend a special thank you to Jim Keogh for his outstanding developmental editorial skills.

Finally, we would like to thank all the creative men and women who have contributed to the disciplines of invention development all around the world. It was all these brilliant minds that made this book so rewarding and enjoyable to produce.

Craig Fellenstein
Jaclyn Vassallo
Rachel Ralston

[1] For information on *Grid Computing*, please reference http://www.amazon.com/exec/obidos/tg/detail/0131456601/ qid=1088124390/sr=1-1/ref=sr_1_1/002-7981399-5750431?glance&s=books.

Table of Contents

About the Author

Craig Fellenstein is an IBM Services Senior Executive Consultant. He holds 68 patents pending in the U.S. Patents Office, and 13 inventions publications in *Journals for IBM*. Fellenstein currently serves as IBM Global Services Integrated Technology Services Chief Architect and Senior Executive Consultant, working with leading IBM customers worldwide in the IBM Center of Excellence for On Demand Business.

Foreword

The Inventor's Guide to Trademarks and Patents is a particularly timely, unique, and valuable book. It is certainly not a book that should be read just one time and then placed on a shelf. Instead, it should be kept close at hand as a trusted resource and guidebook. It is an easy-to-follow reference for the application of creative problem solving that leads to innovation and invention—the two signposts of the 21st century. Whether you are an individual employee, an owner of a small business, or an executive managing a large global enterprise, *The Inventor's Guide to Trademarks and Patents* will become an essential resource for some time to come.

The development of critical and creative thinking is extremely important in order to continue to introduce, develop, and manage global innovations effecting economic growth across all regions of the world. If research and development, technology transfer, and commercialization are the pillars supporting innovation, then critical and creative thinking provide the foundation upon which those pillars rest. We live and work in an age where intellect has become property, where ideas have become raw material, and where knowledge has become the critical asset in any "knowledge economy" enterprise. This book addresses these important themes in very creative and thought-provoking ways.

In September of 2004, the lead author, Craig Fellenstein received a special congressional award from the U.S. Congress for his outstanding achievements as a volunteer educator and the "Inventor Mentor" for the Information Technology Leadership Academy (ITLA), a unique inquiry-based high school program in Connecticut. Throughout his career, Fellenstein has been a prolific inventor and a very effective teacher of the same to many others outside of industry, as demonstrated in his community services volunteer work as a business development leader and master inventor. He has not only demonstrated this unique ability in the United States, but also throughout India, Vietnam, Korea, Japan, New Zealand, Argentina, Brazil, and other countries as well. As a result, this book targets a global audience, without preference to any global location, government, or economic development situation. In simple terms, this is a book about critical thinking—*how* to think like an inventor.

Fellenstein has worked with hundreds of young adult leaders and senior business leaders for several years in the areas of inventions and new business development. He delivers this book with Ms. Vassallo and Ms. Ralston, young adult leaders who have recently completed the innovative workforce skills development program delivered through ITLA. Fellenstein is the honorary co-founder of the ITLA and has worked with business leaders, teachers, and students in the pursuit of developing and strengthening the critical and creative thinking necessary for innovation and global economic and workforce competitiveness.

This book describes a unique "invention development" practice utilized by Fellenstein in many high schools in the state of Connecticut. Using his trademark innovative style, Fellenstein provides the reader with information and techniques that he has used to covey ideas around new business development, innovation, and invention to audiences throughout Connecticut. Information in this book will allow the reader to harvest his own critical skills and to position and strengthen his own business and career development needs in the context of a knowledge-based economy.

Fellenstein reinforces the importance of establishing knowledge-based, workforce competitiveness skills and does so in an interesting and power-packed manner. Developing these skills is not always a simple task. The authors guide the reader through a cognitive journey, developing and cross-training critical skills in many areas of intellectual property management and innovation. This is a great book for all ages and for individuals across all career levels: from line employees of worldwide companies to managers and senior executives of both small and large enterprises around the world. It is very readable and well suited for the casual reader, the expert inventor, or those simply interested in how inventors think. Fellenstein, et al. prove that you too can refine your own creative-thinking skills and add your own inventions to those listed in patent offices around the globe.

This is an essential book for anyone interested in understanding and developing the critical and creative-thinking skills that are key to competing in today's knowledge-based economy. In today's highly productive and competitive global economy, none of us can afford to become complacent in our careers. Today, innovation and invention have to be nurtured and advanced with increasing frequency just to stay competitive. This book addresses this critical need in a variety of ways, while addressing the increasing commerce in intellectual property and critical-skills management, which together, comprise the new operating paradigm for competitiveness in the global marketplace.

There are many practical lessons from the authors presented in this book, many of which can change the way you view and think about problems in everyday life—indeed, how you view the very future.

Rob Keating
Director
Workforce and Knowledge Economy Programs
Governor's Office for Workforce Competitiveness
Hartford, Connecticut USA

Preface

The *Inventor's Guide to Trademarks and Patents* is a unique book that provides readers with insights to creating trademarks and inventions. As the book opens, it guides you through some interesting inventions of the past. This book explains in simple, yet detailed terms what defines intellectual property. This book, like no other on the market, then begins to unveil an invention that the reader may discover and wish to pursue. In fact, this book attempts to give away one or more inventions. This book then explains in simple terms how to file your new inventions.

The co-authors have delivered an unprecedented book that explains how and what to consider related to intellectual property development and protection practices. The reason this book is so unique is that it not only explains how to create trademarks and inventions, but it suggests and gives away one or more inventions. This book then closes with instructions on exactly how to file these inventions and discussions of authoritative sources of reference.

What Is the Importance of This Book?

The co-authors have developed this book as a document of interest and advanced learning for a global reading audience. No book in the global market today teaches you how to create an invention, leads your thinking into a new invention, and then explains exactly how to file it. Furthermore, if the idea is not an invention, then it is no doubt some other form of intellectual property, which is also explained in this book.

PROPER LEGAL ADVICE IS IMPORTANT

All legal advice must be tailored to the specific circumstances of each individual case. It is important to understand that none of the information provided in this book should ever be utilized as a substitute for advice of competent legal counsel.

This book presents simple exercises in both print and thought that are intended to expand thinking around intellectual property. Aspects of intellectual property are explained in easy-to-understand terms, yet in-depth enough to provide a full basis of understanding. Patents, trademarks, service marks, trade secrets, and copyrights are all simply explained, and most important, this books explains how to identify them and properly use them for protection purposes.

The information provided in this book is helpful to readers familiarizing themselves with intellectual property issues that may affect them. What is a trademark versus a service mark? How do I file a copyright? That said, as all legal advice must be tailored to the specific circumstances of each individual case, it is important to understand that nothing provided herein should be used as a substitute for advice of competent legal counsel.

In addition, it is important to understand that intellectual property law varies considerably from jurisdiction to jurisdiction (and even between states in the U.S.). Therefore, some information described in these pages may not be applicable to your jurisdiction. You also should be aware that we (the co-authors) could not promise that everything in this book is complete or up to date, due to the dynamic nature of the content.

All these matters are important to understand as you read this book.

What You Can Expect From This Book

We want to set the stage for what you will find interesting while reading this book. Expect to find a thought-provoking experience throughout the middle chapters of this book. Do not expect that you need to be a Ph.D. or be a college graduate to understand and practice the principals discussed in this book: That would be a mistake. The *Inventor's Guide to Trademarks and Patents* is written in easy-to-understand language and allows for readers of all ages to be able to learn from the information provided.

In this book, readers are introduced to basic invention principles and several important discussions surrounding intellectual property. Readers will find these discussions interesting, with a passive-progressive evolution of cognitive thinking. Expect to learn specific expertise and skill development in the areas of creating patents and trademarks. One most interesting concept will teach the readers how to create their own invention "spawning" teams. This is a very effective approach to problem solving.

These discussions are delivered in a concise, hard-hitting, and to-the-point fashion. Using this delivery approach, we believe this will help readers more clearly understand the basic principles of patents, trademarks, trade secrets, and copyrights, plus, their respective implementation, utilization, and filing models.

Readers of this book should expect to explore the following:

- **The basic concepts of inventing:** Explaining how the inventor thinks. This book walks you into an example of inventing and discovering other inventions that may relate to the solution thinking prescribed in this book.

- **How the patent evaluator thinks:** The inventor and evaluator protocol is described. Workshop examples are established for practicing this interchange. The end result is strengthening the invention and developing critical skills.

- **The influence of intellectual property:** Exploring the cultural aspects of intellectual property, incentives to create these types of assets, aspects of harvesting intellectual property, and commercialization of these kinds of assets.

- **The new world commerce and intellectual property:** Special treatment is provided to other countries and their respective involvement in the fields of intellectual property.

- **The most prominent positioning of intellectual property as assets with an associated value:** Approaches to asset commercialization, incentives, and building invention teams all contribute to developing large numbers of patents and other types of intellectual property. Managing innovation to a common end point is the focus in the teaming discussions of this book.

How This Book Is Organized

The Inventor's Guide to Trademarks and Patents contains nine chapters, which are organized into interesting discussions across several different dimensions of intellectual property management:

Chapter 1, "Patents, Copyrights, and Trademarks—A Look Back," provides an interesting history of innovative inventions, copyrights, and trademarks. In addition, this chapter discusses early inventions, showing examples of how inventors thought during these periods. This chapter closes with informative discussions.

Chapter 2, "Formulating the Idea," provides a unique approach to thinking about a new idea. This chapter accounts for the fact that a problem will have a novel solution. Essentially, this chapter guides you through cognitive processes involved in formulating new ideas, based upon problems trying to be solved. This chapter introduces a patent uniqueness and novelty test, which is paramount in any patent. Discussions related to management of innovation are discussed in the closing pages of this chapter.

Chapter 3, "Search Strategies, Techniques, and Search Tools to Validate the Uniqueness of any Invention," provides simple exercises that will develop critical skills related to searching and researching various topics on the Internet. Discussions of "prior art" are introduced and how to determine if anyone has ever thought about a new idea you might have in mind.

Chapter 4, "Invention Teams," provides fabulous insights on how to establish and engage productive invention teams out of small numbers of individuals. This is a great chapter for understanding key aspects of teaming, as it reaches back to the days of Thomas Edison and his invention teams. This chapter explores the dynamics of certain members on these types of teams, the roles and responsibilities of members, and important elements of invention mentoring.

Chapter 5, "Invention Evaluation Teams," provides a robust view of critical skills involved in evaluating the strengths of invention ideas and other intellectual property assets. The underlying premise in this chapter surrounds the ability to understand values in solution ideas and other forms of intellectual property.

Chapter 6, "Defining a Patent: The Problem, Solution, and Novelty," introduces you to the act of creating a patent. This chapter explores what's involved in defining appropriate problems with solutions that are novel for inventions, while also addressing key aspects of other types of intellectual property. Critical skills for harvesting these types of assets are explored.

Chapter 7, "Mining Intellecutal Property Assets," builds on the previous chapter and addresses key aspects of filing multiple ideas as bulk submissions.

Chapter 8, "Intellectual Property," provides insights to definitive discussions on the various types of intellectual property.

Chapter 9, "Property Protection: Copyrights, Trademarks, Trade Secrets, Patents, and Publishing Intellectual Property," provides an in-depth view on how to file various types of intellectual property. This chapter also identifies authoritative sources to assist in the formalization process of intellectual property.

Appendix 1, "Case Study Patents for Further Research," contains listing of the example patents used in the prior arts study in this book. This clearly shows how claims are written in patents, and more.

Appendix 2, "Trade Secrets," explains additional details surrounding the topic of trade secrets.

Appendix 3, "Inventor Resources," provides an extremely valuable list of resources that any inventor can utilize while engaged in the invention process.

CHAPTER 1

Patents, Copyrights, and Trademarks—A Look Back

Patents, trademarks, and copyrights have an extensive history dating as far back as 5,000 years ago when the Neolithic man marked cave walls to show that he owned the cave. These marks are the predecessor to today's trademarks. Inventors, authors, and others who develop ideas and inventions that have potential commercial value petitioned lawmakers over time to enact regulations that classified their ideas and inventions as assets. Those regulations are known as patents, trademarks, and copyrights.

The differences among patents, copyrights, and trademarks can be confusing. A *patent* grants an inventor sole rights to a new idea, new method, or new process. A *copyright* grants authors, musicians, and artists the exclusive rights to publish and sell literary, musical, or artistic works. Copyrights cover artistic, dramatic, musical, literary, and other scholarly works—both published and unpublished. A *trademark* is a word, phrase, slogan, design, or symbol that is used to identify merchandise and is used to distinguish merchandise from competing products. Trademarks indicate the source of a product (i.e., brand names).

A trademark was the first way a tradesman identified his goods and services. Greeks, Romans, Egyptians, and the Chinese used these markings to identify the maker of a product so that a buyer would know the workmanship of the goods or services that he or she was buying.

One of the first trademark laws was *The Bakers Marking Law* passed in England in 1266 under the reign of King Henry III. The Bakers Marking Law required bread makers to mark their work with either pinpricks or stamps. Nearly a century later in 1363, silversmiths were required to mark their products as well. Soon after, bottle makers and porcelain manufacturers were also obligated to mark their products.

Nearly four centuries after The Bankers Marking Law was enacted, one of the first cases of a trademark infringement appeared before the courts in England. A *trademark infringement* is an action of another that violates the trademark of a trademark holder. In the 1618 case, a company that made a lower-quality cloth tried to pass their product off as their higher-quality competitor's in the marketplace through the use of their markings.

The History of Inventions

An *invention* has three distinct characteristics. These are

1. **Problem.** Every invention (including patents) has to solve a specific problem.
2. **Solution.** An invention must solve a specific problem using an idea that those skilled in the art have not yet considered, which is subjective and the basis for many legal challenges to an invention.
3. **Novelty.** The solution to the specific problem must be novel.

The first patents were granted during the Renaissance period in Italy. Venice granted ten-year patents on silk making devices as far back as the 1200s.

Britain has the oldest formal patent system. During the fifteenth century, the government granted patents to specific persons or groups. The earliest known English patent was given to Flemish-born John of Utynam in 1449 for a method of making stained glass that had not previously been used in England. To receive a patent was to receive a favor from the ruling monarch. In exchange for Utynam's patent, he was to teach craftsmen in England his method. The practice of teaching others and passing on information continues today as part of the patent process (see Chapter 4, "Invention Teams").

A patent in the fifteenth century was different than a patent today. The word "patent" originally came from the Latin "litterae patentes," meaning open letter. Patents during the Middle Ages were literally letters stamped with the king's seal of approval. They were left open so that anyone could come and read them and see or challenge their validity. This was the state of Utynam's patent. The state of being of a simple, literal letter has changed drastically since that time, but the meaning also has changed.

During the fifteenth century, receiving a patent also meant that the person received royal consent for a monopoly on that product. (A monopoly is when a group has exclusive control over certain manufactured goods or services.) This was a problem because merchants were granted patents for common products that were already in existence such as soap, glass, iron, and paper.

An Example of an Early Patent

Let's take a look at an example of a patent granted in 1915, a life-saving device invented by Michael Kispeter,[1] to see how patents were conceived and documented during that time.

---

[1]   Refer to http://colitz.com/site/1143835/1143835.htm.

LIFE-SAVING APPARATUS; MICHAEL KISPÉTER

Patented June 22, 1915

To all whom it may concern:

Be it known that I, Michael Kispéter, a subject of the King of Hungary, residing at New York, in the county of New York and State of New York, have invented new and useful improvements in Life-Saving Apparatus, of which the following is a specification.

This invention relates to life saving apparatus and its object is to provide means whereby the life of a person dropping from an aeroplane or airship either over land or over water may be saved.

I attain my object by means of an outfit consisting of a life jacket, lined with airtight inflatable cushions, a spring helmet removably attached to the jacket and a parachute fastened to the body over the jacket, adapted to be opened and shut at the will of the wearer thereof.

In the accompanying drawings: Figure 1 is a partly sectional, partly elevational view of my device in operation, showing a person fitted out therewith. Fig. 2 is a side elevation of a part of the device. Fig. 3 is a plan of part of my device, partly broken away. Fig. 4 is a section taken on the line a-a of Fig. 3. Fig. 5 is a section taken on the line c-c of Fig. 4, on an increased scale. Fig. 6 is a detail sectional view. Fig. 7 is a sectional view of another detail.

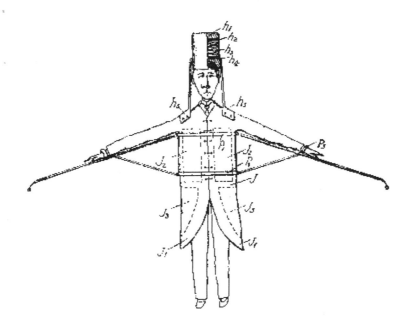

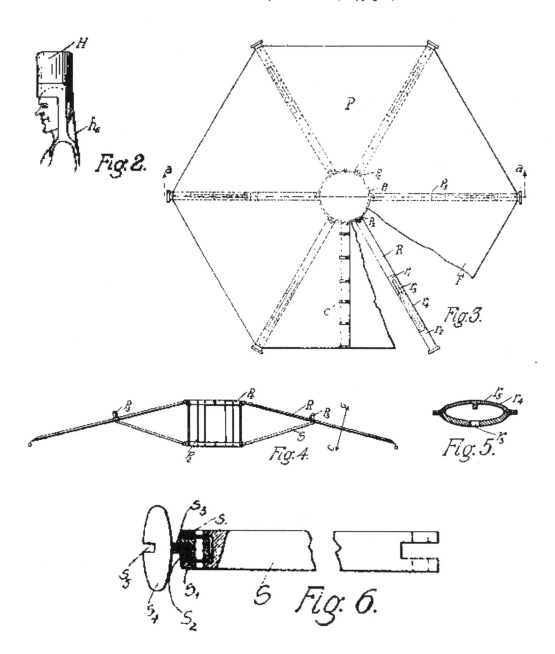

Fig. 2.

Fig. 3.

Fig. 4.

Fig. 5.

Fig. 6.

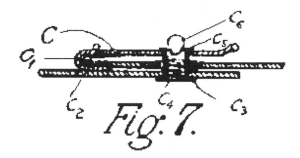

The same reference characters refer to the same part throughout the several views. Fascinating . . . you may do this already, but it would be interesting to understand how the expectations of patent documentation have changed over the years.

Drawing J is a jacket substantially of the shape of an ordinary coat, having two side tails j1, the front and rear part being cut away below the waist. This jacket is lined at the inside with air-cushions j2 made of rubber, two at the front and two at the back of the body portion and one on each side tail, j3. The jacket J is buttoned at the front from neck to waist and if the wearer thereof falls into water, the two coats will, on account of the buoyancy of the air cushions, float on the surface of the water, coacting with the air cushions in the body part of the jacket to keep the wearer afloat.

Over the jacket J is strapped a parachute P consisting of two parallel cylindrical hoops p1, each of two parts hinged together at the back and having means for closing or opening it at the front. The two hoops p1 are connected with each other by six vertical bars p2 placed equidistantly around their periphery. Hinged to the top end of each bar p2 are ribs R and hinged to the lower end of each bar p2 are stays S. On top of the ribs R is conveniently fastened at a substantially circular cover F of some suitable fabric, with a circular opening at its center around the hoops p1. The cover F is slit at the front, the edges overlapping each other and held together by clasps C.

The ribs R are halfround metal bars, having a concave portion from r1 to r2 slotted as at r3 and covered by a convex lid r4 removably secured thereto and forming an elliptical channel therewith. The lid r4 has all along its inside a vertical projection or guide rail r5.

The stays S are flat bars of light metal, forked at their outer ends and carrying between the prongs s1 of the fork pivotally mounted swiveling blocks s2, provided with a screw hole each at its outer surface adapted to take up therein the threaded stem of a screw s3, having a head s4 with a groove s5 diagonally to the length of the stays S. The screw s3 is inserted into the slot r2 in the concave portion of the ribs R, when the lid r4 is removed there from and screwed into the swiveling block s2 so that the groove s5 is parallel with the length of the rib R. Then the lid r4 is fastened on, the guardrail r5 engaging the groove s5, which is adapted freely to slide thereon. Straps p3 are provided on top of the two of the ribs diametrically opposite, for slipping the hand into and thereby open or shut the parachute.

The clasping device of the cover of the parachute consists of a metal clasp C of the form shown in Fig. 7 suitably fastened on the fabric at a convenient distance from one edge of same, having a hinge c1 and a spring c2 tending to keep it open. A small metal cup c3 is passed through the fabric near the same edge thereof to which the clasp is fastened. Attached to the bottom of the cup c3 is one end of the helical spring c4 and to the other end of it is fastened a resilient plate c5, integral with a pushbutton c6. The two ends of the resilient metal plate c5 overlie the upper edges of the cup and the edges of the circular aperture in the clasp C, fitting over the cup, thus preventing it to open. The other edge of the fabric is provided with eyelets fitting over the cup c3 and the two edges are clasped together as shown in Fig. 7. If the button c4 is pressed down by a finger, the metal plate c5 will be forced into the cup c3, thereby releasing the clasp C which will then automatically be opened by the action of the spring c2. When clasped together again, the spiral spring c4 will push the metal plate c5 and button c6 out again of the cup c3.

H is a cylindrical metal helmet having a solid rubber lining h1 inside the top and a metal plate h2 under the rubber. To the metal plate h2 is fastened a helical spring h3, resting on another metal plate underneath it, h4, which projects through horizontal slots in the cylindrical body of the metal helmet on both sides and is continued in two bars running down vertically to the shoulders of the wearer and there shaped like epaulets as shown at h5, removably attached to the shoulder portions of the jacket J. At the back the material of the helmet is prolonged to the back of the jacket J, where it is removably fastened to, as seen at h6. The helmet is supported on the shoulders of the wearer by means of the bars h5 just above the head of the person and not resting thereon.

It will be readily understood from this description of my invention that a person falling from the air, equipped with my life saving apparatus, will first open the parachute by means of raising slightly the hands slipped in the straps over the ribs, the rest being done by pressure of the air against the lower surface of the fabric covering the parachute. Should the person fall into water, the air cushions will keep him or her afloat and should the respective person fall on land and the parachute not assure a descent smooth enough to prevent a violent impact with same, the impact will considerably be reduced also by the air cushions. Should the person fall head foremost the sides of the helmet will break on contact with the soil and the resilient means contained in the helmet will mitigate the concussion.

While I have thus shown and described the preferred form of my invention, it is understood that I do not wish to be limited to its mechanical details and may resort to alterations and modifications, which come within the scope of the claims hereunto appended.

What I claim as new and wish to secure by Letters Patent is:

1. A life saving apparatus, for aeronauts, comprising, in combination, a jacket lined with airtight inflatable cushions, a parachute adapted to be easily opened and closed, removably attached to the body over said jacket, and a helmet supported over the head of the wearer by means of supports attached removably to the shoulder and back portions of said jacket, resilient means in said helmet, substantially as and for the purpose set forth.

2. A life saving helmet, comprising, in combination, a cylindrical body portion closed at the top, said top lined at the inside with resilient material, a helical spring between two metal plates within said cylindrical body, projections of the lower of one of said plates piercing the sides of said cylindrical body, adapted to be fastened to the shoulder portions of a life saving jacket, and to support said helmet just above the head of the wearer, and a prolongation of the material covering said helmet adapted to be removably fastened to the back portion of a life saving jacket, substantially as and for the purpose set forth.

In testimony whereof, I have hereunto fixed my signature in the presence of two witnesses.

MICHAEL KISPÉTER.

Witnesses:

ALEXANDER DENES

ABADAR HAMBURGER.

Between the years of 1561 and 1590, Queen Elisabeth I granted about 50 patents on the manufacture and sale of common things (like those mentioned above). During Queen Elisabeth and her successor, King James I's, respective reigns, there were mounting concerns and overall discontent about the state of the patent system. It came to a head in the year 1624 and was resolved by the publication of the *Book of Bounty*, which stated that "monopolies are things contrary to our laws" and "projects of new invention so they were not contrary to the law, nor mischievous to the state by raising prices at home or hurt of trade." The *Statute of Monopolies* was also published in conjunction with *Book of Bounty*. It limited to 14 years the time of power that the state had in giving out monopolies and "manners of new manufacture" (in other words, new inventions).

This reform satisfied the people, and there was no alteration to the English patent law for nearly 200 years. During the reign of Queen Anne, a condition was added to the law stating, "The patentee must, by an instrument in writing, describe and ascertain the nature of the invention and the manner in which it is performed." James Puckle created the first invention with the new required specifications in 1718. It was for a machine gun.

Article I, section 8 of the United States Constitution says: "The Congress shall have power . . . to promote the progress of science and useful arts by securing for limited times to authors and inventors the exclusive right to their respective writing and discoveries." In 1790, two years after the ratification of the U.S. Constitution, the newly formed United States as a nation passed its first patent statute.

A Timeline of Inventions

1. **287–212 BC, ARCHIMEDES:** Many of the great minds of history not only invented machines but made important discoveries as well. The Greek, Archimedes, invented the simple, practical water screw for raising irrigation water short distances—and these screws are still in use in parts of the Middle East. However, it was also Archimedes who explained the principles of the lever and made the great discovery that since bodies of equal volume displace equal amounts of water, it is quite simple to find the relative density—and thus purity—of many substances. (One simply compares its weight with the volume of water it displaces.)

2. **400 BC, THE NUT AND BOLT:** The nut and bolt, two of the most important discoveries in the history of engineering, were not invented at the same time. Their origins are lost in antiquity, but it is certain that the bolt or screw came first. The Greek mathematician, Archytas of Tarentum, probably invented it about 400 BC. The first recorded securing with nuts seem to belong to the middle of the fifteenth century when they were used to secure parts of suits of armor. One of these bolted suits can be seen today in the Tower of London. All kinds of complex nuts and bolts are now commonplace, including explosive bolts fitted to the escape hatches of spacecraft.

3. **500 BC, THE PLOUGH:** Crude wooden ploughs were used in Egypt and Mesopotamia around 2000 BC, although it is likely they were known of a thousand years earlier. The first iron ploughshares were found in Palestine and in other ancient Mediterranean countries. Both the Romans and Greeks used them, and the Chinese used a wooden plough in about 500 BC. Surprisingly, the plough was not introduced into Europe until the twenty-second century AD. David Ramsey and Thomas Wildgoose patented an English plough machine in 1619. There are many types of modern ploughs, yet some of the ancient designs are still in use.

4. 500 BC, THE WHEEL: The origin of the wheel is lost in the mists of time. However, it is reasonable to suppose that the first "wheels" were roughly hewn tree-trunks used as rollers. The unknown builders of Stonehenge probably used this method to drag the huge stone blocks on to Salisbury Plain. Wooden disc wheels on axles were in use in Sumeria between 2000 and 3000 BC. Carved seals and painted clay models found in Mesopotamia, dated about 1600 BC, show spoke wheels. Celtic wainwrights in Europe made spoke wheels in 500 BC.

5. NINTH CENTURY AD, HISTORY OF PRINTING: The oldest known printed book was produced in China about the middle of the ninth century AD. Early books were called "block" books because they were printed from letters carved of wood, in reverse, which were inked and stamped on cloth and paper. These block books first appeared in Europe about AD 1350, but printing as we know it today really began with the invention of movable type by a German named Johann von Gutenberg, born about AD 1400, whose printed Bibles are now worth a fortune. England's first printer was William Caxton of Kent, who learned the printing trade in Germany and returned to England in 1476.

6. THIRTEENTH CENTURY, MEASUREMENT OF TIME: The first time measuring devices were sundials, water clocks (allowing water to escape at a fixed rate), and candle-clocks. In the thirteenth century came the first true mechanical clocks. Because reliable springs did not yet exist, weights were used for power. However, the early regulating mechanism—a *"foliot,"*[2] or weighted arms rotating backwards and forwards—was still inaccurate by modern standards, and even good clocks of this type could lose ten minutes or so each day. Only with the invention of the pendulum and then the balance wheel was real accuracy attained.

---

[2]   Making for the first mechanical escapement clocks, a foliot mechanism consists of a crossbar with a weight on either end operating in conjunction with the verge, a vertical shaft upon which the foliot sits.

7. 1452–1519, LEONARDO DA VINCI: Leonardo da Vinci has been called the greatest genius who ever lived. He was certainly a most remarkable man with an incredibly inventive and versatile mind. Apart from being a highly talented artist and producing such masterpieces as the Mona Lisa, he had one of the keenest minds in the realms of science and engineering. Drawings and sketches show that he had ideas for submarines, tanks, and other weapons of war, which did not come to fruition until some 400 years after his death. He designed a diving dress, a parachute, and a helicopter and produced superbly accurate anatomical drawings.

8. 1495, FLOATING DOCK: A Floating Dock is in general appearance something like a huge box without ends or top. The bottom consists of a tank or pontoon; by filling this with water the dock is sunk sufficiently to allow the ship, which requires docking, to be floated in. The water is then pumped out from the bottom by means of powerful machinery, the dock rising until the ship is clear of the water. Some of these docks will raise a ship that weighs up to 36,000 tons.

9. 1590, THE MICROSCOPE: The simplest microscope is merely a powerful single convex lens or magnifying glass. The compound or multi-lens microscope opened up an entire unseen world of microbes to Man. The first to achieve this was a spectacle maker of Middelbug, Holland, by the name of Zacharias Janssen in 1590. Dubbed the "father of micro-scopy," Dutch scientist, Anton van Leeuwenhoek, not only created the first high definition instrument but also studied tiny life forms under it.

10. 1608, THE TELESCOPE: Although it is quite easy to magnify close objects with a simple lens, bringing distinct objects close baffled many minds—including that of the famous English scientist, Roger Bacon. Eventually, a Dutch spectacle-maker, Hans Lippershey, solved the problem with a practical two-lens telescope. The great Italian scientist, Galileo, quickly recognized the true value of this invention to astronomy and became the first man to see the craters on the moon and the moons of Jupiter. However, Galileo's telescope aided his then revolutionary theories about the universe to such an extent that eventually his church denounced him as a heretic.

11. **1610, EARLY REFLECTING TELESCOPE:** Telescopes were being made in considerable numbers in Holland around 1610 and were much improved by Galileo, Kepler, and other scientists. One telescope of notoriety was Sir Isaac Newton's (1642–1727): It was a reflecting telescope, the image viewed through a compound eyepiece placed at the side. It magnified from 50 to 800 times according to the size of the parabolic mirror. The mounting was of the "Equatorial" type.

12. **1643, SYPHON BAROMETER:** Torricelli first discovered the pressure of the atmosphere in 1643. The barometer is not really a weather glass but an atmospheric pressure measurer, the column of mercury in the tube rising or falling as the pressure of the air on the mercury at the open end of the tube becomes heavy (as in fine weather) or light (as in wet or windy weather).

13. **1706–1790, BENJAMIN FRANKLIN:** More than 200 years ago, there was much argument as to the nature of lightning, and Benjamin Franklin, who about the year 1746 had begun to be interested in electricity, devised a simple way to "trap" some lightning. It was already known that certain materials when rubbed together would emit a spark. The question was, however, was lightning the same kind of energy? Franklin flew a kite into a thunderstorm and showed that by bringing his knuckles near to a key at the lower end of the kite string an electrical spark could be produced. It was a dangerous experiment. Some of those who later tried it were electrocuted.

14. **1709, THE PIANO:** A whole family of stringed instruments preceded the modern piano, but the two that most closely resembled it were the harpsichord and the clavichord. Both these instruments had keyboards, but they differed in that the harpsichord had strings, which were plucked by quills or pieces of

leather, while the clavichord's strings were struck by brass wedges. Bartolommeo Cristofori, an Italian harpsichord maker, developed a keyboard action, which transmitted the player's true touch on the keys to the felt-covered hammers. Hence, the pianoforte was able to play PIANO (soft), or FORTE (loud) with so perfect an action that every shade of expression could be reproduced.

15. **1712, THE STEAM ENGINE:** Although Giambattista della Porta (1538–1615), Denis Papin (1647–1712), Thomas Savery (1650–1715), and other inventors produced suggestions on how steam could be used to work an engine, it is generally accepted that Thomas Newcomen built the first practical steam engine in 1712. His engine was the "atmospheric" type in which the condensation of steam created a partial vacuum in a cylinder so that the pressure of the atmosphere forced the piston down. These engines were used to pump water out of mines, and some were still in use many years after James Watt's pressure steam engine was invented more than 60 years later.

16. **1714, PRATT'S TYPEWRITER:** As early as 1714, Henry Mill invented a machine for impressing letters on paper, but the first machine to really demonstrate the possibility of producing writing by mechanical means faster than by the pen was that patented by John Pratt in 1866. In 1878 a firm of gun manufacturers in America called E. Remington and Sons brought out their Remington typewriter (the design having come from C.L. Sholes, an American journalist), and since then the use of typewriting machines in business houses has become almost universal.

17. **1731, MARINER'S SEXTANT:** After the compass this was the most important invention for navigation. It simply measures the altitude (number of degrees) of the sun above the horizon. Before reliable ships' clocks existed, this was done at midday when the sun was highest in the sky, and by checking from a table of the sun's altitude on each day, the Equator was quickly found. However, longitude East or West was still largely a matter of guesswork until Harrison, some two hundred years ago, produced a remarkably accurate chronometer unaffected by the motion of a ship. Only then did navigation become a science.

18. 1734, THE FIRE EXTINGUISHER: It is possible that in very early times when humans first became aware of the danger of fire, they kept containers of sand or water near at hand when they kindled cooking fires. However, what might be called a true fire extinguisher did not appear until the eighteenth century when M. Fuchs of Germany invented the idea of glass balls filled with water, which could be thrown on the fire. Then, in 1762, a Dr. Godfrey of London used sal-ammoniac-filled round containers burst by gunpowder. Two Swedes, Von Ahen and Nils Moshein, designed a water-chemical extinguisher in 1792. Some of today's complex extinguishers are computer-controlled.

19. 1763, CUGNOT'S TRACTION ENGINE: The first practical horseless vehicle was the steam "lorry" (or truck) built by Cugnot in 1763. Its success induced the French Government in 1770 to order a steam traction engine for the transportation of artillery, which could carry a load of $4 \frac{1}{2}$ tons at about $2 \frac{1}{4}$ miles per hour on level ground. The traction engine had then become a familiar and almost essential part of the then modern road locomotion.

20. 1768, THE SPINNING MACHINE: Until the invention of the spinning machine, yarn for the making of cloth had for centuries been spun by hand in people's homes. It was a "cottage industry." By the time of the Industrial Revolution, the output was too small to meet the needs of weavers who made cloth. Sir Richard Arkwright's famous "Spinning Frame," which he made at Bolton in Lancashire, was able to spin strong warp yarn or "twist" a better product than the slightly twisted yarn produced by a machine invented by Lewis Paul in 1738. In 1769, Sir Richard Arkwright patented his cotton-spinning frame and established factories at Cromford. He was the first to employ machinery on a large scale for textile manufacturers.

21. 1776, MODERN SUBMARINE: The first submarine to actually go into action was built by David Bushnell in 1776. In 1880–1887, several submarine boats were built; however, these proved to be unstable when submerged. In 1891, the Gustave Zede was built, displacing 266 tons and having a speed of 8 knots when submerged. The modern submarine has a displacement of nearly 1,000 tons and a submerged speed of over 10 knots.

22. 1784, THE LOCK: No one is certain where the first locks were invented, but they are usually attributed to the Chinese. It is known that the ancient Egyptians used locks with movable tumblers. Some early ones were designed to chop off the hand of anyone who fumbled with them without having the right key. The Greeks also had tumbler locks that were opened with a key. A number of Roman locks have been found that had keys to raise levers or lift pins in order to release the bolt. The first modern compound lock was invented by Joseph Bramah of Britain and officially patented in the year 1784.

23. 1785, LIFEBOAT: In 1785, Lionel Lukin, a London coachbuilder, fitted up a Norway yawl with air-boxes at the stem and stern and fixed a best of solid cork along the outside of the gunwale, thus making the first in submersible boat. In 1824, the Royal National Lifeboat Institution was founded, and its fleet later consisted of over 280 boats. The modern lifeboat is virtually unsinkable, is self-righting, and may even have its own radar.

24. 1790, THE SEWING MACHINE: In 1790, Thomas Saint, a cabinet maker who lived in London, invented a machine for sewing leather that produced a chain stitch—a stitch that "locked" itself and prevented running—and so led the way to the modern sewing machine. It incorporated other features of the modern machine such as the vertical needle, the over-hanging arm that carries it, and the feed plate that moves the material along under the needle. Earlier attempts at a stitching machine had been made, such as Englishman Charles Weisenthal's device with its double pointed needle, but none were successful.

25. 1795, HYDRAULIC PRESS: The credit of the invention of the hydraulic press belongs to Joseph Bramah and Henry Maudslay. Wherever an enormous sustained effort is required for lifting heavy loads, bending steel plates, or compressing metal, the hydraulic press was a potential solution. This huge press was also used for consolidating steel ingots for armor plating. It was 33 feet in height, weighed 1,280 tons, and exerted a pressure of 12,000 tons. Today, hydraulic power is indispensable.

26. 1797, PARACHUTE DESCENT BY GARNERIN: In 1785, Blanchard lowered dogs and other animals from a balloon by means of a parachute, and a few years later he made a descent. It was, however, reserved for M. Garnerin in 1797 to make the first descent that attracted public attention. Ascending in a hydrogen balloon to a height of 2,000 feet, he cut himself adrift and descended in perfect safety. He afterwards made other equally successful descents, both in France and London.

27. 1799, THE ELECTRIC BATTERY: Although scientists had known about the strange power of electricity for centuries, the first man to "'capture" it, so to speak, was an Italian chemist named Alessandro Volta. Volta, from whose name we get the term, "volt," discovered that electricity could be produced by chemical means. He made his first electric cell—a "wet" cell—in 1799 by using a zinc plate for the negative terminal and a copper plate for the positive terminal, immersed in a solution of sulfuric acid. "Dry" cell batteries work on much the same principle today, known as the electrochemical generation of power.

28. 1800, FIVE-NEEDLE TELEGRAPH INSTRUMENT: The discovery by Volta in the year 1800 of current or low-tension electricity resulting from chemical action and the introduction of the electro-magnet in 1824 led to the invention of the magnetic receiving instrument. The first needle telegraph was made between 1825 and 1832. Then in 1838, a line of galvanized iron wire, six miles in length, was laid and proven to be satisfactory for transmission purposes. Messrs, Cooke, and Wheatstone invented this five-needle instrument in 1837.

29. 1801, ELECTRIC LIGHT: There are two kinds of electric lamps employed—the arc lamp and the filament lamp. Of the two, the arc lamp was invented first by Sir Humphry Davy in 1801. The filament (incandescent) lamp was developed in 1860.[3] In the arc lamp, two carbon rods are placed with their points almost touching. The electric current sparks across the

---

[3] While the design of the filament was made in 1860, it was not until 1880 when Thomas Edison teamed with Swan that an operative lighting system was achieved.

gap, and an arc of glowing vapor is formed, the carbon points becoming white hot and a dazzling light produced. In the filament lamp, the electric current passes through an extremely fine wire, which creates so high a resistance as to become white hot, thus giving out light.

30. **1802, SPECTROSCOPE:** When a beam of light passes through a glass prism it is broken up into a band of colors called the "spectrum." Light from different substances will give different kinds of spectra, and the spectroscope is an instrument for studying and analyzing the spectra of luminous bodies. The dark lines in the solar spectrum were first observed by Wollaston in 1802, were mapped out by scientists in 1815, and numbered over 2,000.

31. **1802, THE CAMERA:** The principle of photography was acknowledged as early as the sixteenth century. In 1802, Thomas Wedgewood wrote a paper on "An account of a method of copying paintings upon glass and making profiles by the agency of light upon nitrate of silver." In 1824, Daguerre commenced his experiments, and in 1839, Mr. Talbot published a method of producing prints from a negative. Dry plates were introduced in 1874 and, in 1893, Lumiere produced photographs in natural colors.

32. **1804, JACQUARD LOOM:** The credit of introducing the Jacquard Loom and of making it a commercial success, if not of actually inventing it, belongs to Joseph Jacquard, a native of Lyons. This apparatus is one of the most ingenious and important appliances used in the art of weaving, for by its aid the most complex and intricate patterns can be produced with as much certainty and almost as rapidly as plain cloth.

33. 1804, STEVENS' SCREW PROPELLER: Colonel John Stevens built a vessel propelled by twin screws that navigated the Hudson River and attained a speed of nine miles per hour, but for many years, the idea of screw propulsion was abandoned by engineers in favor of the paddle-wheel. The first large sea-going screw steamer was the ARCHI-MEDES of the 232 tons register. The vessel was built in 1838 and proved to be a complete success.

34. 1815, SAFETY LAMP: Although it was well known that the air of coal mines contained gas, which caused explosions upon coming into contact with naked lights, it was not until 1815 that a practical safety lamp for miners was invented. Sir Humphry Davy found that a tube of wire gauze so cools a flame attempting to pass that it prevents the ignition of inflammable gas on the other side, and this principle is embodied in the "Davy" lamp. Only when battery lamps were introduced were the Davy lamps superceded.

35. 1816, HOBBY HORSE: Amazingly, what may have been the first bicycles appear on bas-reliefs from Babylon and Egypt: two-wheeled machines with no pedals and no means of steering. The Hobby Horse—or Dandy-Horse—the forerunner of the modern bicycle, was introduced by J.N. Niepce, a Frenchman, in 1816 and Karl von Drais, a German nobleman in 1817. With the ability to steer, the rider propelled it by a tiptoe running action. The pedal-driven "velocipede" was invented in France in 1865. In 1888, Dunlop invented the pneumatic tire, and the introduction of the free wheel and two and three speed gears finally gave us the bicycle of today. Simple though it may seem, the bicycle is one of the most efficient machines created by man.

36. 1829, GEORGE STEPHENSON'S "ROCKET": The Stephenson's—George and Robert, his son—were undoubtedly the fathers of the modern efficient steam train, although engineers such as Trevithick had had some success earlier. In 1814, George Stephenson's first locomotive pulled several trucks at four mph. His second engine marked a milestone: It forced the exhaust steam up the chimney and thus greatly increased the draught for the fire. His engine, "Locomotion No. 1," opened the world's first fare-paying railway for freight and passengers between Stockton and Darlington. Four years later, his "Rocket" easily won the important Rainhill Trials. One of the Rocket's competitors was disqualified, as it's "engine" was a horse on a treadmill.

37. **1829, READING FOR THE BLIND:** Blindness is a condition that can lead to a terrible sense of isolation. Little had been done to help the blind until the nineteenth century, when Louis Braille, a Frenchman, invented the first specially designed reading system for the sightless in 1829. His system of raised dots, read by touch, is still used today, and automated printing processes now produce Braille books. A new method of blind "reading" utilizes a TV camera, which scans every letter and is linked to a small panel of studs. By placing a palm on the panel, the blind person can feel each letter pattern being raised as it is scanned.

38. **1830, HOWE'S SEWING MACHINE:** In 1830, a successful chain stitch sewing machine was invented and constructed by Thimmonier, who started a factory in which many of these machines were employed. In 1845, Elias Howe constructed the first lockstitch sewing machine, using an eye-pointed needle and an independent shuttle, each of which was threaded. In 1851, Singer patented his first machine and did much to accelerate the commercial introduction of this most useful invention.

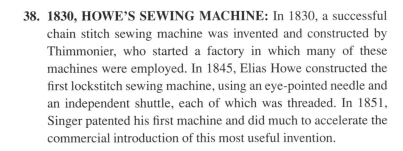

39. **1831, THE DYNAMO:** Although it was known that moving a coil of wire across the force field between the poles of a magnet could produce an electrical current, it was not until 1831 that Michael Faraday set about making practical use of the knowledge. Faraday experimented with a copper disc that could be turned between the poles of a horseshoe magnet, with thin pieces of metal connecting both the center and outer edge of the disc to a galvanometer. When the disc was spun an electric current was generated. Faraday had designed the first dynamo— today it is the world's main source of power.

40. 1834, THE REFRIGERATOR: For many centuries, large numbers of country houses had specially built "ice-houses," which were low buildings with thick walls where ice from frozen winter ponds was stored and covered with layers of straw until it was needed in summer for cooling drinks. By the early nineteenth century, methods had been found to make ice artificially with huge, if rather crude, refrigeration plants, and this ice was sold to householders with ice-boxes, helping to keep fresh vegetables crisp in the summer's heat. It was not long before a home refrigerator was on sale—by Jacob Perkin of America.

41. 1835, THE REVOLVER: For centuries, man tried to develop a small, fast-firing gun, and Samuel Colt was the first to effectively solve the problem. The story goes that the inventor of the famous Colt revolver ran away to sea at the age of 16. His ship was going to India, and while on the voyage, Colt carved a wooden revolver. Realizing its possibilities, Colt then had a number of metal models made between 1831 and 1835 and worked on his idea until he could construct a patent. The American government ordered a thousand Colt revolvers for the Army when the U.S.–Mexican War broke out in 1846, the age of the revolver had arrived.

42. 1837, MORSE CODE: Samuel Finley Breese Morse left his home in America to study art in London when he was 24 years of age. He returned to America on board a ship in 1832, and during this voyage, he spent some time discussing electricity and magnetism with other passengers. Suddenly, Morse thought of the idea of what he called "transmitting intelligence by electricity." He sat on the deck of the ship and worked out the details of his idea, but it was five years later before he was able to apply for a patent. Contrary to general belief, the famous "S.O.S." signal does not mean "Save Our Souls" but was adopted because of its unmistakable character in Morse Code.

43. 1838, STEAM HAMMER: James Nasmyth, a Manchester engineer, invented the Steam Hammer in 1838. Robert Wilson, his partner and successor, improved upon his invention in 1853. While these immense machines can give a blow of enormous energy, so delicately are they adjusted and so perfectly controlled, that they can by made to tap the shell of an egg without breaking it, and some of these hammers can deliver a blow equivalent to 4,000 tons.

44. 1842, ELECTRIC LOCOMOTIVE: The first attempt to use electric power for railways was in 1842 when an electric locomotive was constructed, weighing five tons, which attained a speed of four miles per hour. The powerful Electric locomotive was used for conveying trains throughout the Simplon Tunnel—connecting Iselle, Italy, to Brig, Switzerland. It could draw a train of 300 tons throughout a tunnel in 18 minutes at an average speed of 42 miles per hour.

45. 1845, THE PNEUMATIC TIRE: Although R.W. Thomson, a Scotsman, is credited with inventing the pneumatic tire, it was a fellow Scot, John Boyd Dunlop, who first made it a successful commercial proposition in 1890. Thomson's tires consisted of tubes of rubber protected by an outside casing of leather, and many of these were used on early bicycles. Solid rubber tires were widely used before the arrival of the pneumatic tire. The greatly increased comfort of the pneumatic tire was a great stimulus to the sales of bicycles, and, in fact, this kind of tire with its built-in "shock absorber," is much safer than solid tires.

46. 1847–1931, THOMAS ALVA EDISON: Anyone who worries about not doing well at school may feel encouraged by what happened to Thomas Alva Edison, who was perhaps America's most prolific inventor. His teacher considered him stupid—he had only three months' official schooling. His mother knew he was far from stupid and so took him away from school to teach him herself. Young Edison went on to invent not only the forerunner of the gramophone, but even a successful electric filament lamp in 1880. He also invented an early form of a radio tube and a method of telegraphy between moving ships or trains.

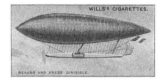

47. 1852, RENARD AND KREBS' DIRIGIBLE: The first airship to be propelled by an engine was built by Giffard in 1852 and attained a speed of about six miles per hour, but the first really successful dirigible was that constructed in 1884 by Captains Renard and Krebs of the French Army. This was of a more scientific design than any of its predecessors and traveled at the rate of 14 miles per hour, overcoming winds of considerable strength.

48. 1860, AUTO-PIANO: As early as 1860, a patent was filed in the United States for a keyboard piano-player, and the first pneumatic keyboard was made in France in 1863. With its many ingenious contrivances for bringing out the melody of a piece, regulating the time and expression, and accentuating any notes desired, the modern Piano-player can be made to exactly reproduce the playing of a master, even though the operator himself be entirely ignorant of piano technique.

49. 1860, THE WASHING MACHINE: The laborious washing of clothes by hand is still the only laundering method available in many parts of the world. Many methods have been used, from banging the clothes on flat stones by a river's edge to an old seaman's trick of dragging them behind the ship to force water through them. Modern washing machines evolved from an idea that appeared in the 1860s when the British firm of Thomas Bradford built the first working model, a hand-turned device. It was made of wood and quite primitive, but modern machines still use much the same principles of mechanical agitation, freeing women from backbreaking labor.

50. 1863, WILDE'S DYNAMO: In 1863, Dr. Wilde invented the first separately excited Dynamo, demonstrating that the feeble current from a small magneto-electric machine could be made to produce currents of great strength from a large dynamo. Wilde's Dynamo weighed $4 \frac{1}{2}$ tons, and when driven at 1,500 revolutions per minute, the current fused 15 inches of round iron $\frac{1}{4}$ in diameter with an expenditure of about 10 horsepower. This machine was used for electro-plating purposes, depositing 20 ounces of silver per hour.

51. **1865, ROCK DRILL:** The Rock Drill differs from most other Rock Drills in that it really bores and does not merely peck its way into the rock. The hollow drill stem, furnished with three or four splayed-out teeth, is driven by means of high-pressure water. The drill is pressed against the face of the rock by a hydraulic ram with a force of 10 tons. To sink a hole 39 inches deep took from 12 to 15 minutes with this method.

52. **1866, TRAFFIC SIGNALS:** The first traffic signals were invented by a man named Hodgson and were of the semaphore type. However, they were actually copied from railway signal-arms. A set of traffic signals was first erected near Westminster Abbey in London in 1868 as an experiment. They had two sem-aphore arms, one for Stop and one for Go, with red and green gas lamps for night use. The modern type of light signal was not introduced until early in the 20th century, the first ones being in use in New York about 1918. They are now sometimes linked to tubes in the road and to computers so that the signals take into account the traffic requirements for the time of day.

53. **1874, VACUUM BRAKE:** By means of the communication cord, a train can be stopped from a compartment. Under each carriage is a cylinder in which a vacuum is created from the engine by an air-ejector. When the cord is pulled, air is let into the cylinder under the piston. This pushes the piston up, and by means of levers immediately puts on the brakes, automatically stopping the entire train.

54. **1874–1937, GUGLIELMO MARCONI:** Marconi was inter-ested in anything electrical when he was a young boy. At Bologna, Italy, he watched Professor Righi doing experiments with electromagnetic waves. In 1895, the young Marconi began his own experiments and soon was able to send Morse code messages more than a mile with a tapping device but with no wires connecting transmitter and receiver. In 1897, the Marconi Wireless Telegraph Company was formed, and in 1899, a wire-less message was sent across the English Channel. Strangely, even before this, an article in *The Strand Magazine* in London had discussed the possibility of television.

55. 1876, THE TELEPHONE: The first words ever to be spoken over a telephone were, "Mr. Watson, come here. I want you." They were spoken by the inventor himself, Alexander Graham Bell, in a hotel in Boston, Massachusetts, where he had been conducting experiments with the help of Thomas Watson, his assistant. Bell was born in Edinburgh in 1847 and studied at both Edinburgh and London Universities. His father was a teacher and elocutionist, and Bell came to realize that the pressure of sound waves in a thin plate held the key to the electrical transmission of sound. Yet even he was surprised by the high quality of sound reproduction he quickly achieved this way.

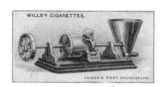

56. 1877, EDISON'S FIRST PHONOGRAPH: In 1877, Edison held the patent for an instrument capable of automatically registering sounds, known as the phonograph. This consisted of a grooved metal cylinder covered with tinfoil on which the sounds were registered and afterwards reproduced by means of a steel needle. A conical mouthpiece was attached to concentrate the reproduced sounds.

57. 1879, CASH REGISTER: The modern cash register, now to be seen at work in almost every store worldwide, has taken the place of the old-fashioned open till. This marvelous mechanism keeps a record of all transactions, indicating the value of the purchase and printing the figures and nature of business done on a ticket for the customer and also on a roll of paper tape for the proprietor.

58. 1882, ELECTRIC TRAM: The electrically driven car entirely superseded the old-fashioned horse-drawn tram. The first electric tramcar was operated at Leytonstone, Essex, in 1882. The trolley pole at the top of most electric cars during this period had nothing to do with the actual driving of the car but simply conducted the electricity from the overhead wire, through the motorman's switchbox, to the motor beneath the car.

59. 1884, STEAM TURBINE: Invented by Charles Parsons, the steam turbine engines were at first used for driving electric-dynamos at very high speeds and generating electric power. Pressure from steam of boiled water is used to turn a turbine. This mechanical action is converted into an electrical energy through the use of a dynamo.

60. 1885, THE MOTOR CAR: Like many great inventions, the motor car was not the result on one man's effort. Nobody can be certain who built the first working petroleum engine road vehicle, but the credit is usually given to two Germans—Carl Benz and Gottlieb Daimler. Benz used a tricycle to which he fitted a $^1/_4$ horsepower engine in 1885; while in 1887, Daimler built the first four-wheeled road vehicle with a more powerful four horsepower petroleum engine. Daimler's invention was the more successful of the two, and his machine incorporated many of the features of the modern car.

61. 1888, PLATE AND ROLL-FILM CAMERA: During the first half-century of photography, pictures were made on plates—originally metal Daguerreotypes, but later glass. The early glass plates, even in such processes as the collodian method, had to be coated with the light-sensitive material just before the photograph was taken—a tremendously complicated task. Obviously, anyone who could invent a simple method of photography could command a huge market for his method, and the honor fell to George Eastman, whose early Kodak roll-fill cameras—at first using a paper roll-film with room for 100 negatives—in 1888 gave photography to us all.

62. 1889, THE MOVIE CAMERA: The origin of motion pictures is obscure, and a number to men were working at more or less the same time on the idea of taking a continuous series of photographs on one length of film. There seems little doubt, however, that an Englishman, William Friese-Green, was the first man to project a film onto a simple screen. He achieved this success in January 1889 after a number of experiments. The American inventor, Alva Edison, also designed an apparatus called a "*kinetoscope*," a kind of moving-picture viewer. However, Friese-Green's invention had gone even further and featured an attempt at 3-D movies.

63. 1889, STEEL-FRAME BUILDING: Owing to the high cost of building sites in the large cities of the United States, the method of the steel-frame building has been adopted. The skeleton of the building consists of steel girders, the walls being comparatively thin, and inserted like panels in a door. Brick and stone buildings cannot be taken more than 12 to 14 stories high, owing to the thickness of the walls required, but steel-frame edifices allow people to produce buildings of astounding heights.

64. 1892, EDISON'S KINETOSCOPE: The cinematograph is really a development of the "zoetrope," or "wheel of life." In 1877, E. Muybridge obtained successive pictures of a running horse by means of a row of cameras, but Edison invented the first practical moving picture apparatus in 1890. In 1892, Edison brought out the kinetoscope, a combination of photography and electricity, by means of which the voice of a phonograph worked synchronously with the action of the figures on the screen.

65. 1894, LEVASSOR'S MOTOR CAR: The first important motor car race took place in July 1894, from Paris to Rouen (France), and in 1895 the Automobile Club de France was established. The famous race from Paris to Bordeaux and back, a distance of some 732 miles, originated in 1895 and was won by M. Levassor, who covered the distance in 48 hours and 48 minutes, at an average speed of about 15 miles per hour; the highest speed in the race being about 20 mph.

66. 1895, MARCONI TRANSMITTING APPARATUS: The outstanding figure in the realm of wireless telegraphy is Guglielmo Marconi. He commenced experimenting in 1895, and when only 22 years of age, he sent wireless messages across the Bristol Channel. In 1901, the first wireless telegraph was sent across the Atlantic, and messages can now be sent from 2,000 to 3,000 miles. Almost all large liners, battleships, and cargo boats are now fitted with wireless apparatus, and the distress call of "S.O.S." has been the means of saving numerous lives.

67. 1895, THE SAFETY RAZOR: Razors with crude guards to prevent deep cuts have been tried out for many centuries past, but the man who gave the world a razor that was not only safe, but also had a separate disposable blade, was an American named King Camp Gillette. Gillette is said to have gotten the idea while shaving with one of the dangerous old "cut-throat" razors one day in 1895. His American Safety Razor Company was formed in 1901, and by 1904, it had sold 90,000 razors and 12,400,000 blades. Today, this kind of razor has hardly changed and is still the most popular shaving method in the world.

68. 1895, X-RAY APPARATUS: X-rays were discovered in 1895. Their discovery has given a great impetus to the progress of science and surgery and has had far-reaching effects in saving human and animal life and the alleviation of pain. Initial descriptions said that the bones of the living body could be seen (or photographed) by means of these rays, flesh being almost transparent to them, while bones being almost opaque.

69. 1902, THE VACUUM CLEANER: Dirt not only makes carpets filthy but also sinks into the carpet backing and cuts the fibers. In the past, the only way to get rid of this dirt was to hang the carpet up and give it a hard beating—a tiring and dirty business. It occurred to inventors a long time ago that the best solution was to collect the dirt up and out of the carpet, where it laid flat, via principals of vacuum. The solution—the vacuum cleaner—began life as a much different machine from the trim "Hoover" of today. It was actually a huge piece of equipment that sat outside the house, and hoses were put through windows to collect the dirt via the vacuum.

70. 1906, SANTOS-DUMONT'S AEROPLANE MOTOR: M. Santos-Dumont built a small flying machine fitted with an Antoinette motor, and on August 22, 1906, he made the first flight in Europe to be officially recorded. On October 23, he made a flight of 25 meters, and on November 12, succeeded in flying 200 meters, winning the prize offered for the first flight of 100 meters.

71. 1920, MODERN LIGHTHOUSE LANTERN[4]: In the earliest types of lighthouses, open wood or coal fires were used as lights for the guidance of navigators. In due time, these were replaced by tallow candles, but as their range was extremely limited, attempts were made to intensify their light by means of reflectors. The modern lighthouse is illuminated by huge "hyper radiant" lanterns, lit by means of incandescent petroleum vapor, sometimes exceeding 1,000,000 candle power, and weighing as much as 20 tons.

72. 1923, THE HEARING AID: Humans probably discovered at a very early stage that they could hear distant sounds better by cupping a hand to their ear, which may later have led them to use animal horns as ear trumpets. Specially made metal horns were later used, but no electronic device appeared until the Marconi Company produced the valve-operated otophone in 1923. It was cumbersome and weighed 16 pounds, including its sturdy case. Some modern hearing aids, far more efficient, weigh only one-thousandth of this.

73. 1925, TELEVISION: A number of men contributed to developing a practical method of transmitting pictures by wireless. Dr. L. Weiller, a German, invented a drum of mirrors used to "scan" the scene to be viewed, and an Englishman, A.A. Campbell Swinton, thought of using electronic tubes for transmission and reception. However, it was a Scotsman named John Logie Baird (1888–1946) who began experimenting in 1922, who built the first practical TV system. Baird used a

---

[4] Although the signaling strength of a lighthouse advanced mostly during the 20th century, lighthouses have been in use as far back as 280 BC.

disc scanning system and saw his first TV picture, a Maltese Cross, in 1925. The picture was very blurred—but it was true television. And a few years later Britain had the world's first TV service.

74. 1930, THE JET ENGINE: Jet engines and rocket engines work basically the same way—a high velocity gas stream is emitted, which produces a thrust in the opposite direction. While a rocket carries all its combustible materials with it, a jet engine sucks in air at the front and mixes it with a suitable fuel. The first man to successfully produce an efficient engine of this type was Sir Frank Whittle, whose early turbojet engine powered the famous Gloster E 28/39 jet in 1941. However, the German designer, Heinkel, had already flown a jet plane in 1939—the He178. Whittle's engine, however, was superior in design, and modern jet engines are based on it.

75. 1934, CATS EYES: Percy Shaw, the inventor of those tiny reflectors that are sunk into the center of roads, was born in Yorkshire. He used to run a road repair business, and as a young man he realized how dark and dangerous unlit country roads could be at night. On his way home one night, he noticed reflectors on a poster by the roadside. This gave him the idea for "cats eyes" in the road. His first road reflectors were used in 1934, and the design has barely been altered in 40 years, including the simple, effective, automatic collapse of the reflector system when a wheel runs over it.

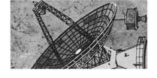

76. 1935, RADAR: Radar is one of those inventions that came about largely by accident, but which nature had already created in a slightly different form—in this case, the bat's method of avoiding obstacles in the dark. Sir Robert Watson-Watt, a member of a British scientific team studying radio reflections from the upper atmosphere in 1934, noticed a strange echo on his cathode ray tube. It turned out to be from a distant building. Once it was realized that distant objects could be found, located, and "ranged" by radio waves, the idea was used to track enemy aircraft and then to make air and sea navigation much safer.

77. **1947, THE POLAROID CAMERA:** The Polaroid camera does not actually use polarized light. It gets its name from the fact that Edwin H. Land, its inventor, created the company that made Polaroid sunglasses. However, his camera is an achievement photographers had dreamed about for a whole century—instant pictures without the trouble of separate developing and printing. In fact, these processes are carried out not in the Polaroid camera itself, but in its film pack. After exposure, the negative, in contact with the positive, is drawn through rollers, which break a pod of developing chemicals, squeezing them on to the sensitized surfaces. In ten seconds, the print appears—developed and fixed.

78. **1947, THE TRANSISTOR:** Three Americans are jointly credited with the invention of the transistor—William Shockley, John Bardeen, and Walter Brattain. Their invention was first demonstrated in 1948 at the Bell Telegraph Laboratories in the United States. Transistors have brought about a revolution in radio and electronics and have almost completely replaced the old radio valve because of their remarkable reliability, toughness and incredibly small size. In fact, without the transistor, the computers used in manned spacecraft would have been so heavy that the rockets might never have been able to get off of the ground.

79. **1954, THE HOVERCRAFT:** In 1953, Sir Christopher Cockerell became interested in the problem of 'drag' on ships' hulls as they travel through water. He experimented unsuccessfully with air films under model boats to give a kind of lubricated surface. In 1954, he tried using fixed sidewalls with water-curtains and also hinged end-doors with air pumped into the center. This led him to consider using air-curtains, and one Sunday he made a model out of two empty coffee tins and a small industrial fan-dryer. It worked, so in December 1955, Cockerell applied for his first "hovercraft" patent. The full-size SRN-1 soon showed that the craft could easily travel over land and marshes as well as over water.

80. 1958, HYDROFOIL SHIPS: The idea of building small vessels that used underwater "wings" to lift the hull above the surface of the water, seems to have originated in France around 1850 when a priest named Ramus demonstrated a model hydrofoil. It failed because he had no way of moving it fast enough through the water. An Italian named Enrico Forlanini built the first successful hydroplane in 1905. It was moderately successful because he used a petrol engine for power. Hydrofoils today offer a simple way to achieve high speed with small vessels without excessive "'wash," which can damage riverbanks and wash levees away.

81. PRESENT, A PEEK INTO THE FUTURE: It's an intriguing thought—what inventions would a "Famous Inventions" picture card series published in AD 2075 include? Or one published in AD 2975? Matter transmitters? Faster-than-light spaceship drives? Tele-transporters? Instant health dust? Certainly, some inventions of the future will be as far beyond our present understanding as the transistor would have been even to a keen mind like Faraday's. However, the steps along the way will be marked with the useful, everyday products of inventions—like a shaving cream that dissolves whiskers, perhaps, or a cheap, truly pocket-sized color TV set. One thing is certain: The future holds inventions galore—just waiting to be invented.

In 1899, Charles Duell, head of the U.S. Patents Office, suggested that his office be abolished, stating that "everything that can be discovered, has been discovered." Clearly, Duell's recommendation was premature, but his statement reflects the attitude from much of society during his time in office. Life expectancies were rising thanks to the development of better public health practices. Incomes throughout the U.S. were rising due to the increased production afforded by industries. Electricity was being made available throughout the country as a "utility," further symbolizing the increased quality of life for the newly affluent country. Very soon, the Internet will be delivered as a broadband solution from our utility companies through the power plugs in our walls. We will (no doubt) then somehow be billed according to our "utility" use of the Internet. We can suppose, then, there is more to be invented.

Conversely, says Rick Hamilton (Master Inventor at the IBM Corporation), it might be convincing to debate this thought from 1899. Consider that perhaps certain more established societies did not have intellectual property protection mechanisms. Could they have suffered from this abundance of innovative disincentives?

The History of Copyrights

Copyright law originated in England. Before the year 1710, there was a monopoly on printing presses and therefore heavy censorship. That year, however, Parliament ratified the Statute of Anne to address mounting concern about ownership and censorship. This act gave the authors of works a 14-year term of fixed protection that could be renewed and extended.

American Copyright Law Was First Seen in the Copyright Act of 1790

The following timeline is presented by the Association of Research Libraries, Washington, DC as noted at http://arl.cni.org/info/frn/copy/timeline.html. *The timeline is a work-in-progress and said to be frequently updated. The original author recognizes Stanley Katz, Director, Princeton University Center for Arts and Cultural Policy Studies, for reading and offering valuable advice on this timeline.*

The history of American copyright law[5] originated with the introduction of the printing press to England in the late fifteenth century. As the number of presses grew, authorities sought to control the publication of books by granting printers a near monopoly on publishing in England. The Licensing Act of 1662 confirmed that monopoly and established a register of licensed books to be administered by the Stationers' Company, a group of printers with the authority to censor publications. The 1662 act lapsed in 1695 leading to a relaxation of government censorship, and in 1710 Parliament enacted the Statute of Anne to address the concerns of English booksellers and printers. The 1710 act established the principles of authors' ownership of copyrights and a fixed term of protection of copyrighted works (14 years—and renewable for 14 more if the author were alive upon expiration). The statute prevented a monopoly on the part of the booksellers and created a "public domain" for literature by limiting terms of copyright and by ensuring that once a work was purchased, the copyright owner no longer had control over its use. While the statute did provide for an author's copyright, the benefit was minimal because in order to be paid for a work an author had to assign it to a bookseller or publisher.

Since the Statute of Anne almost three hundred years ago, U.S. law has been revised to broaden the scope of copyright, to change the term of copyright protection, and to address new technologies. For several years, the U.S. has considered and acted on copyright reform. The Canadian government is considering copyright reform as well.

1787: U.S. Constitution

According to Article I, Section 8, Clause 8 of the U.S. Constitution, " . . . the Congress shall have power ... to promote the progress of science and useful arts, by securing for limited times to authors and inventors the exclusive right to their respective writings and discoveries."

1790: Copyright Act of 1790

The First Congress implemented the copyright provision of the U.S. Constitution in 1790. *The Copyright Act of 1790, An Act for the Encouragement of Learning by Securing the Copies of Maps, Charts, and Books to the Authors and Proprietors of Such Copies*, was modeled on the

[5]   For more information, please refer to http://arl.cni.org/info/frn/copy/timeline.html#Bib.

Statute of Anne (1710). It granted American authors the right to print, reprint, or publish their work for a period of 14 years and to renew for another 14. The law was meant to provide an incentive to authors, artists, and scientists to create original works by providing creators a monopoly. At the same time, the monopoly was limited in order to stimulate creativity and the advancement of "science and the useful arts" through wide public access to works in the "public domain." Major revisions to the act were implemented in 1831, 1870, 1909, and 1976.

1831: Revision of the Copyright Act

The term of protection of copyrighted works was extended to 28 years with the possibility of a 14-year extension. Congress claimed that it extended the term in order to give American authors the same protection as those in Europe. The extension applied both to future works and those current works whose copyright had not expired.

1834: Wheaton v. Peters

The case arose from a dispute between the official reporter of U.S. Supreme Court decisions, Richard Peters, and the previous reporter, Henry Wheaton. Peters began publishing "Condensed Reports" of cases decided during Wheaton's tenure, and Wheaton sued. The case went before the U.S. Supreme Court. Peters argued that Wheaton had failed to properly obtain copyright, while Wheaton argued that authors were entitled to perpetual property rights in their works. Justice McLean delivered the majority decision stating that "since the Statute of Anne, the literary property of an author in his works can only be asserted under the statute . . . That an author, at common law, has a property in his manuscript, and may obtain redress against any one who deprives him of it, or by improperly obtaining a copy endeavors to realize a profit by its publication cannot be doubted; but this is a very different right from that which asserts a perpetual and exclusive property in the future publication of the work, after the author shall have published it to the world." The decision struck a decisive blow against the notion of copyright as a perpetual natural right, and the utilitarian view of copyright embodied in the U.S. Constitution prevailed, i.e., "that patents and copyrights are exclusive rights of limited duration, granted in order to serve the public interest in promoting the creation and dissemination of new works." See the amicus brief submitted to the U.S. Supreme Court by Tyler Ochoa and Mark Rose in the case of *Eldred v. Ashcroft,* May 20, 2002.

1841: Folsom v. Marsh

In a case brought before the Massachusetts Circuit Court in 1841, the owner and editor of a multivolume collection of George Washington's letters sued Charles Upham for using hundreds of pages of the letters in their entirety in a volume on the life of Washington. Justice William Story found that Upham had infringed the owner's copyright in publishing some 350 pages of Washington's letters in his 866-page book. Upham argued that Washington's letters were not "proper subjects of copyright" because their publication would not harm the deceased author and because they were not literary in nature. Story disagreed and held that letter writers and their designated heirs, not the persons to whom the letters are addressed, possess copyright in the letters they had written, no matter the content.

Upham also argued that he had "a right to abridge and select, and use the materials . . . for [his] work, which . . . is an original and new work, and that it constitutes, in no just sense, a piracy of the work of the plaintiffs." Again, Story disagreed, saying that Upham's work was "a selection of the entire contents of particular letters, from the whole collection or mass of letters of the work of the plaintiffs . . . [and] that these letters are the most instructive, useful and interesting to be found in that large collection." In explaining the nature of the infringement, Story said, "It is certainly not necessary, to constitute an invasion of copyright, that the whole of a work should be copied, or even a large portion of it, in form or in substance. If so much is taken, that *the value of the original is sensibly diminished,* or *the labors of the original author are substantially to an injurious extent appropriated by another*, that is sufficient, in point of law, to constitute a piracy pro tanto." The court's definition of what constituted a "justifiable use of the original materials" formed the basis of the "fair use" doctrine. Put another way, Story said that "the question of piracy, often depend[s] upon a nice balance of the comparative use made in one of the materials of the other; the nature, extent, and value of the materials thus used; the objects of each work; and the degree to which each writer may be fairly presumed to have resorted to the same common sources of information, or to have exercised the same common diligence in the selection and arrangement of the materials."

1853: Stowe v. Thomas

Harriet Beecher Stowe sued F.W. Thomas, publisher of a German-language periodical, *Die Freie Presse,* in 1853. Thomas translated *Uncle Tom's Cabin* into German and sold it in the United States without the author's permission. Judge Robert Grier of the Third Circuit Court of Appeals explained in the decision that once an author published her or his work "and given his thoughts, sentiments, knowledge or discoveries to the world, he can have no longer an exclusive possession of them." With regard to translations, he continued, "the same conceptions clothed in another language cannot constitute the same composition; nor can it be called a transcript or 'copy' of the same 'book.'" According to Siva Vaidhyanathan,[6] the "antiproperty" rhetoric in the decision encouraged many American authors to take a stand in favor of copyright as property until the copyright law was revised in 1870.

1870: Revision of the Copyright Act

The administration of copyright registrations moved from the individual district courts to the Library of Congress Copyright Office. The term of protection was not extended in this revision.

---

[6] Siva Vaidhyanathan is currently an assistant professor in the Department of Culture and Communication at New York University. Dr Vaidhyanathan's work is referenced throughout this chapter. For more information on Dr. Vaidhyanathan's works, please reference http://www.nyu.edu/classes/siva/.

1886: Berne Convention

The goals of the Berne Convention provided the basis for mutual recognition of copyright between sovereign nations and promoted the development of international norms in copyright protection. European nations established a mutually satisfactory uniform copyright law to replace the need for separate registration in every country. The treaty has been revised five times since 1886. Of particular note are the revisions in 1908 and 1928. In 1908, the *Berlin Act* set the duration of copyright at life of the author plus 50 years, expanded the scope of the act to include newer technologies, and prohibited formalities as a prerequisite of copyright protection. In 1928, the *Rome Act* first recognized the moral rights of authors and artists, giving them the right to object to modifications or to the destruction of a work in a way that might prejudice or decrease the artists' reputations. The United States became a Berne signatory in 1988.

1891: International Copyright Treaty

Because American copyright law applied only to American publications, European authors were unable to profit from the publication and sale of their works at extremely low prices during the nineteenth century. The so-called "cheap books" movement, spread rapidly by small upstart publishers after the Civil War, threatened the "courtesy principle" of gentlemanly price-fixing adhered to by the large, established publishers such as Henry Holt. By the 1880s cheap books flooded the American market. By 1890, author, publisher, and printer unions joined together to support an international copyright bill.

1909: Revision of the U.S. Copyright Act

A major revision of the U.S. *Copyright Act* was completed in 1909. The bill broadened the scope of categories protected to include all works of authorship and extended the term of protection to 28 years with a possible renewal of 28. Congress addressed the difficulty of balancing the public interest with proprietor's rights:

"The main object to be desired in expanding copyright protection accorded to music has been to give the composer an adequate return for the value of his composition, and it has been a serious and difficult task to combine the protection of the composer with the protection of the public, and to so frame an act that it would accomplish the double purpose of securing to the composer an adequate return for all use made of his composition and at the same time prevent the formation of oppressive monopolies, which might be founded upon the very rights granted to the composer for the purpose of protecting his interests" (H.R. Rep. No. 2222, 60th Cong., 2nd Session, p. 7 [1909]).

1973: Williams and Wilkins Co. v. United States

Williams and Wilkins, publishers of specialized medical journals, sued the National Library of Medicine (NLM) and the National Institutes of Health (NIH), charging that the agencies had infringed copyright by making unauthorized photocopies of articles featured within their publications and distributing them to medical researchers. The U.S. Court of Claims held that finding an infringement in the case would harm medical research, and since the *Copyright Act* was under revision by Congress, it was better to allow the status quo to continue in the interim. In the decision, Judge Davis stated, "the court holds, based on the type and context of use by NIH and NLM as shown by the record, that there has been no infringement, that the challenged use is 'fair' in view of the combination of all of the factors involved in consideration of 'fair' or 'unfair' use enumerated in the opinion, that the record fails to show a significant detriment to plaintiff but demonstrates injury to medical and scientific research if photocopying of this kind is held unlawful, and that there is a need for congressional treatment of the problems of photocopying."

1976: Revision of the U.S. Copyright Act

The 1976 revision was undertaken for two primary reasons. First, technological developments and their impact on what might be copyrighted, how works might be copied, and what constituted an infringement needed to be addressed. Second, the revision was undertaken in anticipation of Berne Convention adherence by the U.S. It was felt that the statute needed to be amended to bring the U.S. into accord with international copyright law, practices, and policies. The 1976 act preempted all previous copyright law and extended the term of protection to life of the author plus 50 years (works for hire were protected for 75 years). The act covered the following areas: scope and subject matter of works covered, exclusive rights, copyright term, copyright notice and copyright registration, copyright infringement, fair use and defenses and remedies to infringement. With this revision, for the first time the fair use and first sale doctrines were codified, and copyright was extended to unpublished works. In addition, a new section was added, Section 108, that allowed library photocopying without permission for purposes of scholarship, preservation, and interlibrary loan under certain circumstances.

In addition to Section 108, Section 107 is important to libraries because it contains an exception to the exclusive rights of owners to make and distribute copies of their works. It states that "the fair use of a copyrighted work, including such use by reproduction in copies or phonorecords or by any other means specified by that section, for purposes such as criticism, comment, news reporting, teaching (including multiple copies for classroom use), scholarship, or research, is not an infringement of copyright." To determine whether the use of a work is a fair use, the following four factors are to be considered: purpose and character of the use, nature of the copyrighted work, the amount and substantiality of the portion used in relation to the whole, and the effect of the use on the potential market. See Title 17 of the U.S. Code.

1976: Classroom Guidelines

In addition to legislative reforms, private negotiations between owners and users of copyrighted materials resulted in guidelines for classroom and educational use as well as reserve room use. These guidelines were not part of the statute but were included in the House report accompanying the 1976 act. The 1976 *"Agreement on Guidelines for Classroom Copying in Not-for-Profit Educational Institutions with Respect to Books and Periodicals"* was adopted by 38 educational organizations and the publishing industry. According to the text of the guidelines, the purpose was "to state the minimum and not the maximum standards of educational fair use under Section 107 of the [*Copyright Act of 1976*]. The parties agree that the conditions determining the extent of permissible copying for educational purposes may change in the future; that certain types of copying permitted under these guidelines may not be permissible in the future; and conversely that in the future other types of copying may be permissible under revised guidelines."

1976: CONTU Process

The National Commission on New Technological Uses of Copyrighted Works (CONTU) was appointed by Congress in 1976 to establish guidelines for the "minimum standards of educational fair use" under the 1976 act. "The CONTU guidelines were developed to assist librarians and copyright proprietors in understanding the amount of photocopying for use in interlibrary loan arrangements permitted under the copyright law." Guidelines were established for copying for interlibrary loan purposes.

1983: Encyclopedia Britannica Educational Corp. v. Crooks

Encyclopedia Britannica sued the Board of Cooperative Educational Services, a consortium of public school districts, for systematically taping educational programs that were broadcast on public television stations and making copies available to member schools. The court found that the actions of the school board would have a detrimental effect on the market of the commercially produced programs and that the use was not a fair use.

1986: Maxtone-Graham v. Burtchaell

Maxtone-Graham wrote a book containing women's stories of unwanted pregnancy and abortion in 1973. She denied Burtchaell's request to use excerpts from her published interviews. He published them anyway. The Second Circuit Court of Appeals found that quoting 4.3% of an author's work was not excessive and that Burtchaell's use of the narratives was a fair use.

1987: Salinger v. Random House

After an initial decision in favor of J.D. Salinger's unauthorized biographer, Ian Hamilton, the Second Circuit Court of Appeals found that quoting or paraphrasing from unpublished materials (Salinger's letters) in an unauthorized biography was not fair use, and the book was never published.

1988: Berne Convention

The United States became a Berne signatory in 1988. The major changes for the U.S. copyright system as a result of Berne were greater protection for proprietors, new copyright relationships with 24 countries, and elimination of the requirement of copyright notice for copyright protection.

1990: Circulation of Computer Software

Congress amended the *Copyright Act* to prohibit commercial lending of computer software. The amendment noted that libraries could lend software, provided the "copy of a computer program which is lent by such library has affixed to the packaging containing the program a warning of copyright." The amendment was a modification of the first sale doctrine.

1991: Basic Books, Inc. v. Kinko's Graphics Corp.

A Federal District Court in New York ruled that Kinko's Graphic Corporation infringed copyrights and did not exercise fair use when it photocopied coursepacks that included book chapters and then sold them to students for class work. The court found that most of the fair use factors worked against Kinko's in this case, especially given Kinko's profit motive in making the copies. Additionally, the court found that the classroom guidelines did not apply to Kinko's. The court did not rule that coursepacks could not constitute fair use in other circumstances.

1991: Feist Publications v. Rural Telephone Service Co., Inc.

The U.S. Supreme Court found that the U.S. Constitution requires that for a work to receive copyright protection, it must reflect creative expression or originality. Thus, the compilation of a telephone directory by Feist was not an infringement even though it was compiled from the information in the Rural Telephone Service White Pages. The information in the white pages was not copyrightable because it comprised "comprehensive collections of facts arranged in conventional formats."

1992: American Geophysical Union v. Texaco

American Geophysical Union v. Texaco resulted from a class-action suit brought by six scientific publishers (on behalf of other publishers registered with the Copyright Clearance Center). In July 1992, a U.S. district judge ruled in the seven-year-old copyright case that a Texaco scientist violated copyright law when he copied complete journal articles without providing the appropriate fee to the publishers. Texaco argued that the copying fell within fair use. The court ruled that the profit motive of the company was a relevant consideration in the analysis of the purpose of the use. They also found against Texaco in considering the amount of the work used and found that the market was affected because Texaco could have paid royalties through the CCC.

In 1994, the Second Circuit Court of Appeals upheld the lower court decision. In April 1995, Texaco petitioned the Supreme Court to review the case. On May 15, 1995, Texaco and a steering committee representing the publishers announced that they had agreed upon terms to settle the case. Texaco, which conceded no wrongdoing in the proposed settlement, paid a seven-figure settlement and retroactive licensing fee to the CCC. In addition, Texaco entered into standard annual license agreements with the CCC over the following five years.

1992: Amendment to Section 304 of Title 17

Congress amended Section 304 of Title 17 making copyright renewal automatic. The amendment dramatically curtailed the entry into the public domain of works protected by copyright before 1978.

1993: Playboy Enterprises Inc. v. Frena

The Florida Northern District Court held that Frena, an electronic bulletin board operator, had violated *Playboy's* copyright when one of its photographs was digitized and placed on the bulletin board system by one subscriber and downloaded by another subscriber. According to the decision, "it does not matter that Defendant Frena may have been unaware of the copyright infringement. Intent to infringe is not needed to find copyright infringement. Intent or knowledge is not an element of infringement, and thus even an innocent infringer is liable for infringement; rather innocence is significant to a trial court when it fixes statutory damages, which is a remedy equitable in nature."

1993: NII Initiative

The Working Group on Intellectual Property Rights was established to explore the application and effectiveness of copyright law and the National Information Infrastructure. The NII was described as "a seamless web of communications networks, computers, databases, and consumer electronics" (Information Infrastructure Task Force, National Telecommunications and Information Administration, *National Information Infrastructure: Agenda for Action,* 1993).

1994: Campbell v. Acuff-Rose Music Inc.

The Supreme Court ruled that 2 Live Crew's parody of Roy Orbison's song, "Pretty Woman," was a fair use. The Court found that a commercial use could be a fair use especially when the markets for an original work and a transformative work are different (Vaidhyanathan, 148-49).

1994: Working Group's Green Paper

The Working Group on Intellectual Property Rights sponsored a series of activities to solicit input on copyright issues and the NII. These included public hearings and, in June 1994, a draft NII report was circulated for comment and review (the *Green Paper*). Part of the review process included three hearings (held in Los Angeles, Chicago, and Washington, DC) hosted by the Working Group, where members of the stakeholder community presented reactions to the *Green Paper*.

1994: CONFU

The Working Group on Intellectual Property Rights sponsored the Conference on Fair Use (CONFU). Established in September 1994, CONFU was the venue for a discussion of issues of fair use in the electronic environment. CONFU participants developed guidelines for fair use of educational multimedia and *proposed* guidelines in a number of areas including interlibrary loan, electronic reserves, digital images, and distance education. According to the final report, issued in 1998, "it was clear that fair use was alive and well in the digital age, and that attempts to draft widely supported guidelines will be complicated by the often competing interests of the copyright owner and user communities."

1995: Religious Technology Center v. Netcom

A federal judge in the Northern District Court of California ruled that Netcom, an Internet Service Provider (ISP), was liable for contributory infringement (as opposed to direct infringement) of copyright because the company did not remove copyrighted materials posted by a subscriber. Justice Whyte found that "mere possession of a digital copy on a [server] that is accessible to some members of the public" may not constitute direct infringement of the exclusive right to publicly distribute and display. The case was significant for its implications for Internet Service Providers' knowledge of and liability for infringers' activities, as well as their use of the fair use doctrine as an affirmative defense against charges of contributory infringement. In 1998, the DMCA limited the liability of "Service Providers" for some forms of infringement. For more information on ISP liability, see the Copyright Crash Course, "Is Your Library an Internet Service Provider Under the DMCA?" *<http://www.utsystem.edu/ogc/intellectualproperty/l-isp.htm>*.

1995: Release of the White Paper

The culmination of the NII Working Group's efforts was release of the *White Paper* in September 1995. The *White Paper* contained recommendations to amend the *Copyright Act of 1976* and presented a lengthy legal analysis of current copyright law. The *White Paper's* legislative amendments and recommendations were introduced in Congress as the *NII Copyright Protection Act of 1995* (S. 1284 and H.R. 2441).

1996: TRIPS Agreement

In December 1994, President Clinton signed the *Uruguay Round Agreements Act (URAA)*, which implemented the *General Agreement on Tariffs and Trade (GATT)* including Trade-Related Aspects of Intellectual Property (TRIPs). Provisions in the URAA amended U.S. copyright law. On January 1, 1996, copyright for works from eligible countries was restored.

1996: Database Protection Legislation

In May 1996, Rep. Carlos Moorhead (Chair, House Judiciary Subcommittee on Courts and Intellectual Property, R-CA) introduced the *Database Investment and Intellectual Property Antipiracy Act of 1996* (H.R. 3531). The legislation was comparable to a European sponsored initiative to protect databases for 15 years from unauthorized extractions of more than an insubstantial part of the database contents. A variety of bills were introduced until 1999. Discussions on this extremely controversial legislation continued throughout 2002, with Congressional staff trying to craft a compromise bill.

1996: Princeton University Press, MacMillan Inc., and St. Martin's Press v. Michigan Document Services, Inc., and James Smith

In November 1996, the Sixth Circuit Court of Appeals decided in an eight to five ruling in favor of publishers who sued Michigan Document Services (MDS). MDS was an off-campus, for-profit photocopy shop whose owner, James Smith, made coursepacks that included substantial portions of copyright protected books and sold them to students. Smith claimed his use of the material was a fair use, and in February 1996, the same court had ruled in his favor. However, in April 1996, the judges of the court voted to rehear the case *en banc,* leading to the November ruling. MDS appealed the case in January 1997; however, the U.S. Supreme Court refused to hear the case.

1996: World Intellectual Property Organization

Delegates from 160 countries considered two treaties on international intellectual property law during a Diplomatic Conference convened in December 1996 in Geneva, Switzerland. The delegates adopted new versions of the proposed treaties resulting in a new approach to copyright issues. The Conference adopted a statement ensuring the two treaties would "permit application of fair use in the digital environment." The treaty language emphasized "the need to maintain a balance between the rights of authors and the larger public interest, particularly education, research, and access to information."

1998: Sonny Bono Copyright Term Extension Act

On October 7, 1998, the House and Senate passed S. 505, the *Copyright Term Extension Act (CTEA).* The law extended protection from life of the author plus 50 years to life of the author plus 70 years. President Clinton signed the measure into law on October 27, 1998 (P.L. 105-298). The law's provisions applied to works under copyright on the date of its implementation. An exception permits libraries, archives, and non-profit educational institutions to treat copyrighted works in their last 20 years of protection as if they were in the public domain for noncommercial purposes, under certain limited conditions. See the ARL Federal Relations site for updates.

1998: Digital Millenium Copyright Act

President Clinton signed the *Digital Millenium Copyright Act (DMCA)* into law on October 28, 1998 (P.L. 105-304). The law's five titles implemented the WIPO Internet Treaties; established safe harbors for online service providers; permitted temporary copies of programs during computer maintenance; made miscellaneous amendments to the *Copyright Act,* including amendments that facilitated Internet broadcasting; and created *sui generis* protection for boat hull designs. A controversial title establishing database protection was omitted by a House-Senate Conference.

Among the most controversial provisions of the DMCA is Section 1201. According to Jonathan Band of Morrison & Foerster, LLP, Section 1201 "prohibits gaining unauthorized access to a work by circumventing a technological protection measure put in place by the copyright owner where such protection measure otherwise effectively controls access to a copyrighted work. This prohibition on unauthorized access takes effect two years after enactment of the DMCA." Over the next two years, the Librarian of Congress conducted a rulemaking proceeding to determine appropriate exceptions to the prohibition. Additional rulemakings will occur every three years.

For more information on the DMCA, please reference:

http://www.arl.org/info/frn/copy/dmca.html

http://www.hrrc.org/html/DMCA-leg-hist.html

1999: Bender v. West Publishing Co.

The U.S. Supreme Court denied *certiorari*, or refused to hear, two cases under appeal by West Publishing Company. By rejecting the request, the Court let stand two decisions by the Second Circuit Court of Appeals in favor of Matthew Bender & Co. and Hyperlaw, Inc.

The Second Circuit Court of Appeals limited the ability of West Publishing Corporation to copyright legal decisions. In two rulings, *Matthew Bender v. West Publishing Co.* and *Matthew Bender Co. and Hyperlaw Inc. v. West Publishing Co. and West Publishing Corporation,* the court determined that the changes that West Publishing made to judicial opinions were not sufficient to warrant additional legal protection of the decisions. The court noted that "all of West's alterations to judicial opinions involve the addition and arrangement of facts, or the rearrangement of data already included in the opinions, and therefore any creativity in these elements of West's case reports lies in West's selection and arrangement of this information. In light of accepted legal conventions and other external constraining factors, West's choices on selection and arrangement can reasonably be viewed as obvious, typical, and lacking even minimal creativity. Therefore, we cannot conclude that the district court clearly erred in finding that those elements that Hyperlaw seeks to copy from West's case reports are not copyrightable, and affirm."

1999: UCITA Passed by NCCUSL

In July 1999, the National Conference of Commissioners on Uniform State Laws (NCCUSL) passed the *Uniform Computer Information Transaction Act* (UCITA, formerly UCC 2B). UCITA is a proposed state law that seeks to create a unified approach to the licensing of software and information.

1999: Digital Theft Deterrence and Copyright Damages Improvement Act of 1999

Congress approved a significant hike in the minimum statutory damages for various types of copyright infringement in the *Digital Theft Deterrence and Copyright Damages Improvement Act of 1999* (H.R. 3456). The law increased the minimum statutory damages for infringements from $500 to $750 and increased the maximum from $20,000 to $30,000. The maximum for willful infringement increased from $100,000 to $150,000.

2000: Virginia Passed UCITA

On March 14, 2000, Governor Jim Gilmore of Virginia signed UCITA into law. Virginia was the first state to approve the legislation. Maryland passed it in April 2000. The highly controversial legislation is under consideration in several state legislatures.

2000: Librarian of Congress Issued Ruling on DMCA

The Anti-Circumvention Provision of the DMCA, Section 1201(a)(1), allows exemptions from the prohibition on circumvention of technological protection measures for "persons who are users of a copyrighted work which is in a particular class of works, if such persons are, or are likely to be . . . adversely affected." Congress directed the Register of Copyrights to review the section and to issue recommendations to the Librarian of Congress on "classes of works" that should be exempt from the ban on circumvention.

Members of the Shared Legal Capability (made up of representatives of the five major library associations: the American Library Association, the American Association of Law Libraries, the Association of Research Libraries, the Medical Library Association, and the Special Libraries Association) had called for a broad exemption from technological protection measures in order to ensure that library users could exercise fair use of protected material. The Assistant Secretary for Commerce, Gregory Rohde, noted that "information crucial to supporting scholarship, research, comment, criticism, new reporting, life-long learning, and other related lawful uses of copyrighted information should never become available only to those with the ability to pay." He called for exemptions "grounded in the principle of fair use" that would allow the public to fully realize their access to lawfully acquired information.

On October 27, 2000, the Librarian of Congress announced the exemption of two narrow classes of works: compilations of lists of Web sites blocked by filtering software applications and literary works, including computer programs and databases, protected by access control mechanisms that fail to permit access because of malfunction, damage, or obsolescence. In issuing the rulemaking, the Librarian of Congress noted several concerns and stated his intent to call upon Congress to reconsider selected aspects of the copyright legislation. In particular, he noted the "potential damage to scholarship" and possible harm to "American creativity" resulting from provisions in the statute.

The full recommendation of the Register of Copyrights and determination of the Librarian of Congress can be found at http://www.loc.gov/copyright/1201/anticirc.html.

2000: Register.com v. Verio

Verio extracted information from the publicly available Register.com WHOIS database for use in telemarketing. In response, Register.com sued Verio and was successful in the New York Southern District Court in December 2000. The judge ordered Verio to stop using customer contact information it had acquired through the WHOIS database for mass marketing purposes. At issue are limits on access to and use of personal information on publicly available online databases.

2001: Greenberg v. National Geographic Society

Two photographers claimed that the inclusion of their photographs in the National Geographic Society's (NGS) CD-ROM version of the NGS magazine violated their copyrights and that the NGS was not exempt under Section 201(c) of the *Copyright Act*. Section 201(c) permits the owner of copyright in a collective work, such as a magazine or encyclopedia, to reproduce and distribute an individual author's freelance contribution "as part of that particular collective work, any revision to that collective work, and any later collective work in the same series."

"The Complete National Geographic," a thirty-disc CD-ROM set, reproduced each monthly issue of the National Geographic magazine from 1888 through 1996. Each NGS magazine included in the CD-ROM is an exact replica of the entire magazine; thus, a user encounters photographs of a freelance author's article in the original context.

2001: New York Times v. Tasini

On June 25, 2001, the U.S. Supreme Court issued its decision in the case of *The New York Times v. Tasini*. In a decisive 7-2 ruling, the Justices upheld an appeals court ruling that the reuse of a freelance author's work on CD-ROMs and in commercial electronic databases without the author's permission constituted copyright infringement. In its ruling, the Court rejected the publishers' argument that a ruling for the authors would have "devastating" consequences, requiring them to delete freelance writers' works in commercial electronic databases. The Supreme Court explicitly noted in its opinion that deletion of the freelance writers' articles was not necessarily the only outcome and that publishers could explore other alternatives. The Justices pointed out that there are "numerous models for distributing copyrighted works and remunerating authors for their distribution" such as the system of blanket performance licenses for musical compositions.

The New York Times now requires permission for electronic republication of works by freelance authors, but this was not standard industry practice until the 1990s. Equally important, implicit in the Court's decision was the recognition that the nation's libraries and archives continue to provide access to the historical record of periodicals and newspapers. In addition, the Court's ruling recognized that certain archival media, such as microfilm and microfiche, do not infringe freelance authors' copyrights. Ultimately, *The New York Times* and other publishers chose to remove the freelance writers' works, as many as 115,000 articles, from Lexis/Nexis and other full-text databases if the writers did not waive their claims for compensation under the decision.

2001: Russian Programmer Arrested for Copyright Circumvention

Among the first challenges to the DMCA was the case of Dmitri Sklyarov, a Russian programmer accused of circumventing copyright protections in Adobe Systems' eBook Reader while working for a Russian software firm, ElcomSoft. Sklyarov was arrested in July 2001. ElcomSoft was charged with one count of conspiracy and four counts of trafficking in technology used to circumvent copyright protections.

On April 2, 2002, Judge Ronald Whyte of the Northern District of California denied a motion to dismiss the prosecution of ElcomSoft. ElcomSoft's attorneys argued that the actions at issue in the case occurred outside of the U.S. and that the law banned tools that consumers could use for legitimate purposes, such as blind people converting e-books to audio files to be read aloud by their computers. Finally, the attorneys argued that computer code is speech and is therefore protected under the first amendment to the U.S. Constitution.

2001: State Sovereign Immunity

According to the Eleventh Amendment to the U.S. Constitution, state entities, including universities and libraries, may not be held liable in federal court cases. After a series of U.S. Supreme Court decisions held that the sovereign immunity clause exempts state entities from adherence to federal intellectual property laws, the Texas Northern District Court took up the question of state immunity from copyright infringement litigation in January 1998. The court concluded that a state agency could not be held liable for copyright infringement in federal court. In April 1998, the Fifth Circuit Court of Appeals affirmed the decision, finding that the University of Houston, a state agency, could not be held liable in federal court for copyright infringements.

On November 1, 2001, Patrick Leahy (Chair, Committee on the Judiciary, D-VT) introduced S. 1611, the *"Intellectual Property Protection Restoration Act of 2001,"* to address what is seen by many as an inequitable situation under which state entities can use federal law to protect their own intellectual property but may infringe the copyright, patent, and trademark laws that protect others' intellectual property. S. 1611 would make the availability of federal intellectual property protection laws contingent upon the voluntary waiver by states of their own immunity from suit under the sovereign immunity clause of the U.S. Constitution.

2002: Consumer Broadband and Digital Television Promotion Act (S. 2048) Introduced in Senate

On March 21, 2002, Sen. Ernest Hollings (Chair, Committee on Commerce, Science, and Transportation, D-SC) introduced the *"Consumer Broadband and Digital Television Promotion Act"* (S. 2048). The goal as stated in the bill is "to regulate interstate commerce in certain devices by providing for private sector development of technological protection measures to be implemented and enforced by Federal regulations to protect digital content and promote broadband, as well as the transition to digital television, and for other purposes." The bill requires that any device that can record, receive, or store copyrighted digital information comply with copy-protections encoded in digital works such as DVDs, CDs, and electronic books.

2002: ABA Issues UCITA Report

The National Conference of Commissioners on Uniform State Laws (NCCUSL), the body that introduced UCITA in 1999 and continues to promote its adoption by state legislatures, met in early August 2002. The UCITA Standby Committee, responsible for drafting UCITA, proposed 38 amendments. Those amendments were adopted despite a lengthy debate in which delegates pushed for additional changes. Forty delegates signed a petition to downgrade UCITA from a "uniform law" to a "model law," a move that would remove NCCUSL's obligation to promote the law in state legislatures. Although the effort was unsuccessful, the debate revealed widespread disenchantment with UCITA within NCCUSL.

On January 31, 2002, the ABA Working Group assigned to review UCITA issued its report to the Board of Governors. UCITA seeks to replace the public law of copyright with the private law of contracts. UCITA was passed by state legislatures in Maryland and Virginia in 2000 but has yet to pass in other states due to significant opposition in the public and private sectors.

As part of the ABA review, NCCUSL, the body responsible for drafting UCITA in 1999, scheduled hearings in fall 2001 and invited interested parties to submit amendments. Representatives from ARL, ALA, and AALL drafted two amendments: 1.) To clarify that terms in non-negotiated licenses would not be enforceable if they prohibited activities normally permissible under federal copyright law; and 2.) To broaden the criteria for declaring such contract terms unenforceable.

2002: U.S. Supreme Court Hears Challenge to 1998 Copyright Term Extension Act

On October 9, 2002, four years after Congress passed the *Sonny Bono Copyright Term Extension Act (CTEA)*, the U.S. Supreme Court heard arguments in a challenge to the Act's constitutionality. Lawrence Lessig, noted legal scholar with the Stanford Law School Center for Internet & Society, represented petitioners in *Eric Eldred v. John Ashcroft*. Passed in October 1998, the CTEA retrospectively extended copyright protection of existing works by 20 years, from the life of the author plus 50 years (as mandated in the 1976 *Copyright Act*) to life of the author plus 70 years. The Act prospectively added 20 years of copyright protection to future works. For works made for hire, the term of protection was extended from 75 to 95 years, thus allowing major corporations such as Disney an additional 20 years of control over their works. In February 2001, a federal appeals court found that retroactive term extensions by Congress were permissible under the Copyright Clause and rejected the argument that the CTEA was unconstitutional. The U.S. Supreme Court is expected to announce a decision in spring 2003.

2002: Senate Approves Distance Education Legislation

The *"Technology Education and Copyright Harmonization Act,"* or the *"TEACH Act"* (S. 287) became law on November 2, 2002. The legislation, supported by members of the higher education and library communities, implements recommendations made by the Copyright Office in 1999. Among the benefits of the Act for distance education are an expansion of the scope of materials that may be used in distance education; the ability to deliver content to students outside the classroom; the opportunity to retain archival copies of course materials on servers; and the authority to convert some works from analog to digital formats. On the other hand, the *TEACH Act* conditions those benefits on compliance with numerous restrictions and limitations. Among them are the need to adopt and disseminate copyright policies and information resources; implementation of technological restrictions on access and copying; adherence to limits on the quantity of certain works that may be digitized and included in distance education; and use of copyrighted materials in the context of "mediated instructional activities" akin in some respects to the conduct of a traditional course.

Additional Reading on Copyrights

1. Patterson, Lyman Ray and Stanley W. Lindberg. *The Nature of Copyright: A Law of Users' Rights.* Athens: University of Georgia Press, 1991.

2. Patterson, Lyman Ray. *Copyright in Historical Perspective.* Nashville: Vanderbilt University Press, 1968.

3. Rose, Mark. *Authors and Owners: The Invention of Copyright.* Cambridge, Mass.: Harvard University Press, 1993.

4. Samuels, Edward. *The Illustrated Story of Copyright.* New York: St. Martin's Press, 2000.

5. Vaidhyanathan, Siva. *Copyrights and Copywrongs: The Rise of Intellectual Property and How It Threatens Creativity.* New York: New York University Press, 2001.

Web Resources on Copyrights

1. Association of Research Libraries, Copyright Web site, <http://www.arl.org/info/frn/copy/copytoc.html>; and Federal Relations E-News Copyright Updates, <http://www.arl.org/info/frn/copy/frncopy.html>.

2. American Library Association, Copyright Web Site, <http://www.ala.org/washoff/copyright.html>.

3. Stanford University Libraries, "Copyright & Fair Use," <http://fairuse.stanford.edu/>.

4. U.S. Copyright Office, "Copyright Law of the United States of America," <http://www.copyright.gov/ title17/>.

5. University of Texas System, "Crash Course in Copyright," <http://www.utsystem.edu/ogc/intellectualproperty/cprtindx.htm>.

The History of Trademarks

The topic of trademark legislation has been an important topic in the United States dating as far back as 1791 when Thomas Jefferson advocated trademark laws. Individual states in the United States then began to pass their own laws (i.e., Michigan in 1842 required that all timber be marked with its origin).

Federal legislation concerning trademarks did not come to pass until July of 1870 with the law on registration of trademarks. This law was soon repealed because it conflicted with Constitutional principals. In 1881, a new law was created, and in 1905, the U.S. Patent and Trademark Office was created, whereby all trademark registrations are (to this day) handled.

TRADEMARKS AND SERVICE MARKS

The symbols (R)—® or TM—™ placed near the trademark indicate that registration is either in force or pending, thus stating that unauthorized use of that mark can lead to legal consequences.

These special symbols warn people that a trademark is registered. A service mark, symbols (SM)—SM—SM, is treated in the same manner as a trademark.

The history of trademarks originates in ancient times. It has, however, been very difficult to determine the exact date when the very first trademark appeared. Although, we know that during the period, 5000 BC, people were creating pottery that had indications of the name of the ruling Chinese emperor, their name as the manufacturer, and information regarding the actual place of creation of the pottery.

When you think about trademarks and their history, consider this: hieroglyphs. As the Hellenistic author, a Greek Egyptian Horapollon, discussed in his book, "*Hieroglyphica*," probably in the fifth century AD, yet this book was published only in the fifteenth century. Horapollon,[7] considered hieroglyphs not as elements of Egyptian language, but as ideograms conveying certain notions. Some of the hieroglyphs from Horapollon's book, for example the Phoenix bird, became a commonplace in emblematic science. As Horapollon describes, demotic script is first encountered at the beginning of the 26th dynasty, in about 660 BC. The writing signs demonstrate the connection with the hieratic script, although the exact relationship is still not yet clear. The demotic characters are more cursive (flowing and joined) and thus more similar to one another, with the result that they are more difficult to read than others. Could this have been the dawning of a trademark in its earliest form, asserting ownership?

Symbolizing and emblematizing were very popular in medieval Europe. In the fifteenth century, the military outfit was very bombastic and rich in emblematical elements: innumerable mottos abundantly decorated the hats, jackets, armors, and the horse harnesses.

Officially in England, they started marking gold and silver in 1300, when King Edward I enacted the law that prohibited jewelers to sell their gold and silver creations without a previous stamping at the Goldsmith's Hall (their office in London); those who tried to counterfeit the hallmarks were sentenced to death.

---

[7] *HORAPOLLON*, of Phaenebythis in the nome of Panopolis in Egypt, Greek grammarian, flourished in the fourth century A.D. during the reign of Theodosius I. According to Suidas, he wrote commentaries on Sophocles, Alcaeus and Homer, and a work on places consecrated to the gods. Photius (cod. 279), who calls him a dramatist as well as a grammarian, ascribes to him a history of the foundation and antiquities of Alexandria (unless this is by an Egyptian of the same name, who lived in the reign of Zeno, 474491). Under the name of Horapollon, two books on Hieroglyphics are extant, which profess to be a translation from an Egyptian original into Greek by a certain Philippus, of whom nothing is known. The inferior Greek of the translation, and the character of the additions in. the second book point to its being of late date. Though a very large proportion of the statements seem absurd and cannot be accounted for by anything known in the latest and most innovative application, there is ample evidence in both the books, in individual cases, that the tradition of the values of the hieroglyphic signs was not yet extinct in the days of their author.

Continuing on this topic, let's explore merchant's marks—these are personal marks that existed since the beginning of the thirteenth century till the end of sixteenth. These marks were widely used by traders and merchants throughout Europe. Merchant's marks can be considered as predecessors of modern trademarks, primarily because they bore names of traders and served as a guaranty that the sold goods were of expected quality. In the fifteenth century, there appeared printer's marks, which were put on books to identify the printer. For example, the famous German printer, Johannes Gutenberg, used the mark representing a double shield, which first appeared in books published in 1462. In the sixteenth century, emblems decorated not only palaces and castles of noblemen, but also inns and taverns, hence were widely used in trade.

The earliest dated printed book known is the "Diamond Sutra," printed in China in 868 CE. It is suspected, however, that book printing may have occurred long before this date. It was in the year 1041 that movable clay type printing was first invented in China. Johannes Gutenberg later invented the printing press with replaceable wooden or metal letters in 1436 (completed by 1440).

The British Parliament adopted the first legislative act concerning trademarks in 1266 under the reign of Henry III, and according to that act, every baker (for example) had to put his or her mark on the breads that were produced.

In Great Britain, the law on registration of trademarks was later enacted on August 13, 1875. This further granted to a trademark holder a monopolistic right for his or her mark and also the right to sue those who infringe upon it. The Department of Registration of Trademarks then opened in London on January 1, 1876. The first registered trademark was the red triangle of the company, "Bass & Co.," which they put on bottles filled with ale.

Although the mark of the "Bass & Co." is still considered to be the oldest registered mark in the world, it was not the first mark among the still existing trademarks. The point here is that the law on registration of trademarks was passed in the U.S. on July 8, 1870, yet marks began registering in the five years prior to 1870.

A pennant with a slogan from the "Averill Chemical Paint Company," which represented an eagle holding in its beak a pot of paint, was the first mark registered in the U.S. However, the Law of 1870 was later repealed as contradicting to the U.S. Constitution; therefore, this first registration was consequently annulled. This new (repealed) law first appeared in 1881.

The trademark of "Pepsi Cola" was registered in 1898, and ever-since, this logo has constantly been changing. The mark has undergone several modifications in the design of typeface. The most notable of these changes occurred in 1905, 1908, and 1940. Then, in 1950, the mark appeared as an image of cap with a logo on it. This cap was then modified several times so that only a circle remained. The final image, the circle, appeared in 1996 transformed into three-dimensional image of a child's ball. Could it be that the developers of this type of symbolism are exploiting our affection for childhood memories and maybe even trying to invoke a subconscious interest?

Heraldry (coat of arms) and heraldic symbols were always in the center of attention—from old ages the displaying of heraldic symbols was seemingly a prerogative of the noble. During times of industrial revolution, there appeared corporate coats of arms, which belonged to guilds of craftsmen.

Among registered trademarks, one can still find many elements of heraldry. Sometimes companies use in their emblems such elements, which are associated with the state emblem. In Russia, for example, there are a lot of trademarks using a stylized double-headed eagle. There is an ambiguous approach to this problem: On the one hand, it is banned to use the state emblem directly; on the other hand, many directors of enterprises are willing to call up associations with state symbols. A possible solution for this dilemma could be a greater degree of stylization of the elements of the coat of arms.

At present special signs warn people that a trademark is registered. The symbols (R)—® or TM—™ placed near the trademark indicate that registration is either in force or pending, thus implying that any unauthorized use of that mark can lead to legal consequences.

In summary, the historical timelines of inventions, patents, copyrights, and trademarks extend far back into ancient history. Since the earliest of times where history can account for the creation or expression of intellectual property, we are able to identify methods of this expression, and protection of these notions of expression.

In the next chapter, we will explore exactly how ideas are formulated, and subsequently, one can begin to look at how to classify these ideas as intellectual property assets.

CHAPTER 2

Formulating the Idea

In order to formulate an inventive idea, you must first identify a problem and then identify a solution to the problem. The solution must be novel in order to be granted a patent. An inventor must apply two tests to determine if the solution is novel:

1. Is this idea one that those *skilled in the art[1]* have **not yet** considered?

2. Is this idea one that those *skilled in the art* **would have[2]** considered?

These two questions have powerful implications when determining if an inventive idea might be granted a patent. The first question tests *novelty* of the inventive idea. The second question tests *non-obvious* aspects of the idea. An inventive idea must pass both tests in order for the idea to be granted a patent.

How does anyone know if they have a valid problem and a solution worthy of a patent? Let's explore a prehistoric invention—fire—to answer this question. The Neanderthal man discovered that fire could solve many problems:

1. Fire provided heat to warm bodies in harsh climate conditions; the problem was that being cold was uncomfortable, and it was discovered that fire emitted heat.

2. Fire burns skin, and with this being discovered by mankind, it causes fear due to this pain. However, due to this pain factor, fire provided a means similar to a weapon, in terms of using it to intimidate and herd animals. With this newly discovered practice,

---

[1] The term *"those skilled in the art have not yet considered"* is key to Intellectual Property Law. Essentially, this means experts have not considered this as a solution.

[2] The question of "would have considered," is very subjective, but suggests that the solution might be obvious to experts and they would have naturally thought of this. The purpose of this test is to establish that the solution is genuinely non-obvious.

man could then force them (through fear) to move to situations causing their death (e.g., driving them over cliffs). The problem invited a solution for hunting food.

3. Fire provided a means for cooking food; the problem was some raw foods were non-palatable, and oddly enough, seemed to have rendered more flavor when heated or cooked.

4. Fire provided a means to see in the dark; the problem was not being able to see in the dark.

5. Fire provided a means to create a charred-coal type or material from wood. This provided for the ability to use this newly discovered dark material for writing symbols and marking on cave walls, a new form of graphical communications. Henceforth, allowing for early mankind to have the capability to mark up, or "trademark," a cave wall or pyramid, thereby stating ownership and certain rights expressed in the hieroglyphics left on the cave walls. The problem this solved was related to not having a satisfactory written means of graphical communications, and expression of thought.

Fire solved problems that those skilled in the art at that time had not yet considered. Were each of these solutions turned into a patent? No—because there was no patent process available; however, fire was an invention.

AN ENGINEERING INNOVATION

An engineering innovation is sometimes mistakenly considered as an invention by new inventors. That is, taking something and figuring out very creative ways to use it, yet using it in the ways that the item (or idea) was intended to be utilized. Compunded with the more obscure drawback, it is likely obvious that the experts would have eventually figured this particular innovation out? If an idea expresses forms of the obvious, it can quickly take on the classification of an engineering innovation.

It is common to confuse this with a patent.

Let's take a closer look at this example. Are these examples of the uses of fire able to show us the difference between an engineering innovation and an invention? An engineering innovation is taking something and figuring out a very creative way to use it, yet using it in the way that the item (or idea) was intended to be utilized. A patent is related to a new idea, using it in ways that those skilled in the art have not yet considered and in non-obvious ways. So was fire used exactly as intended by mankind in prehistoric days? Or, in these examples, was fire used beyond what those skilled in the art might have originally considered?

The discoveries we have just discussed involving fire included a means to warm the body, prepare food, hunt food, fight, provide light to see in dark periods, and communicate. Of course, consider a lightning strike somewhere, which would have obviously shown early mankind the values and effects of fire. One could again argue, however, that the expression of an idea to chase animals over cliffs in order to lead them to their death for purposes of harvesting food—the argument being that this method of hunting was a non-obvious expression of the ideas surrounding fire. This might then constitute the worthiness of a patent (had there been a process during this prehistoric period). Warmth would have also been discovered by anyone including those skilled in the art of fire, simply by stepping within close-range of a fire. The same concepts apply in using charcoal for written communications; it expresses a new and unique idea. Charcoal, created from wood by-products following a fire is a method or expression of it.

An interesting point here is that fire is too broad to be patented; it is not a unique idea. The expressions of the idea and the claims on *how* to use it, however, would be unique, and thus possibly worthy of patent considerations.

Several forms of ideas require special types of attention and protection. For example, copyrights are simple to file and will last from 95 years to 120 years after the inventor's death. If you are the originator of an expression, or a piece of text, you own the copyright. The idea expressed, however, is not protected by the copyright.

A *patent* protects the expressed idea, but there is a procedure to obtain a patent. First, it has to be novel, non-obvious, and useful. Patents last for 20 years and can cost (in the U.S.) from $280 USD to $50,000 USD to file and obtain. There are also patents related to government secrets and/or military secrets, which are handled in very sensitive ways, different from the normal patent process. However, these types of government and military patents are beyond the scope of this book.

Sometimes, litigation costs can far exceed the costs of filing the patent, especially in the case of very high-value patents. The competitive nature of a high-value patent versus a low-value patent invites some intellectual property rights management situations to occur, depending on the strength of the "*claims and teachings*." Obviously, a high-value patent is far more valuable to protect than a low-value patent; a high-value patent may, therefore, be more volatile toward a state of litigations than a low-value patent would be. The claims serve as the basis for any breach of invention ideas, so it is very important how exact the patent claims are written.

Patent claims are written using a specific language[3] style and usually constructed by a patent attorney, or a patent engineer. As a simple example, we might "claim" a vehicle as a unit comprising

1. A chassis

2. A petroleum and/or electric engine connected to the chassis

3. A set of four wheels connected to the chassis and engaged responsive to operations from the gas and/or electric engine

---

[3] TIP: This can be general discussion of the problem, solution, and novelty of an algorithm in a pseudo language of a sort (like items 1–3 in the list). You are not required to supply any "codes" to file a patent; simply identify the problem and the solution, and then begin to explain the logic (if a software program) so a programmer can later write the codes.

There is no specific number of claims that need to be associated with an invention idea; rather, the legal counsel determines the appropriate number. Numbers of claims are always proportionate to the breadth and depth of the idea being described. It is the "claims" that are contested in a court of law regarding infringement on an idea. An infringing device embodies (at least) each and every element and function of the claim. Therefore, infringement would have to invalidate each and every claim, so there is a legal advantage to making broad claims. The goal is to have the broadest claims you establish.

Trade secrets are free to establish and will endure until someone discovers it. A trade secret is a secret you keep and hence has no official status or public view. The recipe for Coke or the recipe for Campbell's Tomato Soup are typical examples of a trade secrets. Only a very few employees of these companies know the secret, and usually the secret is held in high confidence within the company claiming the trade secret.

Registering a trademark can officially protect names, acronyms, or symbols that identify products. Try checking your favorite cereal box or beverage for as many trademark symbols (™) as you can find. Just like copyrights and patents, trademarks can also be licensed and sold. Trademark searches can be performed at numerous sites; one primary site for this is the U.S. Patent and Trademark Office.[4]

Let's take a closer look at the different types of intellectual property and how compare to each other (see Figure 2-1). A copyright simply protects the expression of an idea; a patent protects the idea. A trade secret is an idea that is protected but only if maintained as a secret. A trademark protects the name or the symbol being use and officially restricts its use to the owner.

What Are the Differences?
Copyrights, Trade Secrets, and Trademarks Yield Different Protection

Copyright	Protects the expression of an idea.
Patent	Protects the idea.
Trade Secret	Idea is protected but only if maintained as a trade secret.
Trademark	Protects the name or a symbol identifying a product or a service, officially registered and legally restricted to the use of the owner.

Figure 2-1 Common forms of global intellectual property classifications.

---

[4]   For more information, please reference http://www.uspto.gov.

Ideas: Are They Copyrights, Patents, Trademarks, Trade Secrets, or Engineering Innovations?

There are significant differences in how you must consider new ideas and set forth to manage these innovations in a safe and proper manner.

This section explores the differences of idea formulation as it relates to copyrights, patents, trademarks, trade secrets, and engineering innovations. These are forms of intellectual property, and each is managed in different ways.

Copyrights

Copyright is a form of protection provided by the laws of the United States (title 17, U.S. Code) to the authors of "original works of authorship," including literary, dramatic, musical, artistic, and certain other intellectual works. This protection is available to both published and unpublished works. Section 106 of the *1976 Copyright Act* generally gives the owner of copyright the exclusive right to do and to authorize others to do the following:

- To *reproduce* the work in copies or phonorecords
- To prepare *derivative works* based upon the work
- *To distribute copies or phonorecords* of the work to the public by sale or other transfer of ownership or by rental, lease, or lending
- To perform the work publicly, in the case of literary, musical, dramatic, and choreographic works, pantomimes, and motion pictures and other audiovisual works
- To display the copyrighted work publicly in the case of literary, musical, dramatic, and choreographic works, pantomimes, and pictorial, graphic, or sculptural works, including the individual images of a motion picture or other audiovisual work
- In the case of *sound recordings, to perform the work publicly* by means of a *digital audio transmission*

In addition to this, certain authors of works of visual art have the rights of attribution and integrity, as described in section 106A of the *1976 Copyright Act*. For further information, request Circular 40, "Copyright Registration for Works of the Visual Arts."

It is illegal for anyone to violate any of the rights provided by the copyright law to the owner of a copyright. These rights, however, are not unlimited in scope. Sections 107 through 121 of the *1976 Copyright Act* establish limitations on these rights. In some cases, these limitations are specified exemptions from copyright liability. One major limitation is the doctrine of "fair use," which is given a statutory basis in section 107 of the 1976 Copyright Act. In other instances, the limitation takes the form of a "compulsory license" under which certain limited uses of copyrighted works are permitted upon payment of specified royalties and compliance with statutory conditions. For further information about the limitations of any of these rights, consult the copyright law or write to the United States Copyright Office.

The validity of a copyright, according to the United States Copyright Office, is defined as work that is created (fixed in tangible form for the first time) on or after January 1, 1978, is automatically protected from the moment of its creation and is ordinarily given a term enduring for the author's life plus an additional 70 years after the author's death. In the case of "a joint work prepared by two or more authors who did not work for hire," the term lasts for 70 years after the last surviving author's death. For works made for hire and for anonymous and pseudonymous works (unless the author's identity is revealed in Copyright Office records), the duration of copyright will be 95 years from publication or one 120 years from creation, whichever is the shorter time period.

The way in which copyright protection is secured is frequently misunderstood. No publication or registration or other action in the Copyright Office is required to secure copyright. There are, however, certain definite advantages to registration.

Copyright is secured automatically when the work is created, and a work is "created" when it is fixed in a copy or phonorecords for the first time. "Copies" are material objects from which a work can be read or visually perceived either directly or with the aid of a machine or device, such as books, manuscripts, sheet music, film, videotape, or microfilm. "Phonorecords" are material objects embodying fixations of sounds (excluding, by statutory definition, motion picture soundtracks), such as cassette tapes, CDs, or LPs. Thus, for example, a song (the "work") can be fixed in sheet music ("copies") or in phonograph disks ("phonorecords"), or both.

If a work is prepared over a period of time, the part of the work that is fixed on a particular date constitutes the created work as of that date.

As we can see, the copyright laws are broad, yet a widely used in protecting intellectual property. However, copyright does not and should not be confused with the patent process. The patent and trademark processes are distinctly different from the copyright process and should be utilized carefully, depending on the nature of the intellectual property one is trying to protect.

Patents

A patent for an invention is the grant of a property right to the inventor, issued by the Patent and Trademark Office. The term of a new patent is 20 years from the date on which the application for the patent was filed in the United States or, in special cases, from the date an earlier related application was filed, subject to the payment of maintenance fees. U.S. patent grants are effective only within the U.S., U.S. territories, and U.S. possessions.

The right conferred by the patent grant is, in the language of the statute and of the grant itself, "the right to exclude others from making, using, offering for sale, or selling" the invention in the United States or "importing" the invention into the United States. What is granted is not the right to make, use, offer for sale, sell or import, but the right to exclude others from doing so.

The preceding is the official view of the foremost patent authority in the United States, the U.S. Patents and Trademarks Office.[5] In the later sections of this chapter, we will begin to explore a unique intellectual exercise of creating a new idea, hopefully to become worthy of

---

[5]   For more information, please reference http://www.uspto.gov.

patent considerations, once you finish this book. We will then explore even deeper aspects of this new patent idea in Chapter 3, "Search Strategies, Techniques, and Search Tools to Validate the Uniqueness of any Invention."

Trademarks

A trademark is a word, phrase, slogan, design, or symbol that is used to identify and distinguish merchandise from competing products. Let's explore trademarks by creating a new drink by mixing water, carbonation, sweetener, and food coloring. We'll call it Coke™—a new type of a drink.

The idea to recreate this new drink is fine, but the choice of naming it Coke™ is illegal because the name is a trademark of the Coca-Cola Company and thereby protected by trademark laws. A trademark is a formalized protection practice generally found in cases where advertising and marketing investments surround the particular brand name of a product. For reasons related to competition, a company chooses to protect its own product brand through establishing a trademark.

The differences between Coke™ and Pepsi™ is more than trademark. The difference is also with the trade secret recipes that are used to make each product. A trade secret cannot be patented because claims and teaching requirements of the patent process would divulge the trade secret.

Suppose you wanted to build a specialized biometric or life sciences computers or offer advanced forms of biometric healthcare services. You want to call your company Interpretive Biometric Machines. This name is fine; however, using the acronym IBM isn't a good thing because the acronym violates IBM's trademark.

According to the United States Patents and Trademark Office, a *trademark* is a word, name, symbol, or device, which is used in trade with goods to indicate the source of the goods and to distinguish them from the goods of others. A *service mark* is the same as a trademark, except that it identifies and distinguishes the source of a service rather than a product. The terms "trademark" and "mark" are commonly used to refer to both trademarks and servicemarks.

Trademark rights may be used to prevent others from using a confusingly similar mark but not to prevent others from making the same goods or from selling the same goods or services under a clearly different mark. Trademarks, which are used in interstate or foreign commerce, may be registered with the Patent and Trademark Office.

A trademark is a formalized protection practice generally found in cases where advertising and marketing investments surround the particular brand name of a product. For reasons related to competition, a company chooses to protect its own product brand through establishing a trademark. For more detailed information on this topic, please refer to the following resources:

- United States Trademark Law—An overview, from the Legal Information Institute, Cornell Law School, http://www.law.cornell.edu/topics/trademark.html.

- United States House of Representatives Internet Law Library— Trademarks—A collection of trademark links created for the *U.S. House of Representatives Internet Law Library* and now archived by the LawGuru.com site. All About Trademarks appears in this collection, http://www.lawguru.com.

- USPTO Trademark FAQ—Frequently asked questions about trademarks and U.S. trademark applications, from the United States Patent and Trademark Office, http://www.uspto.gov/web/offices/tac/tmfaq.htm.

- Trademark Basics—Fundamental information concerning marks, including a trademark FAQ, and links to current articles, published by INTA®—the *International Trademark Association*, http://www.inta.org/basics/index.shtml.

- Nolo's Legal Encyclopedia—Trademarks and Copyrights—Basic trademark information (and more) from the Editors at Nolo Press, http://www.nolo.com/category/tc_home.html.

- Trademarks and Business Goodwill—An excellent discussion of what trademarks are; what trademarks are not; why marks are important, and how to choose a "good" mark, by Thomas G. Field, Jr., a Professor at the Franklin Pierce Law Center, http://www.fplc.edu/tfield/Trademk.htm.

- The Intellectual Property Information Mall—Trademark information shopping at the Franklin Pierce Law Center, http://www.ipmall.fplc.edu.

- Yahoo's Trademark List—General trademark links http://www.yahoo.com/Law/Intellectual_Property/Trademarks.

- CataLaw's Trademark Law Links—A collection of links related to trademark, media, and advertising law from CataLaw, a meta-index of law "catalogs" on the Web, http://www.catalaw.com/topics/IP.shtml.

One final point that should be clear is that a trademark extends globally and is protected by international laws.

Trade Secrets

In most states in the U.S., a trade secret may consist of any formula, pattern, physical device, idea, process, or compilation of information that both

- Provides the owner of the information with a competitive advantage in the marketplace
- Is treated in a way that can reasonably be expected to prevent the public or competitors from learning about it, absent improper acquisition or theft

Some examples of potential trade secrets are a formula for a sports drink, survey methods used by professional pollsters, recipes, a new invention for which a patent application has not yet been filed, marketing strategies, manufacturing techniques, and computer algorithms. Unlike other forms of intellectual property, such as patents, copyrights, and trademarks, trade secrecy is basically a do-it-yourself form of protection. You do not register with the government to secure your trade secret; you simply keep the information confidential (a secret). Trade secret protection lasts for as long as the secret is kept confidential. Once a trade secret is made available to the public, trade secret protection (obviously) ends.

Trade secrets often protect valuable technical information that cannot be sheltered under other forms of intellectual property law, such as the formula for Coke.

Engineering Innovations

An *engineering innovation* is the art of creating something that is very innovative, but fortunately or unfortunately, this "something" was created utilizing tools, products, and/or practices in ways this "something" is intended to be utilized for implementations. That is, one utilizes concepts and products in the way that they were intended to be applied and can often come up with very innovative ideas. This may or may not qualify as a patent, based on the novelty and non-obvious tests we have previously discussed.

Problem, Solution, and Novelty and Uniqueness Test

A patent is generally divided into three separate areas: An identifiable problem, a unique solution, and a solution that is novel and non-obvious. This test of being "non-obvious" implies that those skilled in the art would not have naturally thought about this idea.

Perhaps it's a clear and beautiful day in your area. You are relaxing, listening to the daily news on the television as you read this book. Suddenly, a commercial on the television appears within range of your hearing. It is distracting, and you feel like the topic is playing on your intelligence. To many, this is a problem. It is highly probable that many others also can relate to this problem. So let's try to stay with this example for a few chapters and see what we can discover in terms of inventions.

This commercial you may now be in range of is far less than pleasant to listen to, especially while you are trying to think in parallel through this line of thought. Here, you were simply trying to concentrate, while comfortably listening to the news in the background, and this obtrusive commercial on television broke your thought train. What an annoyance, but look closely at the situation. This seems to be the easiest time to invent, when something annoys you and you are able to find a better answer to the problem than what is available today. So you then ask yourself: What might be done to provide an innovative solution to this problem? You also wondered (some lateral thinking) if this holds true with radio as well, but simply leave that thought for now and focus on the TV.

PROBLEM...

Television commercials are sometimes less than desirable for a multitude of reasons, and consumers should be able to choose their own content of advertising.

A second aspect of this problem is that the viewing audience has little to no say as to what network providers serving advertising to viewers transmit on their channels—as it is relates to content.

I could no doubt fix this problem if, on my channel operating device (mine is handheld, but the device could be of many types), I had a one-touch button I could press as soon as I first noted the undesirable commercial. I could press this button just once to begin program sequence to leave this commercial behind, and from then on, my invention would tell my TV to switch every time this commercial comes on my set. For that matter, any commercial I do not want to watch again, I could reprogram to my choice, each time the commercial appears for the first time—never to see it again.

So, let's see...I could press this button and automatically program a path away from this commercial, forever, if I chose to do so. I also could select an alternate switch path, should my first choice channel redirect also have an undesirable commercial on it. But, we then ask ourselves, is this a violation of "rights" or privilege of any sort? In America, freedom of speech is one principle that stands strong. Therefore, commercial advertisers always will have the right to produce content as they wish—as do the networks have the freedom to transmit this content. That is, of course, within the boundaries of Federal Communications Commission laws.

Whatever we end up inventing must have benefits for all three sides, the consumers, the advertisers, and the networks. Yet it is the consumer who is the target of this advertising; therefore, we should enjoy the freedom to pick and chose what advertising content and advertisers we wish to receive.

The solution: How would we do this? We know or can research that a television commercial is delivered to a television set, through a network, probably through some means of network packets. We can assume that a packet has a "header" and a "trailer." And, in this header, the identification of the commercial is data that is known, as is the time or duration of the advertisement. So, in theory, I could change to a different channel as soon as the ID of the undesirable commercial is confirmed and then return to that channel I was watching at the end of the undesirable commercial slot. All this could be done automatically, once programmed into this new invention, the one-touch device.

Now once we convince ourselves this idea might be worth looking into, we want to next make sure that to the best of our knowledge, no one else has thought of this or, if they have thought of this, we are willing and able to invent a way around their prior art in order to create a stronger, yet unique invention of our own. Perhaps I may even reference their ideas in order to establish the grounds of novelty in my idea.

The first step we engaged is a problem in need of a solution. At this stage, there are a few documentation items one may want to consider. What is the problem solved by this new invention? Describe it in clear, concise, hard-hitting, and easy-to-understand terms. Describe known solutions to this problem (if any). Describe the drawbacks of such known solutions or why an additional solution is required. Cite any relevant technical documents, prior art, or references. Explain where the technologies seem to be headed in the areas of your idea.

Next, briefly describe the core idea of your invention (saving the details for the final discussions). Describe the advantages of using your invention, as opposed to using the other known solutions. Review this level of understanding; think in terms of the understanding levels of your audience (e.g., patent engineers and patent attorneys) to make sure they understand what you are describing. Tell them what you have told them for sake of clarity.

Describe how your invention works and how it could be implemented, using textual descriptions, illustrations, and process-flow charts (as appropriate). Focus[6] on the novel aspects of your invention. Resist the urge to begin to wander about marketing aspects of the idea or maybe how something else might do it another way. Focus, focus, focus on your idea and its novelty.

Now that you have focused tightly on the new idea, you might want to consider what is known as the "elevator" presentation style. That is, pretend you are on an elevator (or lift) and, from the first floor, you have pressed the third floor button. You now have to explain to someone your idea so this person understands it before the doors open at the third floor. When a patent attorney first hears your idea, the speed at which he or she can grasp the uniqueness of the idea all depends on how well *you* explain it.

Be prepared to clearly present and defend your idea in a short period of time. Any patent evaluator appreciates a concise, hard-hitting, to-the-point description of new inventions. To be able to explain the problem, the solution, the novelty, and why it is not obvious to those persons skilled in the art is fundamental to being able to sell your idea and getting it properly documented in terms of claims & teachings.

The novelty in the patent is proven by a contrast to that of prior art, in conjunction with clear discussions on how the solution solves the problem. We will explore these aspects in Chapter 3 in greater detail.

Think Beyond Those "Skilled in the Art"

Those "skilled in the art" is an interesting concept relating to expertise. This concept is well known in patent engineering and intellectual property law circles. This phrase simply means that the experts have not yet thought about it.

So how do you take it beyond what those skilled in the art have considered? It is actually often times rather simple to do once you have mastered the skill and, of course, depending on the prior art claims.

Once you determine that the idea is one that the experts have not yet considered, you step back and ask yourself if your idea is obvious to the experts. If it seems that it might be obvious to them, then is it probable they would have thought about it or easily could in the future—which presents problems to any new invention. If this is so, you then need to strengthen your idea and find novelty those skilled in the art would not have obviously considered. If you decide your idea is not obvious to those skilled in the art, you next need to search to find other inventions that may have something close to what you are thinking. This is referred to as "prior art."

---

[6]   TIP: If you can establish an algorithm in your invention, document this algorithm in the write-ups and use a pseudo code descriptive language to explain this algorithm. Often times, generically described algorithms can be utilized as a part of the licensing claims of the patent.

Search using Internet search engines. Creative detailed strategies for searching prior inventions are described in the next chapter of this book, and "prior art" searches are further described in greater details in Chapter 4, "Invention Teams."

Search. Strengthen. Apply forms of "lateral thinking." Think of every possible word that might represent your idea. Take these words and use them as keywords and perform keyword searches on the best-known search engines of your choice. The Google search engine (http://www.google.com) is a good place to search, and the U.S. Patents and Trademarks Office (USPTO) patent search engine facility (http://www.uspto.gov) is a powerful U.S. patents repository for prior art information.

Save references of everything you find that is close to your idea. Be prepared to defend your idea against this newly found prior art and why your idea is different. Any reports, Web sites, books, magazines, and/or documents that discuss aspects of your concepts are also critical and should be considered "prior art."

Locate and compare other similar ideas. Find previous ideas similar to yours but seek to find the unique differences. When you find other ideas that are similar, capture the patent number, the book reference, the report information, and the source of information where the "other" idea can be found. This is proof of the prior art, and it shows the professionalism of the inventor when much of this research has been performed. Finding prior art that has some similarities to your idea (though your idea may have clear and unique differences) is a positive and reinforcing situation for your invention.

Inventors, patent attorneys, and patent agents are obligated to disclose any and all prior art they may be aware of, discovered as a part of their own patents research on the new idea (or current art). Being able to contrast your idea, the current art, to that of any prior art is very important. This is also a fundamental critical-skill of any inventor.

Management of Innovation

The existence of prior art can be a good problem to have. Inventors must openly disclose any prior art they are aware of when they submit inventions. Having prior inventions in areas that are close to your ideas is a good for reasons of endorsement and validation of your idea, but (as we previously mentioned) inventors must now be able to strengthen their idea beyond the prior art. Find ways that your idea is truly unique from the prior art and explain this in writing. State the identification of the prior art; the differences your idea expresses from that of the prior art. This will be extremely helpful towards validating your idea.

Ensure there is a problem you are trying to solve with your idea and that it is the problem you started out trying to solve. Make sure that your solution has significance towards resolving the problem you have identified. At this juncture, you can (in some ways) determine the high/low-value aspects of the new idea and maybe even speculate on the value as it might pertain to justifying a business reason for the idea. A high-value idea would be one that applies to many, and many would be interested in your solution. Sometimes, high-value ideas have associated with them more increased legal expenses, and in fact, sometimes budgets for defending these ideas are set aside, early-on in corporations.

In contrast to the high-value idea is the low-value idea. A low-value idea, of course, has less of a payback than a high-value idea, but nonetheless has a unique value.

Patents are thought of as intellectual property assets, which are (in fact) almost always commercialized with a monetary value. These commercialized assets can now be purchased, exchanged, or traded in complex business negotiations. Patents also can be established to block someone else from gaining a patent on an idea in a specific area. These are referred to as *blocking patents*.

Innovation can be managed in many ways, depending on the strategy and goal. Project where the technology is going in the area(s) of your invention idea and be prepared to discuss where in that continuum your invention idea lies. Understand that it takes (in some cases) years to process a patent submission, so ensure your idea has a "shelf-life" of more than two to three years. Finally, if you want to become an avid inventor, work to establish many inventions across a wide area of interests. Keep a portfolio of your ideas, as one idea may one day lead to another.

Be able to describe your innovation in forms of process flow diagrams, presenting a step-wise discussion of how the novelty occurs in the solution. And finally, consider the problem statement to be absolutely critical. As we mentioned, every invention has to solve a problem, and inventors need to be crystal clear on the problem their invention solves and why it is unique from everything else considered by experts in the field.

The next chapter explores specific "search" strategies to help inventors determine what has and has not been submitted as inventions in the past. Creating inventions that embellish prior art from openly-disclosed pieces of intellectual capital, has to be done in the proper manner. Identifying this information is the first step in this process. We will show you specific research tips on how to construct the most powerful search (syntax) keyword combinations. We will also show you Web sites to execute these types of searches and how to document the results of this important research.

The strategies you choose to use for researching and formulating your invention and comparing it to prior art are very important, as we will explain in the next chapter. We will conclude the following chapter with a fascinating experiment in creating a real invention, searching for prior art, and strengthening to get around some prior art, in order to finally create a new a unique invention. Sit back, relax, and enjoy this next very unique approach to describing how to create a patent.

Search Strategies, Techniques, and Search Tools to Validate the Uniqueness of Any Invention

The invention idea has to be tested against other ideas that may be similar. In order to best do this, it is very important to understand elements of Internet search engine strategies. These searches are commonly referred to as "prior art" searches. The search will resolve that there are or are not any infringing ideas. One needs to make sure the ideas have not yet been previously claimed or implemented.

There are a variety of search engine methods, effective Internet search strategies, syntactical schemes for performing simple or complicated searches, and methods of contrasting these results to the current invention. This new invention or even trademark that the inventor has in mind is often referred to as the "current art."

In this chapter, you'll learn about search strategies and techniques used to validate an inventor's current art and how to search using Boolean operators, phrases, and the unique benefit of using quotation marks.

Finding information on the Internet can seem difficult and overwhelming. Internet search engines perform searches but often return thousands of Web pages. Without a clear Web search strategy, using any search engine can be like wandering aimlessly in the stacks of a library trying to find a particular a word or passage in a book.

Successful searching involves two key steps. First, you must have a clear understanding of *how* to prepare your search. You must be able identify the main concepts in your topic and determine any synonyms, acronyms, alternate spellings, or variant word forms for the main concepts.

In this chapter, you'll learn an easy-to-follow process for using search engines and locating subject directories for finding what you need on the Internet. You'll also explore creative search strategies on how to use the various search engine tools that are available on the Internet. Search engines such as Google, Yahoo!, Kartoo, and AltaVista are very powerful and capable of finding any information that may exist on the Web.

Here's what you learn how to do in this chapter:

- Use subject directories and describe the differences between a subject directory and a search engine
- Use implied and full Boolean search logic, phrase searching, truncation, and field searching effectively
- Identify key concepts, synonyms, and variant word forms in your search topics
- Use key search engines effectively
- Use meta-search engines effectively
- Use specialty databases when appropriate

Although all search engines do the same task, some do it in different ways, which might yield some differences in results. Nonetheless, all search engines are working from the content found on the Web.

A *subject directory* is a catalog type of search engine, consisting of sites collected and organized by employees of the search engine company. The popular search site called "Yahoo!"[1] is a well-known example of a subject directory search site. Subject directories are often called subject "trees" because they start with a few main categories and then branch out into subcategories, topics, and subtopics. Yet, some terms are not intuitively listed in the directory listing.

For example, trying to find the term "inventions" in the Yahoo! directories listing is not easy to do. However, unlike some other directory engines, in the Yahoo! search engine, you also may submit a keyword such as "inventions," which will find the subject of inventions somewhere in their directories, even though this topic is not explicitly shown in the directory list shown on the Yahoo! homepage.

Yet some subjects are actually quite simple and straightforward to find using the directories. For example, to locate the homepage for the New York Yankees at Yahoo!, select "Recreation & Sports" at the top level, "Sports" at the next level, "Baseball" at the third level, "Major League Baseball" at the fourth level, "Teams" at the fifth level, then finally "New York Yankees."

In subject directories, you can often find a good starting point if your topic is included. Directories are also useful for finding information on a topic when you do not have a precise idea of what you need. Many large directories include a keyword search option (e.g., Yahoo!), which usually eliminates the need to work through numerous levels of topics and subtopics potentially found as the result of a keyword search.

Because directories cover only a small fraction of the pages available on the Web, they are most effective for finding general information on popular or scholarly subjects. If you are looking for something more specific, use a search engine's keyword search capability.

---

[1]   For more information, please reference http://www.yahoo.com.

The Yahoo! and Google search engine services are two of the largest subject directories on the Internet, and these are excellent sites for finding topics that appeal to the general public.

For other types of very powerful search engines, try Google or the LookSmart site—other great directories for locating popular sites. The OpenDirectory site lists scholarly and popular Web sites. At About.com, you will find a directory with a unique function: Each topic area has an assigned "Guide" responsible for writing articles and organizing links on the topic one is seeking.

Another unique search service is the Kartoo.com site, where one is able to develop knowledge maps according to topics. Three other useful directories for scholarly research are the Internet Public Library, the Librarians' Index to the Internet, and The WWW Virtual Library.

All of the following sites are excellent examples of Internet search and directory services:

- The Yahoo! search engine site service at http://www.yahoo.com
- The Google search engine site service at http://www.google.com
- The Kartoo search site service[2] at http://www.kartoo.com
- The LookSmart site service at http://www.looksmart.com
- The OpenDirectory site service at http://www.dmoz.org
- The About site service at http://www.about.com
- The Internet Public Library site service at http://www.ipl.org/ref
- The Librarians' Index to the Internet site service at http://www.lii.org
- The WWW Virtual Library site service at http://www.vlib.org/overview.html

Search Engines

The way that some search engines work is very different from subject directory types of search engines. While humans often times organize and catalog subject directories around topics, some search engines rely on computer programs called spiders or robots (a jargon term is bots) to "crawl" the Web and automatically log the words on each page. This is very different from relying on a directory structure to locate information.

With this type of search engine, keywords related to a topic are typed into a search "box." The search engine then typically scans its database and returns a file with links to Web sites containing the word or words specified. Because these databases are very large, search engines often return thousands of results. Without search strategies or techniques, finding what you need will be like finding a needle in a haystack.

---

[2] Kartoo has a unique graphical user interface, search refinement scheme, and search results method; it is worth checking out.

A *search engine* is a searchable database of Internet files collected by a computer program, typically called a wanderer, crawler, robot, bot, worm, or spider. Indexing is created from the collected files, for example, title, full text, size, URL, and so on. There are no selection criteria for the collection of files, though evaluation can be applied to ranking schemes that return the results of a query.

A search engine might be called a search engine service or a search service. As such, this dynamic type of search engine consists of three main components:

- *Spider*: Program that traverses the Web from link-to-link, identifying and reading pages
- *Index*: Database containing a copy of each Web page gathered by the spider
- *Search and retrieval mechanism*: Technology that enables users to query the index and that returns results in a schematic order

There are two major types of commercial search engines:

- *Individual*: An individual engine that utilizes a spider to collect its own searchable index—also, directory search engines consisting of directories and sub-directories assembled by search engine company staff.
- *Meta*: A meta-search engine that simultaneously searches multiple individual search engines. A meta-search engine does not have its own index but uses the indexes collected by the spiders of other search engines. This type of engine is covered later in this chapter under the section "Meta-Search Engines."

To use search engines efficiently, it is essential to apply techniques that narrow the search results and push the most relevant pages to the top of the results list. In the next section, there are a number of strategies for finding what you need quickly and boosting your overall search engine performance.

Identify Keywords

When conducting an Internet search, decompose the search topic into key linguistic concepts (i.e., words and/or phrases). A standard language for performing searches and connecting words and phrases in a search command is known as the *Boolean* operator language. The Boolean operators, AND, OR, NOT (or AND NOT), and NEAR tell search engines which keywords you want your results to include or exclude and whether you require that your keywords appear close to each other.

They are named after George Boole, an Englishman who invented these operators as part of a system of logic in the mid-1800s. (If he could only see what his logic language invention is being used for today.)

Since the Boolean operators are simple English words, they are intuitive, easy to utilize, and even simple to remember—that is, for those individuals able to speak the English language. For example, to find information on what is known about blocking television commercials in the communications industry, a set of primary search keywords might be

television commercial blocking

Boolean AND

Connecting search terms with the AND Boolean operator tells the search engine to retrieve Web pages containing ALL the keywords:

> television AND commercial AND blocking

The search engine will not return pages with just the word television. Neither will it return pages with the word commercial and the word blocking. The search engine will only return pages where the words television, commercial, and blocking appear. These words must all appear somewhere on the page. Thus, the AND operator helps to narrow the search results as it limits the results to pages where all the keywords appear.

Boolean OR

Linking search terms with an OR operator tells the search engine to retrieve Web pages containing ANY and ALL keywords instances:

> television OR commercial OR blocking

When an OR operator is used, the search engine returns pages with a single keyword, several keywords, and all keywords. Thus, OR expands your search results. Use OR when you have common synonyms for a keyword. Surround the entire OR expressions with parentheses for best results. To narrow results as much as possible, combine OR statements with AND statements. For example, the following search statement locates information on television commercial blocking capabilities:

> television AND (commercial OR advertisement) AND (blocking OR filter)

Boolean AND NOT

The AND NOT operator tells the search engine to retrieve Web pages containing one keyword but not the other:

> television AND commercial AND blocker AND NOT (vchip OR "v-chip")

This example instructs the search engine to return Web pages about the first three terms but not about the other vchip or v-chip terms. Use AND NOT when you have a keyword that is ambiguous. The need for AND NOT often becomes noticed after you perform an initial search and realize this ambiguity is an issue. Another non-related example is search the term "Venus." If your search results contain irrelevant results such as Venus the Planet, rather than Venus "The Goddess of Love," then use AND NOT to prune it; you can also consider using AND NOT to filter out any undesired Web sites.

Implied Boolean: Plus and Minus Signs

In many search engines, the plus and minus symbols can be used as alternatives to full Boolean AND and AND NOT operators. The plus sign "+" is the equivalent of AND, and the minus sign "-" is the equivalent of AND NOT. Also note that there is no space between the plus or minus sign and the keyword.

A simple search requires the use of plus and minus rather than AND and AND NOT:

+television+commercial+blocker-vchip
+venus-planet

Use the search engine's simple search capabilities for implied Boolean (+/-) searches, and use the search engine's advanced search capabilities for full Boolean (AND, OR, AND NOT) searches.

> ### EXERCISE IN IMPLIED BOOLEAN SEARCH: PLUS AND MINUS SIGNS
>
> Go to http://ixquick.com.
> Consider the question: Does violence on television have an effect on children?
> Enter query search: +violence+television+children.
> Note that Ixquick will first attempt a Boolean AND search. If this is not successful, it will attempt to find documents with any of your search terms. Putting in the plus signs +s in the actual query should ensure that all of the terms appear in the search results.

Phrase Searching

Surrounding a group of words with double quotes tells the search engine to only retrieve documents in which those words appear side-by-side. Phrase searching is a powerful search technique for significantly narrowing your search results, and it should be used as often as possible:

"television commercial blocker"
"tv commercial blocker"

For best results, combine phrase searching with implied Boolean (+/-) or full Boolean (AND, OR, and AND NOT) logic. The following shows the same example in two different expressions of Boolean:

+"television commercial"+blocker+filter-vchip
(television AND commercial) AND blocker AND filter AND NOT vchip

As you will note, these are identical search command phrases written in two different ways: Implied Boolean and Full Boolean.

Plural Forms, Capital Letters, and Alternate Spellings

Most search engines interpret lowercase letters as either upper- or lowercase characters. Thus, if you want both upper- and lowercase occurrences returned, type your keywords in all lowercase letters, as it does not matter.

Like capitalization, most search engines interpret singular keywords as singular or plural. If you want plural forms only, be sure to make your keywords plural.

A few search engines support truncation or wildcard features that allow variations in spelling or word forms. The asterisk "*" symbol tells the search engine to return alternate spellings for a word, at the point that the asterisk appears. For example, the term advertis* returns Web pages with advertisement, advertising, advertiser, and advertise.

Field Search

Field searching is one of the most effective techniques for narrowing results and getting the most relevant Web sites listed at the top of the results page. A Web page is composed of a number of fields, such as title, domain, host, URL, and link.

The effectiveness of your search increases as you combine field searches with phrase searches and implied Boolean logic. For example, if you wanted to find information about television commercial blocking, try

> +title:"television commercial" WITH blocker AND NOT vchip+device
> title:"Television Commercial" AND Blocker AND Filter

This TITLE SEARCH example instructs the search engine to return Web pages where the phrase Television Commercial appears in the title and the words Blocker and Filter appear somewhere on the page. Also note that in these examples, there is no space between the + or -.

Domain Search

In addition to the title search, other helpful field searching strategies include the domain search, the host search, the link search, and the URL search.

DOMAIN SEARCH allows you to limit results to certain domains such as Web sites from the United Kingdom (.uk), educational institutions (.edu), or government sites (.gov).

> +domain:uk+"Tivo Wireless" +Internet
> +domain:com+"Tivo Wireless" +Internet
> +domain:org+"Tivo Wireless" +Internet

The current, most widely accepted U.S. domains are published as the following:

.com—A commercial business

.edu—An educational institution

.gov—A governmental institution

.org—A non-profit organization

.mil—A military site

.net—A network site

Most Web sites originating outside of the U.S. have a country domain indicating the country of origin. For a current list of all country domains, visit the Internet country-codes site.[3]

---

[3] For more information, please reference http://ftp.ics.uci.edu/pub/websoft/wwstat/ country-codes.txt.

Link Search

Use LINK SEARCH when you want to know what Web sites are linked to a particular site of interest. For example, if you have a home page and you are wondering if anyone has put a link to your page on his or her Web site, use the LINK SEARCH command. Researchers use link searches for conducting backward citations:

>   link:www.ibm.com

Performing a "Search" in Five Easy Steps

Let's prepare a simple search to execute in almost any search engine. If you have not done so already, please review the previous discussions on search engines in this chapter prior to proceeding. This discussion intersects with the next discussion on performing a search.

By spending a few extra minutes up front thinking about your search, clarifying your search, and planning your search strategy—you can increase your percentages of finding more of what you need on the Internet and finding this information in much less time. In this section, we will discuss five simple steps to performing an effective Internet search.

Taking 5–10 minutes in preparing for a search turns out to be much faster and absolutely more effective than wandering in an unprepared search approach such as surfing the Web.

Consider that when a person walks into a library to find a book, he or she has two choices: to (a) randomly wander up and down book isles until he finds the book he is seeking; or (b) going to the card catalog or computerized index and searching through the catalog using exact key words, finding references to what's being sought, then walking directly into that isle of the Library, tracking the bookshelves, and, finding the book. Which makes more sense—(a) or (b)?

The answer to this question is that it depends on what you want. You might have the time and wish to wander up and down isles to see new things, perhaps in somewhat of a random learning mode; or, you may need the information right then so that you can leave the library as soon as possible. Either way, the search preparation is different depending on your goals.

A secondary benefit to this refined search preparation method we are about to explore is found in the by-product of this activity. The documentation assembled in preparation for the search can later be used when the inventor meets with patent agents or patent attorneys during later stages of the patent life cycle where the specification and prior art is being reviewed. Likewise, printed results from the search will also serve useful in defending the differences of "prior art" to the "current art" of the new invention. These concepts of "art" and their differences will be discussed in greater details in Chapters 4, "Invention Teams," and Chapter 5, "Invention Evaluation Teams," of this book.

This prepared search activity and the proof set of search materials ascertained during the search is a value-add during the final patent law search phases. This also shows that the inventor is a highly skilled inventor due to the fact he or she worked diligently to identify any pertinent prior art related to his or her invention.

Let's explore an actual strategy for a rather simple Internet search and the preparation phases being considered prior to beginning this search. This simple search preparation applies to our previous searches, and for continuity purposes, we will use the subject of "television commercial blocking" for our example.

Following this simple example (and in Chapters 4 and 5), we will begin to explore a typical patents prior art search, which is significantly more complex than a simple search.

Step 1: State What You Want to Find

First, in one or two very concise sentences, state in the form of a question what you would like to find in the Internet search. For example

- What alternatives are available for television commercial blocking?
- What are the best television commercial blocking features?

For this particular step, think in terms of unique words or phrases associated with television. Also, think in terms of semantic meanings and information specificity. Modifiers to the keywords are also acceptable, especially if it helps in pruning or refining the search to a more detailed result.

Step 2: Identify the Keywords

Next, underline the main concepts in the statement:

- What alternatives are available for television commercial blocking?
- What are the best television commercial blocking features?

Step 3: Select Synonyms and Variant Word Forms

List any known synonyms, alternate spellings, and variant word forms (perhaps even common misspellings) of each keyword you are considering in your search:

- television TV tele tube
- commercials advertisements promotions promos sales
- blocking blocker filter

Note the variants of the words associated with, for example, *commercials*. Also, think about any words with ambiguity and try to disambiguate them. This combination or synonym-like approach to searching is a common strategy.

Step 4: Combine Synonym, Keywords, and Variant Word Forms

Combine synonyms with the Boolean OR operator and place parentheses around the complete compound OR statements. Truncate compound variations of words using an * symbol. Mix and match operators.

Combine keywords with Boolean AND:

- +television+TV+tele
- (television OR tv OR tele) AND (characteristics OR features OR functions)
- (commercials OR advertisements) AND block* AND program*
- (television AND commercial AND blocking) AND NOT vchip

Use truncation search techniques on varying forms of words with an asterisk symbol * to truncate then allowing a combinatorial search on the variant word forms:

- television AND commercial AND block*
- tv AND television AND (advertis* OR commercial)

This way, you are sure to find any form of the pattern of the words you are seeking to find. In this example, the search would include: commercial AND block, blocks, blocking, and blocker; or, in the case of advertis* the search interprets advertise, advertisement, advertiser. Masking search terms with a * delivers a broadened search result.

Step 5: Check Your Spelling

Inspect all the search terms for spelling accuracy; ensuring the exact spelling of the term is meaningful. Even intentionally misspelled words are acceptable for some types of searches. For example, diamond AND daimond. These types of misspelling mistakes are sometimes searched as keywords, as certain words are commonly misspelled.

Meta-Search Engines

Meta-search engines simultaneously search many search engines, handing the search request to the other engines for execution in parallel. Meta-search engines are also referred to as parallel search engines, multi-threaded search engines, or mega-search engines.

These tools offer very powerful search capabilities across a wide variety of global Internet content. Generally speaking, there are two types of meta-search engines that can be easily found on the Internet today.

The first type of meta-search engine involves a *separate retrieval for relatively comprehensive results*. This type of engine searches a number of other search engines and does not collate the search results. What this means is that you must then sort through a separate list of results from each engine that was searched; you will often see the same result more than once, across the different search engine results.

Some meta-search engines require you to visit each site to view your results. With this type of meta-search engine, you can retrieve comprehensive and sometimes overwhelming results. Other meta-search engines retrieve the results back to their own sites and give you somewhat more limited views of the results. An example of this type of meta-search engine is *wy metasearch*.[4]

The second type of meta-search engine involves *collated retrieval for selected results*. This type is the more common meta-search engine and returns a single list of results, often with the duplicate files removed. This type of engine always brings the results back to its own site for viewing.

In these cases, the meta-search engine retrieves a certain maximum number of files (allowed by the individual search engines) it has searched, limited after a certain point, as the meta-search is processed. The number of documents retrieved may determine the "limit" or it may by the amount of time the meta-search engine spends at the other sites. Some of these services give the user a certain degree of control over these factors.

All of this power and capability to search the Internet has two implications:

1. These meta-search engines *return only a portion* of the documents available to be retrieved from the individual engines they have searched.

2. The results retrieved by meta-search engines can be *highly relevant* since they are usually retrieving the first items from the relevancy-ranked list of hits (or retrievals) returned by the individual meta-search engines.

Meta-search engines interact with several commercial search engines all at once. Meta-search engines and do not "crawl" the Web, or maintain a database of directories and Web pages. Meta-search engines act as a middle-agent of sorts, presenting the query to the other commercial search engines, acting as one of its service agents, only to deliver back to the meta-search engine the final search results for that specific search engine. Because these commercial meta-search engines can sometimes produce very different results, these engines provide a quick way to determine which independent engines are retrieving the most results for your information gathering needs.

META-SEARCH ENGINES HAVE PROS AND CONS TO CONSIDER

Pros:

Meta-search engines are very useful when you want to retrieve a relatively small number of relevant search results. Meta-search engines are also an excellent choice for retrieving information about obscure topics. Utilizing meta-search engines is a good option when you are not having much success finding what you are searching for on the Internet using traditional search engines. Meta-search engines are appropriate when you want to get an overall picture of what information is available on the Internet that is related to your search topic.

---

[4]   For more information, please reference http://www.yurweb.com.

> *Cons:*
> The usage of a meta-search engine is limited to simple queries. There is very limited (sometimes none) field searching functionality available in meta-search engines. Most meta-search services return a limited number of results that do not represent the "totality" of results from any source or search engine. The results from meta-search engine services do not limit or collate results and, therefore, can become redundant and overwhelming.

Some search engines may vary in their capability to receive and interpret complex searches into generic terms that they, as one of many search engines, will understand. For this reason, meta-search engines will operate most efficiently with simple searches. The issue surrounds the query language interpretation capabilities of the search engines, parsing capabilities, and performing in a very specific search syntax language (or programmatic) translation recognized by the search engine. So, given this, what is most effective in a meta-search engine is the "least common denominator" of the search parameters—in other words, a simple search.

What follows are several good examples of meta-search engines:

- *Dogpile* searches eight (or more) search engines and subject directories as well as news-groups, business news, and newswires. Dogpile supports full Boolean logic and phrase searching.[5]

- *Vivisimo* clusters results from eight (or more) search engines and subject directories into convenient topic categories. Utilize implied Boolean logic (+/-) and phrase searching.[6]

- *MetaCrawler* submits queries to seven (or more) search engines and subject directories. Utilize implied Boolean logic ((+/-) and phrase searching.[7]

- *Fazzle* searches several search services on the Web; Fazzle also offers specialty searches of downloads, images, videos and other topics from the deep Web.[8]

- *Profusion* allows the results to be sorted by relevance, title, URL and source; this offers a customizable advanced search form, enabling the search services to better match the search style. This also offers topical searches across the deep Web.[9]

- *Query Server* offers queries of the general Web, health, financial, or government sites—and organizes results by concept, site, or both.[10]

You can see a larger list of commercial meta-search engines by visiting the Internet Search Engines Web site.[11]

---

[5]   For more information, please reference http://www.dogpile.com.
[6]   For more information, please reference http://vivisimo.com.
[7]   For more information, please reference http://www.metacrawler.com.
[8]   For more information, please reference http://www.fazzle.com.
[9]   For more information, please reference http://www.profusion.com.
[10] For more information, please reference http://www.queryserver.com.
[11] For more information, please reference http://library.albany.edu/internet/meta.

Specialty Databases

Sometimes, a specialty database will be more effective at finding what you need than a general search engine or meta-search engine. Specialty databases are dedicated to collecting relevant sites and content for a particular subject area.

For example, Findlaw targets[12] legal resources, and Achoo! collects[13] health and medical sites. Beaucoup lists[14] more than 1,200 engines, directories, and indices from around the world. At Search.com, you will find a search service[15] with access to more than 100 specialized content databases.

Specialty databases are a powerful way to find specific information you need quickly and efficiently.

U.S. Patents and Trademarks Office Search Example

Today, over 170 countries grant some type of intellectual property protection, such as patent, design, trademark, and copyright.

Intellectual property law is designed to safeguard creators of intellectual assets, goods, and services, by granting the creators certain time-limited rights to control the use made of these productions. Statutes or laws by the individual countries that grant intellectual property protection establish these rights. The rules and procedures for each country can and do, however, differ. It should be emphasized that patent rights enforcement is up to the owner of the intellectual property and the independent intellectual property laws of the country in which the invention was born. The owner must be his or her own policeman: This is true in every country.

Clearing the inventor's idea of any prior artwork conflicts is fundamental to establishing novelty in any invention idea. The inventor should begin this process before tremendous time is spent in thinking of the idea or documenting aspects of the idea. This not only helps the inventor in clarifying his or her own thoughts, as compared to others with similar thoughts, but also helps to strengthen the idea. This becomes most evident by adding new thoughts or discoveries stimulated by the prior art. We will begin to explore these "strengthening" phenomena in the following discussion.

The results of prior art searching of intellectual property of every kind can and does have legal implications on new inventions. The best guideline regarding intellectual property rights preservation is to perform initial prior art searching to rule-out any prior art. It also may be a good idea to contact a competent patent agent, patents attorney, or an attorney who specializes in intellectual property when you are ready to begin the patent filing documentation process.

[12] For more information, please reference http://www.findlaw.com.
[13] For more information, please reference http://www.achoo.com.
[14] For more information, please reference http://www.beaucoup.com.
[15] For more information, please reference http://www.search.com.

An Example of a U.S. "Prior Art" Search Site

Following the same search example of a television that blocks and reprograms TV commercials broadcasts, let's now see what has been done on this topic (before now) by performing an actual prior art search. To do this search, we will utilize the U.S. Patents and Trademarks Office Web site.

For this short prior art search exercise, open your Internet browser and go to the USPTO homepage. This Web site can be found at http://www.uspto.gov:

1. From the USPTO homepage, click "Search" under the "Patents" heading that appears on the left side of the homepage screen. The next page displayed, provides two searching areas: Issued Patents (PatFT) and Published Applications (AppFT).

2. On the Published Applications (AppFT) side, the upper-right side of the page, click the "Advanced Search" option.

3. This section provides access to the newest patent application filings (i.e., the "Applications") in the USPTO databases. These are the "patent pending" applications. As an experiment, type (in double quotes) "blocking television commercials" into the "Query" input box, and click the "Search" button. Note the results unveil four patent applications related to this keyword phrase. (We will explore this search result in the next section.)

4. Repeat this same search access path (beginning on the USPTO homepage), only from the upper-left section of the search screen (not the upper-right side of the screen, new "Applications"). The upper-left side of the homepage is the *Issued Patents* database. This alternative search path (Issued Patents) now provides the widest prior art search coverage (not the most recent) of the USPTO databases because these are the issued patents.

Entering Query Terms into the USPTO search engine. Following our previous generalized Internet search examples, let's assume now that televisions with user programmable commercial-blocking capabilities are really not widely available on the markets today. We suspect that there could be some prior art on this, however, and that must always be further investigated. This deep search will unfold in this section, as we continue to describe a prior art search.

Now, we switch gears just a little and begin thinking about how we can invent a way to block undesirable television commercials, and allow television viewers to essentially the simple ability to self-program their own personalized TV commercial markets.

In the next section, we will explore what has been applied in the U.S. patents database on these same search items (i.e., "blocking television commercials").

A Simple Prior Art Search

As we continue to follow this same search example of blocking television commercials—let's now conduct an actual "prior art" search, utilizing the U.S. Patents and Trademarks Office databases, and this same example.

In order to perform this short exercise, open your Internet browser, and go to the USPTO homepage—http://www.uspto.gov:

1. As previously described, in the upper-left side of the USPTO home page, note the "Patents" and then select the "Search" option.

2. Again, please note the two different alternatives for searching: On the left side are the "Issued Patents (PatFT)," which are full-text since 1976 and full-page images since 1790. On the upper-right side of this same homepage, note the "Published Applications (AppFT)" that are published submissions since March 15, 2001. These are the patents pending issuance from the USPTO.

3. Select "Quick Search" on the right side under "Published Applications (AppFT)."

4. In the Query box, type in your search terms. For example, where the field indicator says "TERM1," type in the query box (in double quotes) "blocking television commercials" and press the Search button. This will return a list of all the patents that have the phrase blocking television commercials anywhere in the indexed text: This is a simple search.

5. Read the abstracts associated with each of these patent applications in order to determine if your idea for blocking television commercials is similar, or not, to these abstract discussions. At this stage, you are contrasting the current art (your invention) to the prior art, which has already been filed. Are the ideas you have to do this close or the same to these abstract discussions? Look beneath the abstract discussion; are there differences in the claims documented in this patent application? You are now evaluating prior art— nice work. Keep records of what you are finding, so when you realize the new invention brought forth (unstated) in this chapter, you can use this detail as prior art findings in your patent package.

Based on your prior art search results, what are you able to determine? Read the Abstracts of the invention. Explore further into the textual descriptions to read the actual claims of the invention. View the graphics. Although we will explore in much greater detail aspects of prior art searching let's take one last look at some of the customizable features of the USPTO patent search site.

An Advanced Prior Art Search

Patent search sites often will offer a number of advanced features to allow for anyone searching for prior art to better isolate specific pieces of information.

There are many other features on the USPTO Web site (and other patent prior art search sites), which make searching a more efficient task for the end user.

Let's take a closer look at a couple of these features. It may be a good idea, considering we just found some prior art surrounding our new invention idea for blocking television commercials, to look more closely at this inventor named "Fellenstein," to see if he may have other applications filed surrounding this same subject of commercial blocking, which may result in additional prior art.

1. Click "Home" (or return to http://www.uspto.gov and go to "Patents" and then "Search").

2. Then click "Advanced Search" and note the table that appears with the variety of advanced search refinement terms (e.g., TTL, IN, etc.).

3. Because patent "Application Publications" are new, these are in fact the inventor's patents pending. From these titles, try to identify any other patent applications he may have filed related to this same subject of blocking television commercials.

Do this to ensure there is no more prior art from this same inventor on the subject. It appears there may be some other prior art this inventor has created related to this same topic of blocking television commercials. Look carefully while taking note of any prior art observation you are able to find.

Now that we have identified the existence of other prior art related to this invention idea, let's now prune this search to what we believe to be the core items of interest.

Return to the database search page and enter the search phrase (in double quotes) "blocking television commercials" and note the search result of four published applications.

Following the results of this search exercise, the list shown in Table 3-1 would be presented to your browser (in some form).

Table 3-1 Resulting Prior Art Search Listings

PUB. APP. NO.		Title
1	20040019905	Apparatus and method for blocking television commercials and providing an archive interrogation program
2	20040019904	Apparatus and method for blocking television commercials with a content interrogation program
3	20030227475	Apparatus and method for blocking television commercials and delivering micro-programming content
4	20030192045	Apparatus and method for blocking television commercials and displaying alternative programming

The next discussion includes excerpts from the USPTO Web site related to the topics we have been exploring. This idea of a television that blocks advertising and/or commercials, although residing as prior art, may have room for improvements. Consider elements of the idea we stated earlier—that is, while allowing an end user to program his or her viewing choices across markets. What can we do with this notion, which the prior art has not yet claimed?

Well, the prior art covers programming of alternative commercial viewing time. It discusses returning to the original viewing channel at the end of the original undesirable commercial that initially triggered the channel selector to switch away. The prior art records this information for later interrogation of the data for a plurality of reasons. Question: How important is this end user data to the television network providers? Do they care about viewers that are electing to depart from their channel due to an undesirable commercial? Well, perhaps not so much if the viewer is returned to them at the end of the commercial segment. But what if the viewer finds alternative content upon the preprogrammed switching occurrence and decides to stay at that new channel? The network traffic would have indeed been diverted due to this undesirable TV commercial. This is now perhaps problematic for the television network service provider. Or is it?

What if the networks have a view of all of this aggregate data, that is, the date related to the television viewers who are switching away from which networks based on which commercial sponsors? Would this information cause the networks to rethink who they are selecting as their advertisers? Additionally, would a view of this information perhaps cause the networks to encourage some of their advertisers to improve their levels of content, thereby attempting to retain the viewing audience?

The Actual Prior Art Search and Evaluation

At this stage (on your computer) using the example search terms, you can explore the individual titles and read the abstracts for each of the patent filings. This allows you to now determine for yourself if similarities exist in your idea and the above potential prior art.

Review the patent application claims. Do this in order to determine how deep you need to go in the prior art search to determine if your new idea will infringe in any ways on the claims in the prior art.

Sometimes, the patent Abstract will disclose enough specifics of the invention to conduct the prior art search, but the claims are the most important areas to inspect. Look for the claims in the detailed write-ups, following the Abstract.

Understanding the Patent Abstract

The proceeding text addresses the Abstract you will see at the USPTO site when you perform a prior art patent search on these potential prior art examples. Read it closely to determine if there are similarities. If this seems similar to your new idea for this invention of a TV that blocks commercials and allows the end user to program the TV for personal markets, then further prior art inspection is necessary.

At the USPTO site, anyone can read the associated patent claims, which are always the key part of the patent specification. Anyone can also read the Abstract of the patent, which discloses the nature of the entire idea. This information details the lower-level elements of the invention.

Continuing in this invention exercise and assuming that you constructed your search according to our previous example (i.e., "blocking television commercials"), we have now found four similar titles/abstracts.

Let's now explore these applications one-by-one to see if our idea infringes upon these published applications in any way. It is worthy to note that these are patents (at the time of this book printing), which are pending approval by the USPTO. This is because you began this prior art search from the most recent filings, the patent applications, which are usually in USPTO review stages for several months to years.

The following describes the concepts in the first of the four published applications you found, related to blocking television commercials.

United States Patent Application	20040019905
Kind Code	A1
Fellenstein, Craig William; et al.	January 29, 2004

Apparatus and Method for Blocking Television Commercials and Providing an Archive Interrogation Program

Abstract

An apparatus and method is disclosed for blocking specific television commercials from the viewer's television based upon the characteristics of the television commercial and a program to place the blocked television commercials into an archive. An archive interrogation program then acquires the users search criteria and sends the search criteria to the content search program for a list of matches. The matches are displayed to the user, and the user can select a segment for viewing.

Determine if There Is Prior Art—Using Several Real Examples

By now, you probably discovered your own new idea developing for blocking television commercials (as we continue in this exercise)—an idea that goes beyond what you have read so far as a result of your searching (i.e., the exercises in this book).

If so, you may be wondering if there are potential similarities in your idea, and the patent abstract you just read in the Published Application No. 20040019905. Did you take time to review the claims on application '905? Since your new idea may be close to this idea, you should take time to review these claims.

Are there more patent applications or filings you need to consider? Let's take another step and continue searching in order to determine what might be the "core idea" of these four similar concepts found in the initial prior art search. We need to decide how similar (if at all) these ideas are to your new idea, which you may be considering at this stage.

Again, scanning the returned patent application titles, you notice one particular title, which looks like a controller device of sorts: Application No. 20030192045. Let's take a closer look at this abstract to see what the concepts are in this published patent application.

On your computer, clicking the link to the application title, "Apparatus and method for *blocking television commercials* and displaying alternative programming," for number 20030192045 (also shown next), we will unveil more specifics for this prior art idea. You should also review the claims, which at some point you may need to better understand. To see these, click "Images" and note the "Claims" link on the left side of this page. Or, in some cases, the claims can also be read on the same page, immediately following the Abstract.

At this stage, we need to determine what is the entire idea we have just encountered as prior art and work to invent the new idea around it—free and clear of this prior art: Strengthen your idea to be better than what is already on file. Make it stronger and absolutely unique from what you have found in this prior art.

This next abstract describes yet more detail on the complexities in this prior art invention idea for blocking television commercials. Let's now take a look at how the inventor proposes to allow for viewing audience preprogramming of commercial alternatives. Application '045 that follows describes just this.

United States Patent Application	20030192045
Kind Code	A1
Fellenstein, Craig William; et al.	October 9, 2003

Apparatus and Method for Blocking Television Commercials and Displaying Alternative Programming

Abstract

A logical unit and a commercial blocking program in the logical unit allow alternative viewing options so that the user may define the alternative programming to replace the unwanted communication. The commercial blocking program breaks all incoming television signals into time, video and audio components and is able to recognize specific commercials based on those components. Upon viewing an unwanted commercial, the user indicates that he wants to block the commercial through one of a variety of input methods. The commercial blocking program then prevents the commercial from being displayed on the user's television and causes alternative programming to be displayed instead. The user may configure the alternative programming via the alternative programming logic. The user may configure the alternative programming as a universal television channel, based on the specific commercial, based on the television station, based on the time of day, or based on an elaborate viewing hierarchy. At the end of the blocked commercial, the commercial blocking program displays the television program that was originally displayed on the user's television. Alternatively, the commercial blocking program can buffer the various television programs received from the cable provider and record segments of the cable signal based on certain keywords. The commercial blocking program searches for user-defined keywords, records television programs complying with the search terms, and displays the recorded television programming stored in the memory.

Invent Around the Prior Art While Strengthening Your Idea

A common technique inventors use to strengthen their idea for a new invention is to create an invention around prior art. Rather than devise an entirely new idea, they improve upon an existing idea—building a better mousetrap.

The primary challenge is to exploit the weakness in the prior art idea(s), while stimulating your own line of reasoning. To do this, consider the four abstracts being described in this chapter. What else could you do that this inventor has not yet thought about, in order to create your own novel invention. And, yes, you can reference this prior art as art, which helps to instantiate your idea; however, your idea must be unique from any prior art and especially free and clear of the four Abstracts you have just identified. So, what else can you do, as an inventor, which has not yet been done in this area?

Think at least two years into the future, maybe even more if you can. What will be the state-of-the-art for televisions in the future? Remember, it takes about two years to clear a patent today, so whatever your invention is you must target at least two years into the future.

At this stage in the book, if we were to disclose to you any particular line of thinking about a unique solution, we would be publicly disclosing an invention. If we did this, it might prevent you, the reader, from inventing a solution in this space. Conversely, we can tell you that we have alluded to it now several times in the first three chapters of this book. So it is possible for you to imagine another level of this invention set, which would allow you to be the first to file it as one or more patent applications.

Now, if you want to pursue your own invention at this stage, download or view the full specification patent application information online for these patent application examples—do this at the USPTO Web site we have been discussing. Then, in essence, the goal is to invent around the prior art, such that the current art (your new idea) is strengthened and identifiably more unique and non-obvious.

THE IMPORTANT TEST OF NOVELTY

Seek to make your idea one that those *skilled in the art have never considered*: This is the key to strengthening any invention.

Once you determine it is indeed unique, and those skilled in the art have never considered this new idea you have, ask one final question—would they have ever considered this new idea? This last part of the question addresses the non-obvious requirement of an invention.

In every great idea, solution, or strategy—one or more weaknesses may sometimes be found. This is the starting point the inventor seeks in order to discover a problem in need of a solution. Look hard to find any open questions, weaknesses or flaws in the idea. Incomplete thinking also may sometimes unveil a new idea. Keep in mind that flaws seem to travel in herds; so, if you see one, look closely—there may be several more. Leverage any weakness or shortcoming to your advantage. Use this to find intersections for you to invent around, points of absolute novelty yet to be discovered.

Before we work on any of the idea strengthening, let's be sure there are no other ideas related to your new idea (the current art); you need to be fully aware of all the prior art—locate it and make sure you maintain documented copies.

Let's start a more advanced investigation by going back to the USPTO homepage and taking another look at the inventor of this prior art we have found, to see if he (they) might have other patents on file that could relate to the current art:

1. From the USPTO homepage (www.uspto.gov, left side of page), click "Patent" and then "Search."

2. Next, from the Patent Applications section on the upper-right section of the page, click the "Advanced Search" selection.

3. Note the abbreviated parameter selections on the lower half of this page, in particular, the inventor abbreviation *IN*.

4. In the Query window, enter *IN/fellenstein*.

5. Note the various patent applications listed from the same inventor and look for any other indirect or direct titles, which may suggest additional prior art inspection being required (e.g., App. No. 20030192050).

Repeat these prior art-searching steps on other search engines to ensure you, as the inventor, you are well aware of any conflicting prior art; again, document all of your search activities. You can later refer to the specifications (for example) of these other patent applications, including the following patent filing, No. 20030192050, as what was found at the USPTO site[16] during the prior art search activities.

What follows is the Abstract[17] from another patent application that is also currently categorized as "Patent Pending." This filing was identified in the name search of the author (i.e., IN/Fellenstein) and shows additional details on how to enable this kind of an invention for blocking television commercials. Specifically, the following patent application describes how this invention proposes to search for desired alternative content to display during the period that the undesirable commercial is being broadcast.

United States Patent Application	20030192050
Kind Code	A1
Fellenstein, Craig William; et al.	October 9, 2003

---

[16] To view this patent application specification, please reference http://aiw2.uspto.gov/.aiw?docid=us20030192050ki &SectionNum=3&IDKey=756C15CE5707&HomeUrl=http://appft1.uspto.gov/netacgi/nphParser?Sect1=PTO2%25 26Sect2=HITOFF%2526u=%25252Fnetahtml%25252FPTO%25252Fsearchadv.html%2526r=15%2526p=1%2526 f=G%2526l=50%2526d=PG01%2526S1=fellenstein%2526OS=fellenstein%2526RS=fellenstein.

[17] For more information on this patent application, please reference http://appft1.uspto.gov/netacgi/nph-Parser?Sect1= PTO2&Sect2=HITOFF&u=%2Fnetahtml%2FPTO%2Fsearch-adv.html&r=15&p=1&f=G&l=50&d=PG01&S1= fellenstein&OS=fellenstein&RS=fellenstein.

Apparatus and Method of Searching for Desired Television Content

Abstract

The present invention is an apparatus and method for allowing a user to search for specific content across many television channels in order to locate desirable television shows related to the searched content. Multiplexed cable signals flow thorough a logical unit, which buffers text, associated with the voice stream of each station via the pre-encoded closed-captioning signal or through the real-time voice translation within the logical unit. The user then enters search terms through one of a variety of different input devices. Upon entry of the search terms, the logical unit will compare the entered term with those available keywords stored in each buffer. Lexical parsing associates terms, which may differ from plural to singular forms, or in tense. Additionally, synonym comparisons may be made. The logical unit will return a list of matches for the search criteria and allows the user the option of going directly to the television program. The logical unit also evaluates each returned item for its relevancy to the keywords. When not in use, the logical unit maintains a quiescent but monitoring state permitting continuous creation of lexical buffers. This permits the user who turns the television on to immediately have such search terms available. Alternatively, the logic is implemented at the cable provider and enabled through interactive links to the home. In that case, the home logical unit is unnecessary.

Record Keeping and Invention Strengthening

Keep explicit notes. Copy prior art abstracts, records and applications, and even the patent numbers you have researched—whether they are close to your idea or not. Make a short note as to the results of viewing the other references. Also, make sure you have searched the *Issued Patents* portion of the USPTO site as well as the *Published Applications* area of the site. Both areas can contain prior art. Once you have searched all possible sources, you now have a better idea of any conflicting ideas or existing prior art.

So if you still think you have a better idea or enhancement to an idea you have just read about, be tenacious and keep going. Invent around these types of prior art situations if they exist. Make your idea more novel and absolutely unique from any other prior art.

Use Google and USPTO for prior art searching. Use any sites you can find capable of delivering this type of information. Use any of the search engines we have described in this book, and use as many as you can to identify as much prior art as possible.

This not only shows patent evaluators that you, as an inventor, know how to qualify your ideas, but it also shows them that their job may be simpler, as you have provided some amount of the prior art investigative work. Furthermore, this method will help you to see even more clearly your idea as it relates to other potentially similar ideas. This strengthens your messaging in the overall modeling and descriptions of the novelty in your idea. It may even cause you to discover something you were not originally thinking about in your idea.

There is an unspoken benefit to this phase of prior art searching that is clearly one of the most valuable. I am sure that we would agree that it is human nature to be inquisitive (since prehistoric times). So realize that just perhaps, as you have now been reading other prior art or previously submitted patent applications, and perhaps only the abstracts at that, did you discover anything that you have never considered? If so, does it go beyond what you have just read? And if so, do you have a new and unique idea?

Before you answer these questions, go review the specifications (again), which are also listed online for each of these prior art ideas. Look at the images, too, for they can reveal many important graphic aspects of the intellectual property.

So, what is this "new invention" in your mind? Can you describe it in a paragraph? We are giving away an invention at this point in the book: Can you see it? We cannot state it in any fashion, or we would be creating prior art. This is an invention that has not yet been stated, disclosed or considered by anyone, at least not in the public domain. *Hint: It also satisfies the second part of the problem the original new idea addressed.*

It is common for an individual to be reading other published invention abstracts, in order to clear his or her idea of any prior art, when they suddenly discover something new that is now possibly their own idea—an invention. Call it psychosis, call it insights, or call it discovery, but it is a natural cognitive tendency. Or is it a critical skill? Or is it both? Is it legal? Well, law strictly defines patents, so the inventor always must comply with the patent laws during the inventive stages. This surrounds a problem, solution, and absolute novelty—and then, of course, the non-obvious test.

This new idea you now have, perhaps caused through associations[18] of other ideas, may or may not have been considered by those skilled in the art. What does this mean? Based on earlier discussions in this chapter—it means you must begin this entire prior art evaluation method all over again (only on your new idea) in order to prove the novelty of your new idea. Except now, you must perform this prior art search activity considering only the newly discovered idea—it's search keyword concepts, and everything we have just learned in this chapter, and the last chapter all applies.

Does your new idea pass the invention novelty test yet? Does it need a new prior art test yet—a prior art test not unlike the one that caused you to discover the new idea? If so, apply one last test: Is this new idea something that is non-obvious to those skilled in the art? Is it free of all prior art? If you pass both of these tests with "yes" answers, you may have a new invention idea to explore as a patent.

You want to reference these patent filings as other prior art, in some ways perhaps enabling your new idea. This discovery process can be thought of as a "starburst" effect—where one particular idea causes the discovery of one or more new and distinct ideas. *Hint: One new idea could enable the consumers to begin to program the statistical basis for which commercial networks select their advertising sponsors, based on consumer advertising ratings across a small or large grid of television viewers.*

---

[18] Aristotle [ca. 350 B.C.].

Finally, think about the patent applications (or filed patents) you have just reviewed. Have you come up with a new, absolutely unique, better idea, yet? Have you thought of your own unique solution? If you do not have a new idea in your mind, then try thinking further out of the box—say, three to five years into the future. Revisit the original problem that brought you to this point, stated earlier in this chapter. If you have now conceptualized a new idea, and you can prove this new idea is free and clear of all prior art instances—file it. You may have a new patent.

The Illustration Pages

Do not forget to look at the patents and patent application drawings. These can convey tremendous information about the idea.

Click the "Images" button at the top of the database search page at the USPTO Web site. In order to view these images you will need a specialized TIFF viewer. If you require this viewer, click the "Help" button at the top of the page and then click on the topic "How to Access Patent Full-page Images" to get complete instructions on downloading this free software.

Web Sources for Conducting Patent Searches

We have already identified several very good Web resources for searching information related to patents and trademarks. The following list also identifies additional resources.

1. United States Patent and Trademark Office, homepage (http://www.uspto.gov) links to all of the USPTO sites and search engines. Since it can often be rather difficult to navigate, some of the sites more useful to novice searchers are linked below.

2. General Information about Patents (http://www.uspto.gov/web/offices/pac/doc/general/index.html) is a table of contents to the information that the USPTO site provides about patenting.

3. Patent and Trademark Depository Library Program homepage (http://www.uspto.gov/web/offices/ac/ido/ptdl/index.html) provides useful links within this site include List of PTDLs (http://www.uspto.gov/web/offices/ac/ido/ptdl/ptdllibm.htm), Basic Materials Available (http://www.uspto.gov/web/offices/ac/ido/ptdl/ptdlserv.htm), and Frequently Asked Questions About Patents (http://www.uspto.gov/web/offices/ pac/doc/general/faq).

4. USPTO's list of related sites (http://www.uspto.gov/web/menu/other.html). Most useful in this page is the list of the intellectual property offices of foreign countries. Since U.S. patents only protect intellectual property in the United States and its territories, this is a useful site for inventors interested in patenting in different countries.

5. USPTO Web Patent Databases (http://www.uspto.gov/patft/index.html) provide the user with two databases to search. The bibliographic database contains a complete listing of citations and abstracts from patents issued between January 1, 1976, and the present. The full text database is still incomplete; however, when it is completed it will span the same time period. Both databases are searchable by Boolean expression (simple search), manual field search (advanced search), and patent number search.

6. PTO bulletin (http://www.uspto.gov/web/offices/ac/ahrpa/opa/bulletin/index.html) is a periodic update of happenings connected with the USPTO.

7. List of Patent Attorneys and Agents Licensed to Practice Before the PTO (http://www.uspto.gov/web/offices/dcom/olia/oed/roster/region/). This source provides a geographic listing of patent attorneys and agents registered with and approved by the USPTO.

8. USPTO Forms (http://www.uspto.gov/web/forms/). Current forms for patent and trademark applications, reissues, etc., available from the USPTO.

9. IBM Intellectual Property Network (http://www.patents.ibm.com/). This site provides full text of patents issued between 1974 and the present. Although the time coverage is more extensive than the USPTO site, the quality of the images and the text leave much to be desired. Search capabilities include Boolean searches, text searches, and searches by patent number.

10. Franklin Pierce Law Center U.S. Patent, Trademark & Copyright Information (http://www.fplc.edu/tfield/ipbasics.htm) provides information useful for general patent searchers as well as providing trademark and copyright information. Run by a law school, it is particularly useful in providing information to those interested in becoming patent attorneys.

11. Chemical Patents Plus (http://casweb.cas.org/chempatplus/). This source, maintained by the American Chemical Society, provides access to full-text patent information from 1975 to the present. It is updated weekly, and the texts of the patents listed in the *Official Gazette* on Tuesday are available by Thursday. Although the site requires a CAS user ID and password, registration, searching, and retrieval of patent titles and abstracts is free. There is a charge to display the text of the patents. There is enhanced coverage of the chemical patent literature.

12. Patent, Trademark, Copyright and Intellectial Property (http://fedlaw.gsa.gov/legal23.htm). This site provides links to various laws and regulations surrounding intellectual property, as well as listing various links to related sites.

13. DOE Patent Databases (http://apollo.osti.gov/waisgate/gchome2.html) list bibliographic information on patents issued to the Department of Energy beginning in 1978 to the present.

14. Web Patent Searching Tutorial (http://scilib.ucsd.edu/electclass/patsearch/index.html) from the University of California San Diego. This provides additional assistance in performing basic patent searches, including a valuable comparison chart between the IBM and USPTO search sites.

15. Electronic versions of some basic print sources (http://magni.grainger.uiuc.edu/patents/whery.html). For explanation of the functions of many of these sources, please refer to these patent searching techniques.

16. *Manual of Patent Examining Procedure* (http://patents.ame.nd.edu/mpep). The fore-
    word to the *Manual of Patent Examining Procedure* explains its purpose in the fol-
    lowing words: "This Manual is published to provide Patent and Trademark Office
    patent examiners, applicants, attorneys, agents, and representatives of applicants
    with a reference work on the practices and procedures relative to the prosecution of
    patent applications before the Patent and Trademark Office. It contains instructions
    to examiners, as well as other material in the nature of information and interpreta-
    tion, and outlines the current procedures which the examiners are required or author-
    ized to follow in appropriate cases in the normal examination of a patent application"
    (http://patents.ame.nd.edu/mpep/00/Foreword.html).

17. Index to the *Manual of Classification* (http://metalab.unc.edu/patents/index.html), run
    through the University of North Carolina.

18. Classification Definitions (http://www.uspto.gov/web/offices/pac/clasdefs/).

Patent Law Links

Here are valuable patent and trademark search sites, many of which are related to patent law:

1. U.S. Patent Office Full Text Database, http://www.uspto.gov/patft/index.html.

2. Delphion Intellectual Property Network, http://www.delphion.com.

3. Get The Patent.com, http://www.getthepatent.com.

4. IP-Discover, http://www.ipdiscover.com.

5. SurfIP.com, http://www.surfip.com.

6. IPOrganizer.com, http://www.iporganizer.com.

7. IP Search Engine, http://www.ipsearchengine.com.

8. CASWEB–Chemical Patents Plus!, http://casweb.cas.org/chempatplus.

9. CNIDR U.S. Patent Database, http://patents.cnidr.org:2424/access/access.html.

10. MicroPatent, http://www.micropatent.com.

11. Lexis-Nexis, http://www.lexis-nexus.com.

12. Shadow Patent Office, http://www.spo.eds.com/patent.html.

13. Software Patent Institute, http://www.spi.org.

14. COS US Patent Database, http://patents.cos.com.

15. Questel Orbit Patent Database, http://www.qpat.com.

16. Derwent, http://www.derwent.co.uk.

17. IFI Claims Databases, http://www.ificlaims.com.

18. Chi Research, http://www.chiresearch.com.

19. Fullerene Patent Database, http://www.godunov.com/Bucky/Patents.htm.l

20. Dialog, http://www.dialog.com.

CHAPTER 4

Invention Teams

Throughout history, teams of inventors have been formed to produce large numbers of inventions in a short time period.

Consider Thomas Edison (see Figure 4-1), who expanded his own talent as an inventor by creating a team of inventors to work in his Menlo Park research and development laboratory in what is today Edison, New Jersey. Edison's invention team enabled Edison to receive 1,093 patents—the most of any inventor in U.S. history.

Figure 4-1 Thomas Edison, master inventor with 1,093 patents (photo courtesy of the Smithsonian Institute).

Thomas Edison is the master inventor of many new ideas. Once, Edison told the world that "[My lab will produce] a minor invention every ten days and a big thing every six months or so."

Within six years of the founding of Edison's laboratory (see Figure 4-2), Edison with the help of his team earned more than 400 patents. These inventions included, among others, the phonograph, a carbon telephone transmitter (the microphone in the telephone mouthpiece), the first practical incandescent light bulb, and an electrical generating and transmitting system.

Figure 4-2 The Menlo Park, New Jersey, invention team lab in 1876
(photo courtesy of the Smithsonian Institute).

Shown here are drawings that Edison probably used when working with Alexander Graham Bell to invent the microphone for Bell's telephone. The following illustration Figure 4-3 shows Bell's concept drawing of the telephone.

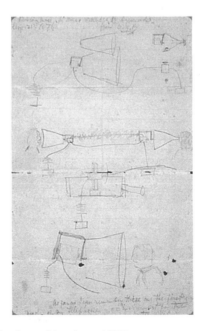

Figure 4-3 Sketch of Bell's telephone idea from 1876
(photo courtesy of the Library of Congress, Bell Papers).

Invention Team Core Members and Objectives

An invention team is a group of interested and skilled individuals who decide to meet regularly to develop inventions. Members of the team have unique skills and capabilities that they draw upon in interacting with each other while working on several different inventions at the same time.

The members of an invention team work closely together, and as shown in the Figure 4-4, they should enjoy spending time with each other testing their inventions and interacting with one another. Team-building interactions and activities, as shown in the Figure 4-5, help to build team spirit among the team members. With practice, refinement, and the right type of environment that fosters thought leadership—productivity of an invention team can soar.

INVENTION TEAM OBJECTIVES

The invention team objective is to identify many new and unique ideas over a relatively short period of time. Then the technical writers can further develop these ideas with collaboration from the core inventors. The invention draft is then created for other key inventors to review (and build upon), possibly incorporating additional intellectual property. In this process, the other co-inventors work to strengthen the idea by adding additional intellectual property not yet considered.

Many times, this will spawn other new and unique ideas.

Figure 4-4 The Edison invention team staff in its Menlo Park, New Jersey, lab in 1880 (photo courtesy of the Smithsonian Institute).

The psychological atmosphere of the place partook of the inspirational, as a sort of reflex of Edison's genius, which was happily joined with a common sense and a commendable human nature that made him . . . "one of the boys." . . . Here breathed a little community of kindred spirits, all in young manhood, enthusiastic about their work, expectant of great results; moreover often loudly emphatic in joke and vigorous in action.

—Charles Clarke, Edison employee.

For relaxation, it has been told that Edison would occasionally play an organ located against the back wall of this lab, especially when the men slowed down for a midnight snack or meal after long evenings of work. There were often energetic sing-along sessions, storytelling periods, and practical jokes and pranks played on each other. Edison would organize fishing trips, sometimes using the lab's experimental electric train for transportation to a local fishing hole.

Let's explore some member roles and team interactions noted in this type of phenomenal teaming approach. The invention team consists of the leadership team, technical writers, technology specialist(s), and patent defense team members. These individuals interact to create new ideas and to develop these new ideas into invention descriptions.

Figure 4-5 The Edison invention team staff members enjoy time together riding their experimental train (photo courtesy of the Smithsonian Institute).

Leadership Team

The leadership team's role is to coordinate the multiple inventions being developed in parallel by multiple team members. Sometimes, an invention team will consciously decide to take on a large number of inventions. Often, when this is done, it is because many of the inventions have causal impacts on the others, so separating the intellectual property is key. Managing the property well is important to keep the team from creating prior art against itself.

When creating bulk invention sets with many inventors, consider doing them all at the same time and compiling a notebook. In this notebook, place all of the details surrounding the problem, the solution, and the novelty of each invention. Be prepared to explain the differences in the claims and how they may or may not relate to each other.

This multiple invention approach will introduce complexities to the teaming effort, but these complexities can be managed. The leadership team will help to manage innovation amongst the team and to ensure that the team is working in healthy ways to achieve the goal.

Technical Writers/Technology Specialists

The invention team technical writer(s) provide very core support to their team by demonstrating their critical writing skills, especially with regard to semantics and understanding of documentation. They participate in inventor exchanges and effectively listen to this interchange of inventors' ideas. They contribute to this intellectual property development activity in their documentation, contextual expansions, and other critical skills areas only excellent writers can provide. This role is also very helpful for individuals who have a desire to learn the inventing process.

In this role of technical writer, one learns how to articulate the claims in such a way that each shows novelty: This is a challenge and nontrivial for even the best writers. This role is very critical to the team, and, generally speaking, this role should involve one or more individuals who are excellent in their expression of language. As an example, the ratio of technical writers on an invention team may be 1:4—that is, one writer for every four inventors. In this same area, an invention team may also want to include one or more inventors with a role of creating/writing marketing collaterals, depending on the nature of the invention. If a team intends to market their invention ideas, this step is a necessity. These collaterals might include a Web site, prototype examples, white papers, and product/services abstracts.

The invention team technology specialists seek to identify new areas of inventor interests related to technologies. These individuals maintain the goal of locating topic areas where many high-value inventions might be found. Often times, new technology can be studied and analyzed, whereby areas of the technology can be identified that require new ideas to efficiently assist the technology in some way. Inventors can pursue these areas with sometimes great results in yielding many inventions in a single topic area.

Patent Defense Members

The invention team patent defense members are critically skilled members who provide defensive thinking when the invention is being challenged, either by a team member, a patent attorney, a patent agent, or simply for reasons of strengthening the idea. The goal is to defend the idea by outlining strengths of the inventions, spotlighting the novelty and non-obvious points—while at the same time articulating the invention's problem, solution, and novelty.

Invention Team Processes

An invention team should consist of between five and ten inventors. Two or more teams can participate together on an invention if each team has few members. This minimizes the churn within the team surrounding innovative ideas.

Brainstorm ideas. See how many ideas the team can list within a given period of time. Do not process these ideas; no idea is considered to be out-of-line or crazy. It is this bundle of ideas that will spawn thinking of other ideas. List them all. Keep notes on comments of each idea, as long as the comments are for purposes of clarification and not determination.

If ideas begin to spawn other ideas around the same subject, bucket them and keep records of each idea. Draw or list them out on a white board where everyone can see them.

WHAT WILL A PATENT GIVE YOU?

A patent will give you the right to exclude others from making, using, selling, and importing a product or process that is covered by your patent. The value is clearly one of protection.

Whether or not you make any money from your patent depends on many factors, primarily relating to your routes-to-markets.

These are two very different topics.

Remember, every invention has to solve some kind of problem. So, the team members should keep track of these problems. If there are multiple problems, a team may want to consider creating a portfolio of problem areas. This way, each idea can be associated within this larger portfolio, and problem areas can better be classified according to some schema. This schema could be related to areas of technology, manufacturing, design, finance, life sciences, and medicine—virtually any topic of importance. Categories of classification for each idea should include consideration of whether or not the idea is high-value or low-value.

Perhaps occasional incentives to the inventors for certain topic areas of interest would be in order. Let's say that due to some external marketing force affecting a particular topic area, it is now inviting intellectual property to be created. This can strengthen your invention portfolio in areas that need more substantiation. These incentives can be monetary awards, specialized monogram clothing, dinner certificates, or online gift certificates—basically anything that might be an appropriate award for the intellectual property contribution of the inventor(s).

An outstanding example of how invention teams can be managed while engaging in practice business development activities is noted at the Information (IT) Leadership Academy, founded and directed by Michael Mino. In the ITLA,[1] hundreds of young people from many different New England High Schools gather each year to explore challenging mock-business development ideas, and at the same time, they develop vast numbers of inventions that help them to expand these business opportunities and ideas. These young adults are instructed on aspects of

[1] For more information on the IT Leadership Academy, please reference http://www.itacademy.org, or contact Mr. Michael Mino directly at mino@educationconnection.org.

becoming inventors, how to define problems and solutions, and how craft these ideas into inventions that those skilled in the art have not yet considered. These young adults are learning about business leadership through technologies and invention approaches. This program is a world-class, role-model program and demonstrates how innovation can be managed to a common end, using invention-teaming approaches.

Organizing an invention team can be a rewarding experience, and at the same time a very engaging process. More good news is that almost anyone can become an inventor. It is our basic human nature to solve problems, and it is this tendency that makes the invention process so natural for many people.

As shown in Figure 4-6, it is the idea that triggers a series of events.

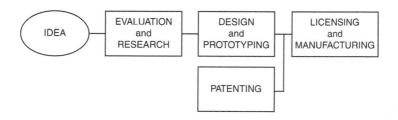

Figure 4-6 The invention team process has many facets, all of which begin with an idea.

Inventor Mentoring and Strengthening of Ideas

The team should consider ideas in a lateral fashion, building on previous thoughts. As a mentor, this means encouraging innovations surrounding a theme. Follow the team's thinking and find areas that as a mentor you are able to increase the teams' level of sensitivity to a design point. Select a point in the invention design that seems weak—solution aspects are broad and unclear. Ask questions around this area, causing the teams to consider points of novelty they had not yet considered in their solution sets. Once they do this, direct the teams back to the problem(s) they are trying to solve and ask each team to think in terms of "how do any new points of novelty we are considering help to solve this problem?" Encourage the teams to collaborate, while teaching them how to develop and manage their own intellectual property as assets.

Be consistent in the theme of invention by reinforcing the notion of something that *"those skilled in the art"* have not yet considered. Guide the teams into and through prior art searches, which will unveil aspects of their reasoning (or show them how prior art may exist and how to find it). Ask questions around these solution areas that may not be obvious but are indirectly related to the core idea. Causal impacts to the core idea are important when new lateral lines of thinking are introduced. If you see aspects of their ideas that have clear relationships to other ideas, point this out. Help the teams to collaborate in business ventures, and whenever possible, teach them how to share or manage their intellectual property in proper ways. Intellectual property asset evaluation and commercialization topics all become interesting discussions at this stage.

While inventor mentoring, always be curious. Ask many questions. Then, listen very effectively to what the individual inventors are saying. Help them to expand their thinking. Help them to see the novelty in their thinking. Help them to establish strength in the descriptions of their ideas. Always try to cross-reference any new lines of reasoning to other previously stated lines of reasoning; thus, strengthening the core of the novelty in the idea.

THE INVENTOR MENTORING ROLE

The inventor mentor works to guide teams to new inventions. He or she fosters the team's innovation towards solving the problem they originally stated, with a solution that is novel and that those skilled in the art have not yet considered. The inventor mentor often finds the need for working from engineering innovations to inventions.

The mentor has to possess patent creation skills and knowledge and have a strong understanding of the evaluation processes. This act of inventor mentoring, when effectively applied, enhances the chances for success across any invention team.

Strengthening ideas will often unveil new aspects of ideas not previously considered. In essence, this is a form of rapid idea generation. During this inventor mentoring process, it is common that new ideas will "starburst" into new, independent inventions. Carefully listen to each person as ideas are generated and begin to burst forth, and as the mentor, when you begin to hear something unique from their original thoughts, build upon what you are hearing. Cause conceptual graphing of sorts to occur in their minds to other new ideas. Guide the team to new discoveries of their own. Foster their innovation towards solving the problem they originally stated with a solution that is novel and that those skilled in the art have not yet considered.

CHAPTER 5

Invention Evaluation Teams

An invention evaluation team has a very valuable role to serve. This team works to create inventions (or intellectual property) and assess it for problems and solutions that suggest new and unique discoveries. This is accomplished by having an understanding of the laws respective to patents, trademarks, and copyrights.

An invention evaluation team is usually a small group of skilled individuals (maybe 5–10). The needed skills are, among others, effective listening and a broad and deep technical understanding across a wide spectrum of topics. The invention evaluation team meets on a regular basis to review patents and explore the development of strength of the invention(s). The most efficient evaluation teams will track and monitor the nature of invention ideas they review, while managing this intellectual property toward a much larger, more complex portfolio of ideas for their enterprise.

This team seeks to understand the problem suggested by each invention, the solution as described by the inventor(s), and the novelty in the solution. Non-obvious aspects of the idea are considered at this stage to ensure the idea fully qualifies as an invention.

The invention evaluation team focuses on prior art. Once the current art is understood, the invention evaluation team members may use a number of techniques for evaluating the idea. For example

1. Real-time Internet searches seeking prior art on other Web sites

2. USPTO adhoc keyword searches using a multitude of search strings

3. Focus on claims to prove or disprove validity

The evaluation team works with the inventor teams and tries to strengthen and prepare the idea for the more formal evaluation process. The evaluators want to cause the inventors to think about the problem and exactly how their solution solves the problem. At this stage, the inventor(s) through their work should be suggesting claims that serve to prove the invention solves the problem; these claims must be unique, original, and non-obvious.

Members of the team armed with defensive line-of-reasoning capabilities may want to be quietly waiting for the exact moment to speak up. To defend a challenge on a particular aspect of the idea is not a simple skill to demonstrate (or describe). Defensive reasoning is as much an interpersonal art form as it is managing a conversation based upon facts.

How to Start an Invention Evaluation Team

Since this is an informal evaluation team that is only created to provide the inventor team with a comparable board of invention reviewers—let's go ahead and draw from among the inventor team. This experience of utilizing inventors as invention evaluators provides great educational experience for inventors as they turn to the role of evaluator.

The evaluation team will focus on the aspects that the formal evaluators will consider. These are the elements of the problem, the solution, and the novelty. The evaluators will focus on what the inventors are claiming: Is it clear, hard-hitting, concise, and to the point? Has the inventor researched the prior art? Can the invention team respond to challenges against the claims with clarity, assurance, and confidence?

The evaluation team is best served when it rotates inventors in and out of the evaluation team process as evaluators. Of course, an inventor is always disqualified to process the evaluation of his or her own invention(s). However, anytime an inventor is available and not acting as an inventor, he or she should participate as an evaluator.

Evaluation Team Roles and Responsibilities

The evaluation team consists of several types of team members. These roles can rotate from member to member as the team sees fit; however, for most participants, several unique skills will be developed over time using this approach.

The evaluation team leader establishes the agenda and ensures regular meetings are conducted to keep the patent evaluation queue manageable. Generally speaking, keeping patent reviews to a minimum of 15 minutes, and no more than 25 minutes is a best practice to develop. The point here is that allowing fewer minutes, as opposed to more minutes, enforces with the inventor(s) to be to-the-point in presenting their ideas. This practice forces clarity in thinking.

The inventor team should agree on a spokesperson for the defense of the invention to the evaluators in the review and a special needs defensive team member, should the invention idea fail to prove its case. This entire exercise can only help to strengthen the skills of the team members and the sharpness of the problem, solution, and novelty.

Inventor and Evaluator Interactions

This collaboration is excellent for strengthening of ideas and building skills on any inventor team. Establish regular review sessions with inventor(s) and evaluators on a team. Consider appropriate protocol exchanges, which can occur between the evaluators and the inventors.

Work together to review the proposed invention ideas, the respective problems, solutions, and novelty associated with each idea. Inventors need to listen closely to the questions the evaluators are asking to determine if their explanations of the invention are coming across in the manner that they intend.

Inventor's Protocol

The inventor(s) must be crystal clear in their thinking. Remember that it is within the first few moments of discussion that an evaluator is looking to try to understand the problem, solution, and novelty the idea addresses. Pick a spokesperson for this role. Back this person up in all cases with additional teaming and support if it becomes necessary during the review; otherwise, let this person carry the role of "lead inventor," for the duration of the review.

Make sure each team member is concise, hard-hitting, and to-the-point as he or she describes elements of the problem, solution, and novelty. Ask the evaluators if they have questions as you progress through your discussions. Make sure that you are being understood in you explanation. Work to establish a warm and friendly review environment. This in itself encourages a welcome learning environment for both sides.

Sometimes if the topic of the invention(s) requires some education up-front of a review, it may be beneficial to send materials to the evaluators ahead of time. This often times can happen with very leading-edge technologies, sciences, and other technical areas.

Evaluator's Protocol

Evaluators (*for purposes as presented in this book*) should always work with inventors to help them strengthen their ideas. This can be accomplished in enlightening ways, which often result in the inventor(s) developing new lines of reasoning—ways for them to better explain exactly what they are thinking when they state the problem, the solution, and the novelty in their ideas. Ask them to explain why this is not obvious to those skilled in the art. Ask them to concisely state what they are claiming to be novel in their idea(s).

Evaluators need to be careful in handling innovative thinking concepts of inventors. Encouraging innovation is the key. Always work to recognize the novelty, relating it back into the solution and ultimately aspects of the problem this solves.

Evaluators may also want to watch carefully for ideas that spawn from other ideas. In some cases, inventors will describe an idea, which actually has more than one valid invention within it. Take time to point out to the inventor the potential of multiple ideas concealed inside a single idea.

Encourage the inventor(s) to contrast the prior art they have discovered with that of the current art—their invention idea(s).

Guidance on Secrecy Practices for Patents

Patents are sometimes classified into government-protected secrets. In these cases, the patents, the evaluators, and the inventors are managed in slightly different ways from normal patent processing methods.

The following discussion outlines the variance in handling secrecy patents, that is, according to the laws of the United States. For other countries and applicability to this subject of "secrecy," please contact the patent authority for your country or geographical region. For additional details on the content described in this section, please reference http://www.rl.af.mil/pls/oradata/show?in_filename=31-401.HTML.

NOTE
This discussion references the U.S. Department of Defense (DOD) 5200.1-R, Information Security Program Regulation, AFPD 31-4, Information Security, and AFI 31-401, Managing the Information Security Program. It sets up procedures for the review of patent applications held by the Security Division, U.S. Patent Office, and Department of Commerce.

A1-1. Patent Applications and Government Security

A1-1.1. A basic "specification" describing the invention

A1-1.2. A set of drawings illustrating the mechanism or apparatus

A1-1.3. An original set of claims (these are numbered, single paragraphs at the end of the specification which set out to define just what the invention is)

Although claims are in a language difficult for the layman to understand, their close scrutiny is not, ordinarily, necessary for a determination of secrecy.

A1-1.4. Correspondence, amendments, and office actions

These need not be reviewed, at least until an understanding of the invention has been secured from the specification and drawings.

A1-2. A Secrecy Order Is Needed When the Application Includes Certain Items

Technical data properly classifiable pursuant to a security guideline of the National Security Executive Order (EO 12358, classified National Security Information, April 20, 1995, effective 180 days).

A1-3. A Secrecy Order Is Not Needed When the Application Includes Certain Items

A1-3.1. Improvements in technique, application, material, or apparatus which basically are already known in the open engineering or scientific literature

A1-3.2. Bizarre, impractical, or technically unsound solutions to actual or imaginary problems

A1-3.3. Merely different arrangements or ways of doing something, where the existing general solution to the problem is well known or established

A1-3.4. Any improvement which has no apparent utility in National Defense effort

A1-3.5. Minor details of material in classified projects, providing the feature or parameters which cause the project to be classified are not disclosed

A1-4. As an Expert in the Technical Area, the Review Should Provide the Following Recommendations

A1-4.1. Whether or not the patent application should have a Secrecy Order issued

A1-4.2. Whether classified material is contained in the patent application

Where there is clear evidence of government property ownership interest (i.e., a statement on the first page of the specification as to an interest-free license to the government, a government contract number, or received with classified marking when filed at the Patent and Trademark Office (PTO)), the Government Technical Representative has the right to classify the patent application. If the patent application does contain classified information, it should be classified per DOD 5200.1-R, that is, classification level, downgrading and classification authority (including the most current security classification guide). If the patent is on microfiche, the envelope must be marked with the proper classification and downgrading. If a hard copy is supplied, all pages and paragraphs must be marked per DOD 5200.1-R. The Business Management Division marks the document based on your recommendation.

A1-5. Some Clarifications Related to Secrecy Orders

A-1-5.1. Any patent application that is found to have classified information contained in it and is subsequently classified automatically has a Secrecy Order issued on it by the Patent and Trademark Office (PTO).

A-1-5.2. Per DOD 5200.1-R, paragraph 2-701, a patent application on which a Secrecy Order has been imposed is handled as though classified CONFIDENTIAL (or some higher classification as determined in A1-4.2, this section).

Intellectual Property Asset Commercialization

Intellectual property assets have an elastic value that will greatly differ over the life of the asset. For example, our last discussion on patents that became government secrets, this becomes very clear. Government assets have a distinctive value set to a specifically defined cultural base.

To determine the value of an intellectual property asset is to say whether it is a high-value or low-value invention idea. Or to sell a trademark or copyright—what value might that bring? These topics are at the core of many large enterprise and country-level discussions today, as these entities aggressively work to bring to global markets their first-of-a-kind products and/or services. This is prevalent in almost every industrial country—none more aggressive than in the United States; however, for the purpose of this example, we will explore an Asian country, China.

China is an excellent example of a country that has demonstrated incredible growth in areas of intellectual property development. One very good example of this is the product approach they have employed to assist them in intellectual property asset commercialization decisions.

Shanghai's Intellectual Property Asset Evaluation System and Its Growth

According to Shanghai's Xinhua News Agency, enterprising organizations in China have created an application environment that evaluates intellectual property for assessing value. This system is described in the following text.

"A system that can evaluate a patent and give a fair price to it has been designed successfully in Shanghai and approved by experts.

The system, designed by the Shanghai Intellectual Property Right Service Center and the Shanghai Lixin Asset Evaluation Company, can store numerous data and patent cases and is equipped with special software for evaluation of patents.

In the past ten years, about 300,000 patent applications have been submitted, but only a small number have been put to commercial use partly due to lack of reliable patent evaluation systems.

The system will accelerate the industrialization process of China's patent achievement, according to the State Intellectual Property Office."[1]

China's Growth in Intellectual Property Areas

It has been noted that more and more patents are being applied for in China, with the total number standing at three million last year. This places China as a world leader in total quantity of patent applications. According to the State Intellectual Property Office, China led the world in 2003 with the largest number of applications filed for Innovation Patent and Patent of Practical New Patterns.

These statistics would, in turn, indicate that China's patent system is (more than ever) playing an increasingly important role in promoting technical innovation in the world.

Shanghai, the leading technology research geography center in China, saw an average of 62 new patent applications every day in 2003; this was an all-time high for them.

Shanghai received 22,374 patent applications in 2003, which was an increase of approximately 12% over the previous year. Patent applications from universities and colleges totaled 1,794, which exceed all other institutes of higher learning in China. Applications from industrial enterprises totaled approximately 15,280 in 2003, which was up 7% from the previous year.

Shanghai has collaborated on a wide-scale to build relationships across 16 provinces and regions. This particular collaboration is (in part) to serve to enhance an inter-regional crackdown on patent infringements.

An expert with the Shanghai Municipal Intellectual Property Rights Bureau claims that a big rise in patent applications now shows that many local technicians have a much stronger sense of intellectual property rights protection.

In recent days, statistics have shown that the average cost of an innovation patent is 42–73 million Yuan in state-owned scientific research institutes; 11–19 million Yuan in colleges and universities; and 3–11 million Yuan in large and medium-sized enterprises. The high cost of state-owned institutes reflected the inefficiency of the government input in technological innovation.

[1]   For more information, please reference Xinhua News Agency at http://www.china.com.cn/english/BAT/94635.htm.

This, however, is changing in very effective ways.

Today, their top priorities are beginning to focus on large enterprises that can achieve place-ment on the list of the world's top 500 enterprises and do so over the next five to ten-year period. And regarding the private technological enterprises with their own intellectual property rights, these organizations will also receive financial support from the government. At the same time, the government should consider an aggressive program providing increased incentives to individual innovators and inventors.

Defining a Patent: The Problem, Solution, and Novelty

The most interesting part of being an inventor is to solve problems that have never been solved. Being able to clearly state the problem that an invention addresses is paramount in any invention case. When an inventor describes his or her invention, the very first item of discussion should be exactly what problem the invention addresses and solves. The next topic should be the solution the inventor is proposing, and finally the novelty (if it did not become clear in the solution description).

This chapter will address the art (perhaps a critical skill) of identifying problems, creating unique solutions, and being able to simply articulate the novelty of these solutions. The underlying theme in this chapter will surround subjects of innovation engineering. The "farming" of ideas will be explored in more detail, unlike what we have been discussing thus far in this book.

The Skill of Problem Identification

Perhaps the most intuitive skill we have is one that has to be conditioned and refined by almost every individual during his or her life. That is the skill of being able to see a problem and to see it clearly enough as to identify its boundaries. Seek to understand what is related to this problem, extensions of the problem, and perhaps extensions *not* part of the problem. Make sure you know when you are looking at. Is it a separate problem in itself?

Problem identification is often most easy to perform when you are frustrated. Anyone who becomes part of a frustrating situation is actually facing an opportunity to solve a problem. While driving, walking, working, or playing—we all experience times that we see something and say to ourselves, "I could have thought up a much better solution to this . . . " Well, at that moment, think about what you are seeing, what you are experiencing, and record mentally what you would do to make it better. Immediately ask yourself, "Do you suppose anyone has ever thought of my idea before?" And if not, why not?

This invention skill can be consciously trained and refined every day if you continuously seek to identify problem areas, new technology areas, new services areas, and new utility areas—virtually any area where problems exist. When you become frustrated, look hard around you to understand why this situation is occurring. Invent a solution right there on the spot.

Seek to identify these problems by understanding the subject matter in greater depth. Separate problems when multiple problems exist. Consider sharing your ideas with trusted others with the sole intention of co-inventing a stronger solution idea. Many ideas can spawn many other ideas. We have discussed the benefit of intention teams; these are "patent spawning teams."[1] These teams record everything that is discussed and keep it as record for future spawning of ideas. Keep records of any and all searches that occur as a result of thinking about the solution space or problem space. Record all prior art that is discovered and note the differences in your idea(s) and the prior art. We discussed this in greater detail in Chapter 5, "Invention Evaluation Teams," and will now explore the skills involved on these teams that work to deliver a successful result.

The Skills of Solution Development

Solution development for creating inventions involves a discreet ability to envision many solutions in rapid-fire order. This, in some ways, resembles a chaotic approach to alternative analysis of many different ideas laterally—all at the same time. Try this, try that, keep thinking of different ways to solution the problem, and there is no possible wrong way to consider it. Then, step back and think about which solution makes the most sense and how novel that solution is.

Two major keys are exhaustive analysis of various solution design points and contrasting the points to specific functional needs in the solution. This type of thinking is done in parallel, and often times some degree of reasoning in uncertainty is involved—uncertain in terms of if I change the way I am thinking about this now, will the outcome be different? This line of reasoning is important to exhaustively exploring the conceptual design space in lieu of the scope of the problem trying to be resolved.

Effective listening is key here since one needs to fully understand where the problem barriers lie and what the boundaries of these barriers are. Understand how to foster and manage innovation, intersecting intellectual property (IP) with other elements of IP. Strengthen the solution to the most practical level and describe it in terms of *problem, solution, and novelty.*

The Skills of Novelty Harvesting

Learning how to spot novelty is sometimes (and only for some) like learning how to enjoy Sushi. Want a clue? Watch for situations that frustrate you. This happens because there is probably a better answer in your mind than to whatever is happening at that moment, and if you cannot think of it—you should quickly invent one.

---

[1]   "*Patent Spawning*" teams can be created and trained for the purpose of harvesting IP and spawning patents, and/or IP assets. This can be done surrounding any subject. Please contact the Author(s) for detailed information related to workshops entitled, "*Patent Spawning Teams*." For more information, e-mail SpawningTeams@yahoo.com.

Usually where you see a problem, look closely because there are probably several problems involved. When you find them, separate them, collect them, and look for relationships in them. Keep the scope of the problem you're attempting to solve in mind and focus on aspects of novelty in that solution. Then move to the next problem and do the same. If, in the course of doing this, you think of other solutions. This is natural; be certain to record these other problems and solutions by making notes.

Now think in terms of invention *claims* in the solution—claims that you can make to introduce and reinforce the novelty. How many different problems do you have? And if you combine some of them, does it then strengthen the original problem you started to solve? Have you harvested all that you can? Are there more? See Figure 6-1.

Figure 6-1 Harvesting intellectual property takes a lot of careful analysis and separation of problems and solutions. While gathering all these assets as new ideas, consider the need for packaging these idea, and how best to do it.

When you are able to associate a problem and a solution, which now seems novel, collect it. Harvest it and place it into the inventor's portfolio. (See Figure 6-2.) See how many other problems might surround that problem. Identify as many problems as possible, and then place these problems and solutions into a new invention portfolio. Now that you are beginning to make a collection of potential new ideas for inventors to review, try to expand them. By reviewing these ideas with the larger team, the team may spawn new ideas. Harvest them.

Classify each of the problems and associate the solutions and their claims of novelty. Collect any documentation or references to this problem that may be of relevance.

Claims are not simple to create. Study how other inventors have made their claims in their patent specifications. Notice the crispness and clarity.

Figure 6-2 Harvesting intellectual property requires precise packaging.

What Are Claims?

This section provides examples of real invention claims. These claims are related to the invention idea we discussed in Chapter 3, "Search Strategies, Techniques, and Search Tools to Validate the Uniqueness of any Invention," for blocking television commercials. Consider the intellectual protection each claim asserts to protect.

Apparatus and Method for Blocking Television Commercials and Displaying Alternative Programming

United States Patent Application	20030192045
Kind Code	A1
Fellenstein, Craig William; et al.	October 9, 2003

A method for blocking television programming comprising: receiving a first television signal; recognizing said first television signal; blocking said first television signal; and displaying said second television signal:

1. The method of claim 1 wherein said first television signal is a commercial.

2. The method of claim 1 wherein said first television signal is recognized by the time, audio, and video components of said first television signal.

3. The method of claim 1 wherein said first television signal is recognized by an identifying tag.

4. The method of claim 1 further comprising receiving user input defining said second television signal.

5. The method of claim 5 wherein said second television signal is defined as universal alternative programming.

6. The method of claim 5 wherein said second television signal is defined as alternative programming based on said first television signal.

7. The method of claim 5 wherein said second television signal is defined as alternative programming based on a television channel.

8. The method of claim 5 wherein said second television signal is defined as alternative programming based on the time of day.

9. The method of claim 5 wherein said second television signal is defined as an elaborate viewing hierarchy.

10. The method of claim 1 further comprising: buffering a third television signal; searching said third television signal; and recording part of said third television signal in a memory.

11. The method of claim 11 wherein said second television signal is defined as the contents of said memory.

12. A method of determining alternative programming displayed during a blocked television commercial comprising: displaying a plurality of alternative programming options to a user; receiving input from said user; blocking a first television signal; and displaying a second television signal based on said input.

13. The method of claim 13 wherein said second television signal is defined as universal alternative programming.

14. The method of claim 13 wherein said second television signal is defined as alternative programming based on said first television signal.

15. The method of claim 13 wherein said second television signal is defined as alternative programming based on a television channel.

16. The method of claim 13 wherein said second television signal is defined as alternative programming based on the time of day.

17. The method of claim 13 wherein said second television signal is defined as an elaborate viewing hierarchy.

18. The method of claim 13 further comprising: buffering a third television signal; searching said third television signal; and recording part of said third television signal in a memory.

19. The method of claim 20 wherein said second television signal is defined as the contents of said memory.

20. A programmable apparatus for blocking television programs comprising: programmable hardware; software; said hardware being directed by said software to: receive a first television signal; recognize said first television signal; block said first television signal; and display said second television signal.

21. The apparatus of claim 21 wherein said first television signal is a commercial.

22. The apparatus of claim 21 wherein said first television signal is recognized by the time, audio, and video components of said first television signal.

23. The apparatus of claim 21 wherein said first television signal is recognized by an identifying tag.

24. The apparatus of claim 21 wherein said software further directs said hardware to receive user input defining said second television signal.

25. The apparatus of claim 25 wherein said second television signal is defined as universal alternative programming.

26. The apparatus of claim 25 wherein said second television signal is defined as alternative programming based on said first television signal.

27. The apparatus of claim 25 wherein said second television signal is defined as alternative programming based on a television channel.

28. The apparatus of claim 25 wherein said second television signal is defined as alternative programming based on the time of day.

29. The apparatus of claim 25 wherein said second television signal is defined as an elaborate viewing hierarchy.

30. The apparatus of claim 21 wherein said software further directs said hardware to: buffer a third television signal; search said third television signal; and record part of said third television signal in a memory.

31. The apparatus of claim 31 wherein said second television signal is defined as the contents of said memory.

32. A programmable apparatus for determining alternative programming displayed during a blocked television commercial comprising: programmable hardware; software; said hardware being directed by said software to: display a plurality of alternative programming options to a user; receive input from said user; block a first television signal; and display a second television signal based on said input.

33. The apparatus of claim 33 wherein said second television signal is defined as universal alternative programming.

34. The apparatus of claim 33 wherein said second television signal is defined as alternative programming based on said first television signal.

35. The apparatus of claim 33 wherein said second television signal is defined as alternative programming based on a television channel.

36. The apparatus of claim 33 wherein said second television signal is defined as alternative programming based on the time of day.

37. The apparatus of claim 33 wherein said second television signal is defined as an elaborate viewing hierarchy.

38. The apparatus of claim 33 wherein said software further directs said hardware to: buffer a third television signal; search said third television signal; and record part of said third television signal in a memory.

39. The apparatus of claim 39 wherein said second television signal is defined as the contents of said memory.

This is an example of a solid set of invention claims for a single patent application: U.S. Patent Application No. 20030192045. A professional patent attorney and/or patent agent have worded these claims, and typically speaking, an inventor wants the claims to be constructed by a professional to ensure the proper protection language is incorporated into the patent application. These claims establish the form of breadth and depth of the idea, constituting the basis for the invention (for more details on this particular invention, No. 20030192045, see Appendix A, "Case Study Patents for Further Research").

Idea Farming

Idea farming is when you recognize that a series of problems exist, but you need to uncover a framework to be sure the scope of the problem series is properly understood (see Figure 6-3). In order to do this, bring together a group of bright minds and begin to foster innovation around topics related to the problem—mining group gold.

Explore the problem. Brainstorm many solutions. Identify unique solutions and find the claims. Capture these claims in writing. Step back, take another objective look at the problem, and ask, "Does this solution seem like something that those skilled in the art have already considered?"

Figure 6-3 Farming intellectual property in the form of problems, solutions, and claims of novelty takes a lot of forethought.

As an example of claims, let's take a look at the claims in one of the main invention ideas that we discussed in Chapter 3—that is, the television commercial blocking device.

The leadership skills necessary for establishing this kind of teaming approach to farming intellectual property are, in fact, less than remarkable. Success for these types of sessions requires a personality that is able to foster innovation by presenting thought provoking challenges to members of a group. If the group is large, keep track of the individual contributions of intellectual property.

Sometimes, the leader can build intellectual intersections between what one person says versus another. Point these out as clear items of novelty whenever possible. Teaming and a bit of cognitive collaboration is the fundamental objective of these types of sessions.

This process serves to identify and strengthen new ideas and perhaps cause the discovery of unique invention claims. With practice, these types of invention teams can grow to become very effective and able to tackle almost any topic.

CHAPTER 7

Mining Intellectual Property Assets

As you have learned throughout this book, the major premise of an invention asserts the fact that the solution to any specific problem must prove to be a unique idea—that is, an idea that those skilled in the art have not yet claimed or considered. Furthermore, there is another premise that proves that it is NOT obvious that these experts would have ever considered this idea. This second premise, although somewhat subjective and awkward, is an important test to apply.

This chapter shows how to file multiple invention ideas and how to be most efficient in this process. This discussion will build upon our last discussions of "mining group gold," and show us how to deliver bulk patents surrounding any area with needs for improvement. (See Figure 7-1.)

Problem, Solution, and Novelty
An Invention Must Address a Problem with a Unique Solution

Problem	The problem addressed by the invention idea is a relevant problem.
Solution	The solution that addresses the problem is a unique solution, one which those "skilled in the art" have not yet considered.
Novelty	The idea expressed by the solution is unique, novel, and non-obvious.
Non-obvious	The solution must be non-obvious in such a way as those skilled in the art would have obviously considered this idea as a solution.

Figure 7-1 An invention idea must represent a problem and yield a solution that those skilled in the art have not yet considered. Non-obvious consideration is the final test. Although subjective in many ways, this is a very important premise.

How to Articulate Multiple Related Problems

Inventing begins with a clear understanding of the problems to be solved. Every invention has at least one associated problem. Find this problem, reduce it to its most common denominator, and begin to solve it. During this problem definition stage, inventors should try to envision any social, technological, and economic positioning of their inventions. Also, inventors should consider the parameters and clear problem boundaries for the invention. Make sure to look at the problems from many different perspectives including that of the end user.

Defining a problem sometimes implies that one is able to determine the limitations and boundaries of reasoning surrounding the problem. For example, the introduction of a new technology. and, let's say you have a financial limit of USD $1,000,000 to introduce the new technology. There may be other limitations such as environmental concerns, cultural issues, government issues, other geographies, or legal issues. So before you begin solving the problem, ensure that all possible factors that could limit your success are well understood.

Considering the problem of trying to introduce a new technology (e.g., grid computing), and making sure any obvious problems are attended to in creative and innovative ways, you begin to identify multiple problem areas. In getting to this stage, the invention team focuses on understanding the problems and any relationships between the problem areas. They explore alternatives by considering lateral lines of thinking as they attempt to provide solution design points and creative ideas. Capturing all the random ideas and documenting any discussions—they begin to see a framework or pattern. This framework then allows solutions to be categorized, considered as independent inventions, and allows the team to work on ideas according to some priority. At this stage, team dynamics are well underway towards "mining group gold."

Another important aspect of defining the problem area is researching what has been done in the past to solve it—that is, the prior art. We have already discussed this topic in great detail. The first step is to do a thorough patent prior art search, much like the example on "blocking television commercials" we explored in Chapters 2 and 3. In addition to thorough patents prior art search, one should also do a literature search and finally a (wider) general Internet search. Keep printed records of your search. Keep these printouts on file with any other documents that may describe prior art that overlaps or comes close to your idea(s). Keep in mind, that even after you complete these in-depth searches, there is no guarantee that you will find all the previous prior art. Nonetheless, this has to be done in order to show due diligence on the part of the inventor(s). There is also a secondary benefit to performing a thorough patent prior art search. That is, by analyzing other inventions close to your ideas you (by default) begin to conceptually strengthen your own ideas. This is a natural defensive tendency that occurs, and yet, the most fascinating part of this process is that it tends to spawn new ideas. Capture these new ideas, as well.

How to Articulate Multiple Solutions for Multiple Problems

Resist the urge to present the "marketing" side of the idea. Almost invariably when invention descriptions are presented this way, they are far too broad to concisely state the problem, solution, and novelty. Patent evaluators are not inclined to be able to easily identify the claims of an invention from these types of broader descriptions. This is especially difficult when multiple patent applications related to a common area are being considered.

Once the multiple problems are clearly defined, the next step is to generate ideas to solve these. Most likely (if you are working with a patent spawning team), the team already has some ideas that seem like winners, but do not close the door on new ideas due to preconceived notions. These preconceived notions are, however, extremely important for all the team members—because to generate their own ideas first, before brainstorming in the larger group, improves the potential for novelty in the end result.

Brainstorming (for those unfamiliar with the technique) is a word that refers to the activity of opening your imagination to produce as many ideas as possible without processing any of them in the first round—just getting them out is the goal. Most of the ideas may end up being not exactly what you are looking for in your mind, but there will be some excellent ideas that you may discover through the process.

Once one or more problems are envisioned and many solution ideas have been generated, try to be more concise, hard-hitting, and to-the-point regarding claims of novelty associated with each of the solutions. Look closely to see what you are claiming to be the problem and its relationship to another problem, and make sure you have made the respective number of proposed claims in your solution(s) to address the proper aspects of the problems. Ensure the defense of these novelty items includes other prior art examples that might be close, or even examples of where the prior art is weak (may be, or may not be related) or the prior art is simply non-existent.

Communicating the multiple ideas clearly is paramount and the single key to success. Think of it like this. The *elevator pitch*: This requires the inventor to verbally articulate the individual idea's in a very few minutes. Imagine you just stepped onto an elevator (or lift), and the person already onboard this elevator is someone you must convince that they need your invention, prior to them arriving at their floor. So you only have a few minutes to convey the problems, solutions, and items of novelty. Prepare yourself for this as the ideas then become clearer in your mind.

Intersect the solutions back to the problems and do this to prove your solutions solve each of the problems in unique and independent manners. Contrast the solutions to what has been done in the past; yet, (most importantly) show without a doubt how your idea is different from what has been previously filed. Show this in such a way as it would not even be obvious to experts in this area. The solutions and claims you make as to how you have solved the problem must be unique, and the inventor has to be able to clearly explain this.

The best disclosures will always give the "big picture," and then they will describe the prior art and the invention with the technical details necessary to articulate the conclusion. Make sure you show how the invention differs from any prior art. In some disclosures, a common problem with an inventor is that he or she sees chunks of the big picture, only a brief discussion of related prior art, and often not enough technical details to clearly articulate the solution(s). All of this is further confused by references to other disclosures. The prior art that needs to be discussed for the invention is how each problem is solved in a systematic way and how it is solved well in this environment. Ensure that the proper level of detail is directly referenced in the disclosure. That is, if this is the level at which the solution differs from the other solution(s), this is the level of technical detail that should be in the disclosure.

The best disclosures focus on the technical descriptions and are not overrun by legal jargon put forth by inventor: Leave the legal descriptions to the patent attorneys. Inventors should focus on writing a good, solid, technical description of the invention. When patent attorneys are forced to read legal jargon (from inventors) in a disclosure, analyze the legal jargon to determine what it means, and then rewrite it—this is counter productive. We have no doubt that many inventors can use proper legal jargon, but at the same time, legal jargon should not be a substitute for a good, solid technical description. This inventor-placed legal jargon adds an extra step of analysis by the patent attorney that is neither productive or of much value.

The best disclosures (when submitted in bulk numbers or as single filings) are concise, hard-hitting, and to-the-point. In some early disclosure drafts of the inventor(s), there may be repetition of the same ideas using different terminology within a single disclosure and across multiple disclosures. What is actually preferred is a more concise definition of the problem(s) and solution(s). This, in turn, leads to a more productive and concise prior art search, which then leads to a better application, which then has the best chance of issuing the strongest and most original claims. One suggestion is that if specific passages of any disclosures are included to answer predicted questions from an evaluation team, then help these teams (or the patent attorney) by including those predicted questions in the disclosure.

When describing multiple, related ideas, the best disclosures have the same technical description of the entire invention but separate titles and intro paragraphs that describe each problem to be solved, as well as how the problem is to be solved. This method more effectively forces all the related disclosures to go through the process together and is more likely to provide an enabling embodiment for the inventor. As you do this, ensure that you know the difference of proposing an engineering innovation, versus a patent. We discussed this in previous chapters. Ensure that all of your documentation is recorded as clear as possible, and shared with the wider team.

In addition, in the case that counsel disagrees with the way that the inventor has defined the multiple inventions, inventor has really only invested a couple of paragraphs worth of time into each disclosure beyond the common description. In our experience, even though an evaluation team may see, let's say, four related ideas as separate, the patent attorney may suggest bringing together of these ideas after seeing the search results—or for other relevant reasons. If the ideas are merged, then when counsel gets the merged ideas, they may not have to merge the description of the invention, which is less work for everyone.

In conclusion, the best invention disclosures are organized for efficiency. Bulk invention disclosure submissions are often created as a package of multiple inventions and considered as a holistic group. In corporate environments with intellectual property incentive programs, patent attorneys, and inventors may sometimes be receiving flat fees for each application they file. Submitting patents in bulk form is often a best practice utilized to address (for instance) a new technology (e.g., biomedicine, grid computing) or a wide area of technologies. This bulk submission process is most efficient, especially when both parties are working towards efficient use of each other's time. This is critical when dealing with many inventions in a single lot; and it is at this stage that you are, in fact, truly "mining group gold."

Intellectual Property

Intellectual property is a consideration of intellectual capabilities that has market value, such as (and perhaps not limited to) inventions, ideas or expressions, business methods, industrial processes, and chemical formula. Intellectual property is an intangible business asset that has elastic value determined by the marketplace.

An intellectual property asset must be protected through an appropriate legal means, such as a patent, trademark, service mark, or copyright. State, federal, and international intellectual property laws provide protection (see Figure 8-1).

What Are the Differences?

Copyrights, Trade Secrets, and Trademarks Yield Different Protection

Copyright	Protects the expression of an idea.
Patent	Protects the idea.
Trade Secret	Idea is protected but only if maintained as a trade secret.
Trademark	Protects the name or a symbol identifying a product or a service, officially registered and legally restricted to the use of the owner.

Figure 8-1 The provisions for providing regulated forms of intellectual property can be thought about in several different ways.

Intellectual property consists of two principal perspectives. These are basically considered to be industrial property and copyrights of literary works, including music and artistic works:

1. **Industrial property:** Patents and other rights in inventions, rights in trademarks, industrial rights, and appellations of origin

2. **Copyrights and neighboring rights:** In literary, musical, and artistic works in films and records

The term "intellectual property" was formally defined in the *1967 Stockholm Convention*, which established the World Intellectual Property Organization. Article 2 (viii) of the *Convention* provides that "Intellectual Property" shall include the rights relating to

- Literary, artistic, and scientific works
- Performances of performing artists, phonograms, and broadcasts
- Inventions in all fields of human endeavors
- Scientific discoveries
- Industrial designs
- Trademarks, service marks, and commercial names and designations
- Protection against unfair competition
- All other rights resulting from intellectual activity in the industrial, scientific, literary, or artistic fields

Protection of intellectual property is the subject of many international agreements. The need for comprehensive international agreements became apparent in the nineteenth century and then resulted in the creation of the Paris and Berne Unions. This subject is also provided full treatment in Chapter 9, "Protection: Copyrights, Trademarks, Trade Secrets, Patents, and Publishing Intellectual Property."

The *Convention for the Protection of Industrial Property*, signed in Paris on March 20, 1883, established the Paris Union. Originally signed by 11 countries, more than 100 countries are now parties to this convention. Its objectives were to secure legal protection for industrial property and to encourage uniformity of law by superseding the system of bilateral treaties. Among the key principles adopted by this convention is the principle of "national treatment," which provides that member states shall accord to nationals of other member states the same advantages under their laws relating to the protection of industrial property as they accord their own nationals. The *Paris Convention* has been revised on seven occasions since its adoption and is now administered by the World Intellectual Property Organization (WIPO).

The Berne Union was established to confront the problem of international editorial and literary piracy in Europe and America in the nineteenth century. The *Convention for the Protection of Literary and Artistic Works*[1] was signed at Berne on September 9, 1886. More than 80 countries

---

[1]   For more information, please reference http://en.wikipedia.org/wiki/Berne_Convention_for_the_Protection_of_Literary_and_Artistic_Works.

are parties to this convention. One of the convention's guiding principles is that member states must accord the same protection to the copyright of nationals of other member states as to their own. It also prescribes minimum standards of protection. For example, copyright protection generally continues throughout the author's life and for 50 years thereafter. The *Berne Convention* has been revised seven times and is also administered by the World Intellectual Property Organization.

Since the creation of the Paris and Berne Unions in the nineteenth century, over 30 global treaty arrangements have entered into force, as well as a variety of regional treaty arrangements, governing different aspects of the intellectual property protection. The development of new technologies involving the semiconductor chip, computer software, and biotechnology has led to the promulgation of such treaties as the *Treaty on Intellectual Property in Respect of Integrated Circuits*, signed in Washington on May 26, 1989, and the *Budapest Treaty on the International Recognition of the Deposit of Microorganisms for the Purposes of Patent Procedure*, signed at Budapest on April 28, 1977.

Because of the increase in international trade in intellectual property over the past decade, it has become apparent that there is a compelling need for greater international cooperation. Protection of intellectual property rights is now the subject of much interest and debate upon the world's intellectual property theater. Let's take a definitive look at the various forms of intellectual property.

Patents

Patents are different from trademarks. Patents provide protection for inventions, processes, formulas, or improvements in one of these areas. Patent protection is a right granted by a government that gives its holder the right to exclude others from making, using, or selling the patented invention "claimed" in the patent deed, provided that certain fees are paid. Part of the intent of patent provisioning laws is to give the developer of a new product or idea time to recover any necessary research and development costs, along with start-up costs, without the normal influence from competition.

Patents may not be obtained for an invention that has been publicly disclosed, is in use, or marketed in this country for more than one year before a patent application is filed. Thus, it is critical to patent an invention before disclosing or marketing it; otherwise, the possibility of obtaining a patent is quickly jeopardized.

Obtaining a patent sometimes can be time-consuming. In fact the process, which includes conducting a search and the application preparation, may take from several weeks up to a year and then another two years for approval by the U.S. Patent and Trademark Office. Patent searches are necessary because these will give the inventor a good indication as to whether the idea has already been patented. This search period will vary, depending on the country, but it will take time. The fact that the idea is not on the market does not mean that has not been patented; therefore, the need for a prior art search exists.

Patent searches can be accomplished in several ways. We discussed formalisms to this process in Chapter 3. The inventor can and should also consult a patent attorney for a legal search. These usually cost several hundred dollars but will provide the best results. The inventor also can visit the publicly available free search sites to try to identify prior art (as shown in Chapters 2 and 3). There is no charge to utilize the free public sites for this assistance, but it will take time and some computer keyword-search expertise on the part of the inventor.

Definition: Patent

pat·ent ('pa-t°nt)—*n.*

1.
   a. TA grant made by a government that confers upon the creator of an invention the sole right to make, use, and sell that invention for a set period of time.
   b. Letters patent.
   c . An invention protected by such a grant.

2.
   a. A grant made by a government that confers on an individual fee—simple title to public lands.
   b. The official document of such a grant.
   c. The land so granted.

3. An exclusive right or title.

pat·ent ('pa-t°nt)—*adj.*

1.
   a. Protected or conferred by a patent or letters patent: *a patent right.*
   b. Of, relating to, or dealing in patents: *patent law.*

2. (also 'pa-t°nt) Obvious; plain.

3. ('pa-t°nt) *Biology.*
   a. Not blocked; open.
   b. Spreading open; expanded.

4. Of, relating to, or being a nonprescription drug or other medical preparation that is often protected by a trademark.

5. Of high quality. Used of flour.

6. (also 'pa-t°nt) *Archaic.* Open to general inspection. Used especially of documents.

pat·ent·ed, pat·ent·ing, pat·ents—*tr.v.*

1. To obtain a patent on or for (an invention, for example).
2. To invent, originate, or be the proprietor of (an idea, for example).
3. To grant a patent to or for.

Copyright

A copyright is a form of protection to the authors of original works including literary, dramatic, musical, artistic, and certain other intellectual works. Examples of copyrightable works include books, music, motion pictures, photographs, and architectural works. Copyright laws give the owner(s) of the copyright exclusive rights to reproduce and to authorize others to reproduce the copyrighted work, to prepare derivative works based on the original(s), to distribute copies of the work, and to perform or display the work into public forums.

Copyright protection begins immediately, as soon as the work is created in a fixed form. It is an incident of the process and becomes the property of the author as it is accomplished. Only the author or those proclaiming their rights through the author can rightfully claim copyright to the work. The employer (and not the employee) is almost always considered the author in the case of works made for hire or if the works were created within the scope of his or her employment.

In the U.S., registration with the U.S. Library of Congress does offer certain advantages. Registration of a copyright establishes the public record of the copyright claim(s), and in the event that the work is infringed, the court will not allow a defendant to claim "innocent infringement" (in other words, he or she was not aware that the work is protected). Innocent infringement claims often reduce the amount of damages that the copyright owner would otherwise receive. Another advantage to copyright registration is that it allows the copyright owner to record the registration with the U.S. Customs Service for protection against the importation of infringing copyright copies. Before an infringement suit may be filed in court, copyright registration is necessary, and if made before the actual publication, this registration establishes solid evidence as to the validity of the copyright.

Any work that is fixed in a tangible form is protected from the point of creation and normally endures for the author's life, plus an additional 50 years after the author's death. For works classified as "made for hire," the protection lasts for a period of 75 years. As with patents and trademarks, the burden of policing copyrighted materials always falls upon the holder of the protected material.

Trademarks, patents, and copyrights often play an important role in a small business enterprise. The processes of obtaining them can be confusing, time consuming, and usually require legal advice. Knowing where to go for information, advice, and assistance makes the copyright process much simpler.

Definition: Copyright

cop·y·right (ˈkä-pē-rīt)—*n. Abbr.* **c.** or **cop**.

> The legal right granted to an author, composer, playwright, publisher, or distributor to exclusive publication, production, sale, or distribution of a literary, musical, dramatic, or artistic work.

> The right of an author (or his/her assignee) under statute to print and publish his/her literary or artistic work, exclusively of all other persons. This right may be had in maps, charts, engravings, plays, and musical compositions, as well as in books. Note: In the United States, a copyright runs for the term of 28 years, with right of renewal for 14 years on certain conditions.

cop·y·right (ˈkä-pē-rīt)—*adj.*

> **1.** Of or relating to a copyright: *copyright law; a copyright agreement.*

> **2.** Protected by copyright: *permission to publish copyright material.*

cop·y·right·ed, cop·y·right·ing, cop·y·rights—*tr.v.*

> **1.** To secure a copyright for.

cop'y·right'a·ble *adj.*
cop'y·right'er *n.*

Trademarks

A trademark is any word or symbol that is consistently attached to certain goods to identify and distinguish those goods from others in the marketplace. In other words, a trademark is basically like a brand name. Trademarks are a means of identification for a product (or services, in the case of a service mark) of a particular individual or company. This mark can be a symbol, slogan, word, design, or a combination of words and designs. Sometimes, trademarks are confused with trade names. *Trade names* only refer to the name of the company that sells the product or service. Trademarks are the name of the product or service that a particular company is offering for sale in the public. Trademarks are protected under federal trademark laws, and trade names are protected under state laws wherein the company resides.

Consumers often purchase a product or service because they associate a certain quality or reputation to the trademark or service mark. Service marks, which are also a form of trademark protection, are a name or symbol that identifies services rather than products provided by a company. Examples of service marks include "Blue Cross Blue Shield," the health-care provider. Certification marks are a specific form of trademark protection, which consists of a name or a symbol identifying a particular group, board, or commission that judges the quality of goods or services. For example, in the U.S., we have power equipment certifications, such as "UL Approved." The final form of trademark protection is referred to as *collective marks*. These consist of an identifying symbol or name showing membership in an organization, such as in the financial industries, the "FDIC."

Trademark rights can last indefinitely; however, five to six years following the initial registrations, the registrant is required to file an affidavit stating that the mark is currently being utilized as intended, and the registrant must renew this mark every 10 years. The registrant and owner of a trademark must police it against infringements and assure that it does not fall into general use by others. Otherwise, the mark could become generic, and the trademark protection is then forfeited.

Obtaining a trademark can be (and often is) a time-consuming task, especially if the owner plans to market products nationally. Any approval of a federally registered trademark will take several months. Existing trademarks can be registered nationally (in the U.S.)—that is, providing the product is being sold through means of interstate commerce (i.e., the mark is utilized in two or more states). A trademark may also be registered within a state in the U.S.

If the mark will be utilized only within the state, then the mark needs only to be registered within the office of the Secretary of State. If the mark will be used in two or more states in the U.S., then it is eligible for federal registration through the U.S. Patent and Trademark Office.

Before one takes the steps to apply for registration of a trademark or service mark, it is paramount to understand if the trademark (or a similar trademark) already exists. This information is available on an individual state basis from the Secretary of State offices and on a national U.S. basis from the U.S. Patent and Trademark Office, within the U.S. Department of Commerce. There are U.S. state agencies that offer assistance by checking for existing trademarks.

Trademark infringement can be problematic whenever people attempt to use trademarks or symbols that closely resemble those utilized by existing companies. Therefore, U.S. state registration of a national trademark "look alike," does not legitimize utilizing it, nor does it offer any protection against claims of the firm that already has the trademark nationally registered. One must check the national registration of existing trademarks before utilizing any trademark.

Although trademark registration is designed to prevent infringement from others, the entire responsibility of policing their already registered mark against infringement or general use is the responsibility of the trademark owner.

Definition: Trademark

trade·mark (trād'märk')—*n.*

1. *Abbr.* **TM** a name, symbol, or other device identifying a product, officially registered and legally restricted to the use of the owner or manufacturer.

2. A distinctive characteristic by which a person or thing comes to be known: *the shuffle and snicker that became the comedian's trademark.*

trade·marked, trade·mark·ing, trade·marks—*tr.v.*

1. To label (a product) with proprietary identification.

2. To register (something) as a trademark.

Trade-mark \Trade"-mark\—*n.* A peculiar distinguishing mark or device affixed by a manufacturer or a merchant to his goods, the exclusive right of using which is recognized by law.

1. *n*: A distinctive characteristic or attribute [syn: hallmark, earmark, style mark].

2. *n:* A formally registered symbol identifying the manufacturer or distributor of a product.

For More Information on Intellectual Property

U.S. Patent and Trademark Office, reference http://www.uspto.gov
Copyright Office, Library of Congress, reference http://www.copyright.gov

Selected References

- *Basic Facts About Trademarks.* U.S. Department of Commerce, Patent and Trademark Office, November 1989.

- *Can You Make Money With Your Idea and Invention?* U.S. Small Business Administration, Management Aids, No. 2.013.

- *Copyright Basics.* Library of Congress, Circular 1.

- Disclosure Document Program. U.S. Patent and Trademark Office, Washington D.C., 20231.

- *General Information Concerning Patents.* U.S. Department of Commerce, Patent and Trademark Office, May, 1992.

- *How to Sell Your Own Invention.* William E. Reefman, Halls of Ivy Press, 13050 Raymer Street, North Hollywood, CA 91605, 1977.

- *Introduction to Patents.* U.S. Small Business Administration, U.S. Department of Commerce, Management Aids, No. 6.005, 1983.

- *Inventors Guidebook: A Step By Step Guide to Success.* Melvin L. Fuller, ILMA Printing and Publishing, P.O. Box 251 Tarzana, CA 91356, 1984.

- *Patent It Yourself: A Complete Legal Guide for Inventors.* David Pressman, NOLO Press, 950 Parker Street, Berkeley, CA 94710, 1985.

- *The Inventors Handbook: How to Develop, Protect, and Market Your Invention.* Robert Park, Betterway Publications, Inc., While Hall, VA.

- *Understanding Patents, Trademarks, and Other Proprietary Assets and Their Role in Technology Transfer.* Homer, O. Blair, 10 Maguire Road, Lexington, MA 02173, 1977.

CHAPTER 9

Property Protection:
Copyrights, Trademarks,
Trade Secrets, Patents,
and Publishing
Intellectual Property

Intellectual property is protected through copyrights, trademarks, trade secrets, and patents, which you learned about throughout this book. In this chapter, you'll learn how to initiate this protection for your own ideas.

Remember that for a patent, your idea must provide a novel solution to a problem, and the solution must be non-obvious based on common legal practices. If your idea doesn't pass this test, then intellectual property patent laws will not protect your idea.

A trade secret is a unique kind of intellectual property that isn't granted official status because, by its nature, a trade secret is out of public view. Your trade secret is protected by secrecy until the secret is revealed or someone discovers it.

What Are the Differences?
Copyrights, Trade Secrets, and Trademarks Yield Different Protection

Copyright	Protects the expression of an idea.
Patent	Protects the idea.
Trade Secret	Idea is protected but only if maintained as a trade secret.
Trademark	Protects the name or a symbol identifying a product or a service, officially registered and legally restricted to the use of the owner.

Figure 9-1 Variety of common intellectual property classifications.

What are the differences between trademarks, copyrights, patents, and trade secrets? They are all generally described as *intellectual property*. These are forms of intangible property because they maintain property rights that cannot be touched (literally speaking) or physically felt like personal property (e.g., a car, a desk) or real property (e.g., land) (see Figure 9-1). However, the actual terms have distinct meanings and define different attributes of property:

- *Trademark* (®, ™, ᔆᴹ) protects a word, phrase, symbol, and/or design that are utilized with a product or service in the open market. A trademark is often referred to as a brand. Trademark rights may continue indefinitely, as long as the mark is neither abandoned by the trademark owner nor loses its significance in the marketplace as a trademark by becoming a generic term.

- *Copyright* (©) protects the original way an idea is expressed, not the idea itself. It includes artistic, literary, dramatic, or musical works presented in a tangible medium such as a book, photograph, or movie. This protection is given to works to prevent unauthorized copying. The general rule for a work created on or after January 1, 1978, is that the copyright lasts for the author's lifetime plus 70 years after the author's death or 95 years after publication for a work made for hire.

- *Patent* protects a new and useful idea, which includes an article of manufacture and composition of matter. It is granted by the government, providing an inventor with exclusive rights to make, use, and sell a patented invention. Patents have a fixed term, 20 years starting from when the patent application is filed. This goes into effect when the patent is issued.

- *Trade Secret* is held as a secret (e.g., Campbell's Soup recipes, the mud at the core of a baseball, etc.) and is only valid until it is divulged or discovered, and at this stage of public discovery, it is no longer a secret.

In this chapter, we will explore all of these concepts and explain in a step-wise fashion exactly how to initiate and complete each one of the protection means in a simple yet legal fashion. Likewise, we will explore the differences in these various types of innovations and how both global societies and businesses typically tend to deal with managing and submitting these types innovations.

The Value of a Copyright, and How to Initiate It

A *copyright* is the legal right granted to an author, composer, playwright, publisher, or distributor to exclusive publication, production, sale, or distribution of a literary, musical, dramatic, or artistic work.[1]

---

[1]   As defined by http://dictionary.reference.com/search?q=copyright.

The values of establishing a copyright, aside from simply protecting the expression of an idea, are several. These values are listed here and are exactly noted (and referenced from) the United States Copyright Office. Subject[2] to Sections 107 through 122, the owner of copyright under this title has the exclusive rights to do and to authorize any of the following:

1. To reproduce the Copyrighted work in copies or phonorecords

2. To prepare derivative works based upon the Copyrighted work

3. To distribute copies or phonorecords of the Copyrighted work to the public by sale or other transfer of ownership, or by rental, lease, or lending

4. In the case of literary, musical, dramatic, and choreographic works, pantomimes, and motion pictures and other audiovisual works, to perform the Copyrighted work publicly

5. In the case of literary, musical, dramatic, and choreographic works, pantomimes, and pictorial, graphic, or sculptural works, including the individual images of a motion picture or other audiovisual work, to display the Copyrighted work publicly

6. In the case of sound recordings, to perform the Copyrighted work publicly by means of a digital audio transmission

Also, as defined very exactly by (and referenced from) the United States Copyright Office,[3] a copyright is a form of protection provided by the laws of the United States (title 17, U.S. Code) to the authors of "original works of authorship," including literary, dramatic, musical, artistic, and certain other intellectual works. This protection is available to both published and unpublished works. Section 106 of the 1976 Copyright Act generally gives the owner of copyright the exclusive right to do and to authorize others to do the following:

- *To reproduce* the work in copies or phonorecords
- To prepare *derivative works* based upon the work
- *To distribute copies or phonorecords* of the work to the public by sale or other transfer of ownership, or by rental, lease, or lending
- *To perform the work publicly,* in the case of literary, musical, dramatic, and choreographic works, pantomimes, and motion pictures and other audiovisual works
- *To display the Copyrighted work publicly,* in the case of literary, musical, dramatic, and choreographic works, pantomimes, and pictorial, graphic, or sculptural works, including the individual images of a motion picture or other audiovisual work
- In the case of *sound recordings, to perform the work publicly* by means of a *digital audio transmission*

[2] For further details, please reference http://www.Copyright.gov/title17/92chap1.html.
[3] For further details on this important topic, please reference the United States Copyright Office, Library of Congress, at http://lcweb.loc.gov/Copyright.

In addition, certain authors of works of visual art have the rights of attribution and integrity as described in Section 106A of the 1976 Copyright Act.[4] Fees for basic registration, document recordation, supplementary registration, search services, certificates, and additional certificates are listed here. The U.S. Copyright Office increased certain fees effective July 1, 2002. For more information, read the *Analysis and Proposed Copyright Fee Schedule*, or see a *fee comparison chart*.

For further information[5] on current fees, call the Copyright Public Information Office at (202) 707-3000, 8:30 a.m. to 5:00 p.m. Eastern time, Monday through Friday, except federal holidays. The TTY number is (202) 707-6737. See also *Circular 4*, Copyright Office Fees.[6] Or, you may write to this address for information:

> **Library of Congress**
> **Copyright Office**
> **101 Independence Avenue, S.E.**
> **Washington, D.C. 20559-6000**

For further information[7] on this specific topic, request Circular 40, "Copyright Registration for Works of the Visual Arts."

It is illegal for anyone to violate any of the rights provided by the Copyright law to the owner of copyright. These rights, however, are not unlimited in scope. Sections 107 through 121 of the 1976 Copyright Act[8] establish limitations on these rights. In some cases, these limitations are specified exemptions from copyright liability. One major limitation is the doctrine[9] of "*fair use*," which is given a statutory basis in Section 107 of the 1976 Copyright Act. In other instances, the limitation takes the form of a "compulsory license" under which certain limited uses of copyrighted works are permitted upon payment of specified royalties and compliance with statutory conditions. For further information about the limitations of any of these rights, consult the Copyright law or write to the Copyright Office. Fair use is an issue with digital material such as video, which is currently not resolved.

The Value of a Trademark (and Service Mark), and How to Initiate It

A *Trademark* is a peculiar distinguishing mark (or device) affixed by a manufacturer or a merchant to his/her goods; it is the exclusive right of using the distinguishing mark, which is recognized by law.[10, 11] A *Service Mark* is a mark used in the sale or advertising of services to identify

---

[4] For further details, please reference http://www.Copyright.gov/title17/106a.
[5] For further details, please reference http://www.Copyright.gov/title17/106a.
[6] For further details, please reference http://www.Copyright.gov/circs/circ04.html.
[7] For further details, please reference http://www.Copyright.gov/circs/circ40.pdf.
[8] For further details, please reference http://www.Copyright.gov/title17/92chap1.html.
[9] For further details, please reference http://www.Copyright.gov/title17/92chap1.html#107.
[10] As defined by http://dictionary.reference.com/search?q=Trademark.
[11] For further details, please reference http://www.uspto.gov/web/offices/tac/tmlaw2.html.

the services and distinguish them from the services of others. The application for a service mark is handled in the same way that an application for a trademark is managed. These two fairly similar terms will be used interchangeably throughout this book.

A trademark can also be thought of as any distinguished word (e.g., Poison), any distinguished name (e.g., Giorgio Armani), any distinguished symbol or device (e.g., the Pillsbury Doughboy), any distinguished slogan (e.g., Got Milk?), any distinguished package design (e.g., Coca-Cola bottle), or any distinguished combination of these that serves to identify and uniquely identify a specific product from others in the market place or in trade. Even an audio sound (e.g., NBC chimes), a color combination, a smell, or a hologram can be registered as a trademark under certain circumstances.

A service mark (e.g., Harrods) is somewhat similar to a trademark, but it is used in the sale or advertising of "services" to identify and distinguish the services of one company from those services of another other company.

The United States Patent and Trademark Office (USPTO) reviews trademark applications for federal registration. This review is performed in order to determine if an applicant meets the requirements for federal registration. The USPTO will not, however, decide whether one has the right to *use* a particular mark (which differs from the right to register a mark). Even without a registration, one may still *use* any mark adopted to identify the source of ones goods and/or services. Once a registration is issued, it is up to the owner of the mark to enforce its rights in the mark, based upon the ownership claims of the federal registration.

The USPTO employees will gladly answer questions about the application process in the United States. However, the USPTO employees cannot

- Conduct narrow or wide trademark searches for the public
- Comment on any form related to the validity of registered marks
- Answer any questions on whether a particular mark or type of mark is indeed eligible for trademark registration
- Offer any form of legal advice (or opinions) regarding common law trademark rights, state registrations, and/or trademark infringement claims

Is the registration of a trademark or service mark always required? The answer to this is no. You can establish rights in a particular trade or service mark, based upon legitimate use of the mark. However, filing and owning a federal trademark or service mark registration on the "Principal Register" provides several advantages, including the establishment of

- A constructive notice to the public of the registrant's claim of ownership toward the exact mark
- A legal presumption of the registrant's ownership of the mark and the registrant's exclusive right to use the mark nationwide on or in connection with the goods and/or services listed in the registration

- The ability to bring an action concerning the mark in federal court
- The use of the U.S. registration as a basis to obtain registration in foreign countries
- The ability to file the U.S. registration with the U.S. Customs Service to prevent importation of infringing foreign goods

When can you use the trademark symbols, ™, ˢᴹ, and ©? Any time you claim rights in a mark, you may use the "™" (trademark) or "ˢᴹ" (service mark) designation to alert the public to your claim(s), regardless of whether you have filed an application with the USPTO.[12] However, you may use the federal *Registration* symbol "®" only after the USPTO actually "registers" a mark and *not* while an application is pending. Also, you may use the registration symbol with the mark only on or in connection with the goods and/or services listed in the Federal Trademark Registration:

- A trademark is a word, phrase, symbol or design, or a combination of words, phrases, symbols or designs that identifies and distinguishes the source of the goods of one party from those of others.
- A service mark is the same as a trademark except that it identifies and distinguishes the source of a service rather than a product. Throughout this entire book, the terms *trademark* and *mark* refer to both trademarks and service marks.

Is there an electronic form on the Internet for filing a trademark application? Yes. Using the *Trademark Electronic Application System (TEAS)* available at the USPTO,[13] you can file the application directly over the Internet. The specialized features of the electronic filing include

- *Online Help.* This provides online hyperlinks that present Help sections for each of the application filing data fields.
- *Validation Function.* This helps avoid the possible omission of important information while filling out the form.
- *Immediate Reply.* The USPTO immediately issues an initial filing receipt via e-mail containing the assigned application serial number and a summary of the submission. This is important time and date information, as a matter of record, in some time sensitive situations of filings.
- *24-Hour Availability.* TEAS is available 24 hours a day, 7 days a week (except 11 p.m. Saturday to 6 a.m. Sunday), so receipt of a filing date is possible up until midnight EST.

---

[12] For further details, please reference http://www.uspto.gov.
[13] For further details, please reference http://www.uspto.gov/teas/index.html.

If you do not have Internet access, it is possible to access TEAS at any Patent and Trademark Depository Library (PTDL)[14] throughout the United States. Many public libraries also provide Internet access.

Are there other ways to file besides the Internet? Yes. While the USPTO greatly prefers that you file electronically (for workload efficiency reasons), using TEAS, you may also either mail or hand deliver a paper application to the USPTO. You can call the USPTO's automated telephone line, at (703) 308-9000 or (800) 786-9199 to obtain a printed form. *You may NOT submit an application by facsimile.* Any individual may also wish to utilize a U.S. Postal System mailing address to file a new application, at the following address:

> **Commissioner for Trademarks**
> **2900 Crystal Drive**
> **Arlington, VA 22202-3514**

Must you hire an attorney? No—however, it is highly recommended. If one prepares and submits his or her own application, he or she must comply with all requirements of the trademark statute and respective rules. If one, in fact, chooses to appoint an attorney to represent his or her interests before the USPTO, then the USPTO will correspond *only* with his or her attorney. The USPTO cannot help any party select an attorney.

International Trademark Association (INTA)

The International Trademark Association (INTA) is a not-for-profit membership association of more than 4,300 trademark owners and professionals[15] from more than 170 countries. The INTA™ is dedicated to the support and advancement of trademarks, worldwide and related intellectual property as elements of fair and effective national and international commerce.

In 1878, 17 merchants and manufacturers who saw a need for an organization "to protect and promote the rights of trademark owners, to secure useful legislation and to give aid and encouragement to all efforts for the advancement and observance of trademark rights," founded the association. After 125 years in operations, the INTA continues its mission to represent the trademark community, shape public policy, and advance professional knowledge and development.

[14] For further details, please reference http://www.uspto.gov/web/offices/ac/ido/ptdl/index.html.

[15] For further details, please reference http://www.inta.org/about/membership.html.

The INTA Mission

INTA's mission is to support and advance trademarks and related intellectual property as elements of fair and effective national, regional and, international commerce. INTA supports this mission and its members through policy development and advocacy, communications, educational programming, and enhanced member services.

INTA's vision is to be the world's preeminent organization devoted to the generation and communication of knowledge in the trademark field and the application of that knowledge to improve legal practices within the trademark community.

Four strategic directions drive INTA's future in meeting its educational, advocacy, and membership objectives:

1. *Internationalization.* Reflect the scope and diversity of the association's membership through expansion of international advocacy, education, information and services, and recruitment of new members and staff.

2. *Policy development and advocacy.* Develop policy and positions on leading and emerging trademark and related issues round the world. Continue to build the worldwide influence of trademark owners and shape public policy by advocating the implementation of association positions and policies in treaties, legislation, regulations, and cases around the world.

3. *Education, information and services.* Provide consistently excellent education, information, and services to association members, industry, trademark professionals, and the general public around the world on trademarks and related issues.

4. *Association governance, membership, and participation.* Continue to strengthen the Association's governance, membership, and staff and its committee operations.

Along with INTA's worldclass leadership team, its most important asset is the talented and committed group of volunteers who serve on its many committees. INTA's goal is to make the best use of these vital resources in order to maintain its leadership position in the worldwide trademark communities. Its purpose, which is so important to global commerce, is to protect and promote the rights of trademark owners and to secure useful legislation worldwide.

For more information regarding INTA, please feel free to contact:

International Trademark Association
1-(212)-768-9887 Telephone
1-(212)-768-7796 Fax

The Trade Secret and How to Exercise Control

Trade Secrets are defined by a number of sources. Under the Restatement of Torts, §757 (1939), "a trade secret may consist of any formula, pattern, device or compilation of information which is used in one's business, and which gives him an opportunity to obtain an advantage over competitors who do not know or use it. It may be a formula for a chemical compound, a process of manufacturing, treating or preserving material, a pattern for a machine or other device, or a list of customers."

Trade secrets are defined under the Uniform Trade Secrets Act as:

A trade secret means information, including a formula, pattern, compilation, program, device, method, and technique or process that:

1. Derives independent economic value, actual or potential, from not being generally known to, and not being easily ascertainable by proper means, by other persons who can obtain economic value from its disclosure or use

2. Is the subject of efforts that are reasonable under circumstances to maintain its secrecy

The Illinois Trade Secrets Act, 765 ILCS 1065/1 et seq. (West 1993), provides that trade secrets are information, including (but not limited to) technical or non-technical data, a formula, pattern, compilation, program, device, method, technique, drawing, process, financial data, or list of actual or potential customers or suppliers, that

- Is sufficiently secret to derive economic value, actual or potential, from not being generally known to other persons who can obtain economic value from its disclosure or use

- Is the subject of efforts that are reasonable under the circumstances to maintain its secrecy or confidentiality

The New Restatement of the Law Third, Unfair Competition defines a trade secret in Section 39 as follows:

- § 39. Definition of Trade Secret. A trade secret is any information that can be used in the operation of a business or other enterprise and that is sufficiently valuable and secret to afford an actual or potential economic advantage over others.

In addition to these interpretations, it is well established that a trade secret can exist in a combination of characteristics and components, each process, design and operation of which, in unique combination, affords a competitive advantage and is a protectable secret. Also, a trade secret need not be essentially new, novel, or unique like a patent.

The trade secret owner may communicate the trade secret to others provided that those to whom the trade secret is communicated pledge not to reveal the trade secret to others.

Unlike other forms of intellectual property protection we have previously discussed, trade secrets are generally protected by state law and not by federal laws. Trade secret protection is in certain cases very limited. A trade secret holder is only protected from unauthorized disclosure and use of that trade secret by others and from another person obtaining the trade secret by some improper means.

Several factors determine if subject matter qualifies as a trade secret. Among the factors considered are the extent of measures taken by the trade secret owner to guard the secrecy of the information and the ease or difficulty with which the information could be properly acquired or duplicated by others. Based on these considerations, the general rule is that subject matter cannot be successfully protected as a trade secret if it is widely distributed. However, if adequate security precautions are taken to ensure that access to the subject matter being distributed is treated as secret, the subject matter may still be considered a trade secret.

Whether trade secret owners distribute their trade secrets through will largely depend on the extent that they believe that the secrecy of the trade secret will not be compromised by such a distribution.

In addition to the concerns regarding security precautions, issues of jurisdiction may also arise. As trade secrets are generally protected by state law, determining which state's law should control in a trade secret disputeis often an issue. This choice of law issue, however, is no more problematic than those issues presently associated with the distribution of trade secrets and can be adequately resolved by the choice of law rules presently codified in state law.

To some degree, whether trade secret owners distribute their trade secrets may also depend on the type of information products and services being disseminated. For instance, it has been suggested that the most common way to protect software is through trade secret protection. Unlike most trade secret information, computer programs can be copied and used without the copier ever understanding or viewing the information in a comprehensible form.

In a trade secret, the actual idea need not be complicated; it may be extremely simple and nevertheless qualify as a trade secret. That is, unless (of course) the idea is common knowledge and known within the public domain. The fundamental notion here to remember is that a trade secret may not be within the realm of general skills and knowledge in one's field of business, and as such, the idea may not be readily duplicated without involving considerable time, effort, and expense. This is a trade secret: Protect it.

The Patent and How to Initiate It

The United States Patent and Trademark Office (USPTO), an integral part of the U.S. Department of Commerce, is the most recognized authority on patents and trademarks in the U.S. The USPTO is also the center for filing of patents and trademarks.

Normally, inventors who file patents will do this through an authoritative source, such as a licensed patent attorney or patent engineer. This intermediate filing source is paramount due to the fact of the specific language that has to be created in order to protect the filing's claims and teachings. For more information on this and how to file, please visit the USPTO at www.uspto.gov for further instructions on how to initiate the filing.

The Significance of Publishing Intellectual Property

Publishing intellectual property has a varied effect on the intellectual property, depending on the type.

If you have an idea that is too broad to patent but you wish to protect the intellectual property in the idea—publish it in a journal or magazine, in turn placing your claim on the idea.

There are legal deadlines that might limit your ability to receive a patent for your idea. If your patent is disclosed (published) publicly and the disclosure was made without protection of a confidential disclosure agreement (CDA), in the U.S., you have 12 months to file for a patent on this idea. You cannot be granted a patent after the deadline has past.

If your idea is disclosed under a CDA, then you still can file for a patent anytime during the one-year period following its disclosure under CDA. A trademark is protected by virtue of its registration in the USPTO. A copyright protects the idea, once published and showing the appropriate copyright statements. So, yes, publishing intellectual property has a variety of significant effects.

The Considerations of Intellectual Property Protection

Any company's intellectual property—whether that's patents, trade secrets, or just employee know-how—may be more valuable than its physical assets. This primer, compiled from *CSO* articles, covers basic and overlooked steps for keeping your secrets secret.

Intellectual Property in Simple Terms

Intellectual property can be descriptive materials from a particular manufacturing process to plans for a specific product launch, a chemical formula, or a list of the countries in which your patents are registered. It may help to think of it as intangible proprietary information. The formal definition, according to the World Intellectual Property Organization, is creations of the mind—inventions, literary and artistic works, symbols, names, images, and designs used in commerce. Intellectual property includes (but is not limited to) proprietary algorithms, concepts or ideas, inventions (products and business methods), industrial solution designs, as well as literary and artistic works (e.g., novels, films, music, architectural designs, and Web site pages).

For many companies, such as those in the biomedical or services business, intellectual property carries much more value than any physical asset. It has been purported across industries that each year intellectual property theft costs U.S. enterprises approximately USD $300 billion dollars. This is a non-trivial amount and partly due to lack of security and business operational practices.

Considering the various types of intellectual property we have already discussed, it is important to ensure that intellectual property is registered according to its respective type. This means it is registered with state, federal, and/or international agencies, and if infringed upon or otherwise abused, those infringing upon intellectual property claims can be prosecuted.

As we have already discussed in previous chapters, the four legally defined types of intellectual property protection are noted in the following review list:

1. *Patents.* When an individual registers an invention with the government, he or she begins an analytical process that can take more than a year or two to complete, once he or she has filed the idea. This analysis period is required for the investigation of the idea, which is how an individual gains the legal right to exclude anyone from manufacturing or marketing his or her idea. Once an individual (or enterprise) owns the patent, others can then apply to the owner to license the idea. Patents remain valid for 20 years.

2. *Trademarks.* A trademark is a symbol, name, phrase, or sound used in association with products or services. It can connect a brand with a level of quality or service, on which companies can build reputations. A trademark protection lasts for ten years after registration, and much like patents, a trademark can be renewed.

3. *Copyrights.* Copyright laws protect written or artistic expressions fixed in a tangible medium—for example, novels, poems, songs, or movies. A copyright protects the expression of an idea, but not the idea itself. Only the owner of copyrighted work has the right to reproduce it, to make derivative works from it (e.g., a movie), or to sell, perform, or display the work to the public. You don't need to register your material to hold a copyright, but registration is a prerequisite if you decide to sue for copyright infringement. A copyright lasts for the life of the author plus another 50 years.

4. *Trade secrets.* A formula, pattern, device, or compilation of data that grants the user an advantage over competitors is a trade secret. State, rather than federal, law covers it. To protect the secret, a business must prove that it adds value to the company— that it is, in fact, a secret—and that appropriate measures have been taken within the company to safeguard the secret, such as restricting knowledge to a select handful of executives. Coca-Cola, for example, has managed to keep its formula under wraps for more than 117 years.

Intellectual property can also be something broader and less tangible than these four protected classes: It can simply be an idea. If the head of your R&D department has a "eureka" moment during his morning shower and then applies his new idea at work, that's intellectual property, too.

Responsible Protection of Intellectual Property

The aspects we have discussed with regards to legal protection of intellectual property are paramount; however, experiencing the theft of intellectual property is extremely difficult, and prosecuting the thieves is even more difficult. A small amount of due diligence is often very helpful. Do not overlook the fact that because some people really are out to comprise competitive information, everyone concerned with protection needs to be aware. As examples, consider the following real-life situations:

- An engineer regularly met for meals with his former manager, who is now working for a competitive company, as opposed to where he used to work managing this engineer. The engineer always felt as though he possessed a critical skill for gathering competitive intelligence information. What this engineer did not realize was that the information he was giving up, in return for this competitive intelligence, caused his current employer (once the market leader) to lose three major bid opportunities in approximately one year. The old cliché here is easy to understand—that is, "loose lips sink ships."

- In the week prior to a company's release of its regular quarterly report, employees across several operating units reporting to the Chief Financial Officer received several hundred calls from individuals claiming to be with a credit-reporting agency. They stated that certain information about the upcoming earnings report (prior to its release) was important for them to be able to better understand. Employees were immediately instructed by management to transfer all such inquiries to the corporate security office, and yet, the calls continued on a regular basis. It was later revealed that all of these calls came from a research company hired by this company's competition.

- Immigrant scientists from areas of Europe were working on an American defense project. These scientists kept getting unsolicited invitations from their home countries to speak at events, or for them to serve as consultants. The invitations appealed to them as scientists and professional speakers—because they absolutely wanted to share information about important work with colleagues. Is it possible that certain countries consider this kind of intelligence gathering facade as cheaper than performing their own research and development?

Is Your Intellectual Property Secure?

Securing intellectual property is a responsibility, or should be, if you are an employee of a company. Securing it as an individual for personal interests is simply a wise practice to perform.

The following items are considered as best practices for securing intellectual property. These are not the only means, but a means for doing this:

1. *Know what information assets are in your possession.* If all employees understand what information needs to be protected and what about these assets is important, they can better understand how to protect these assets. To do this, security officers in a company

must communicate the importance of intellectual property on an on-going basis. They must do this with the responsible executives and other key employees who oversee intellectual capital in the corporation. Security should meet with selected executives and representatives from HR, marketing, sales, legal, manufacturing, and R&D. These individuals should meet at least once a quarter to discuss issues and practices. Corporate leadership must work in concert to adequately protect IP.

2. *Prioritize information assets in your possession.* Security specialists skilled at protecting intellectual property suggest doing a risk and cost-benefit analysis of what is believed to be an information asset or intellectual property asset. Create a map of your corporation's assets, and determine what information, if lost, would impact your company the most. Next, consider which of these assets are at high risk of being compromised. Considering these two factors will help you prioritize where to best apply your intellectual property protection activities.

3. *Clearly identify the intellectual property assets.* If information is confidential to your company, identify it as such. If your company data is proprietary, put a note to that effect on every login screen. This seems trivial, but if you wind up in court trying to prove someone took information they weren't authorized to take, your argument won't stand up if you can't demonstrate that you made it clear that the information was protected.

4. *Secure the intellectual property assets.* Physical and digital protections are very important considerations, with regards to securing intellectual property assets. Ensure that the assets are secured in rooms where sensitive data access is controlled, whether it is a Web server farm, data center, or the long-term storage and retention rooms. Keep auditing track of who has what kind of access to these assets; track their access to each asset, and when they accessed the information. Use effective forms of identification, authentication, and validation. Limit and control every employee's access to important information, and ensure it is only on a "need to know" basis.

5. *Educate and raise the level of awareness of all employees.* Education and awareness training can be very effective ways for protecting intellectual property, but only if it is focused on the specific information that a particular group of employees needs to protect. When one speaks in very specific terms about something that professionals have a vested interested in protecting, you will have everyone's attention.

Often times, speech is the absolute weakest link in the defensive chain of protecting intellectual property. That is why an overall intellectual property protection effort that depends on security practices, firewalls, copyrights, patents, trademarks, and trade secrets are all-important. However, not focusing on employee education and awareness is a recipe for failure in this area.

6. *Understand your security practices, policies, and information protection tools.* There is an increasing selection of software applications available for tracking files, documents, and other intellectual property repository assets. These methods are designed to perform

many types of unique functions, including locating sensitive intellectual property assets, keeping track of who is utilizing these assets, and when they are accessing them. There are also other means of protection, such as patents, copyrights, trademarks, and trade secrets, previously discussed in several sections of this book.

7. *Think in terms of the "big picture."* Information security professionals see how problems can develop if you do not continuously portray the "big picture" view of security. For example, this big picture view includes any situation where someone is scanning the internal network. In this case, the internal intrusion detection systems are triggered, and typically somebody from information technology operations or security calls the employee who is doing the scanning and instructs, "Please stop doing that type of scanning." The employee offers a plausible explanation, and that is the end of that situation. Then later that evening, the night security officer sees an employee carrying out protected documents, and his explanation is perhaps, "Oh . . . I did not realize that document got into my briefcase."

Then, over some period of time, the HR or personnel group, the company audit group, even the individual's colleagues (and perhaps some others) all noticed isolated incidents. However, nobody puts these individual incidents together into a pattern and realizes that this same person perpetrated all these security breaches. Do you suppose this person could be actively engaged in stealing intellectual property assets? What should you do?

The point here is that unnecessary communication gaps between company personnel and corporate security groups can be very harmful. Intellectual property protection requires connections and communication between all the corporate functions. The Legal department has to play a role in intellectual property protection, and so do HR organizations, Information Technology groups, R&D, Engineering, Graphic Design groups; every group is involved. So, think with in terms of the big picture; that is, both to protect and to detect those obvious and non-obvious situations related to information security breaches.

8. *Apply a counter-intelligence mindset and professional function to match.* If one were spying on his or her company, how do you think it would be accomplished? Thinking through such hypothetical tactics will lead you to consider protection of files, phone lists, personnel records, shredding papers, convening an internal council to approve your R&D scientists' publications, and other worthwhile ideas. Ethical hackers are of a great value, providing a highly valued service and in some cases required to ensure the integrity of a large enterprise. All of these tactics may prove extremely useful in protecting a particular line of business—or the entire company.

Offensive and Defensive Security Measures

Security professionals are constantly working to understand the dark sides of people who are that are trying to get information from a company and then piecing it together in a useful way. Some of these forces come disguised as "competitive intelligence analysts" who, in theory perhaps, are governed by a set of legal and ethical guidelines. These individuals may even say they are careful to abide by the Society of Competitive Intelligence Professionals (SCIP). Other individuals are professional spies, hired by competitors, or even foreign governments, who will stop at nothing to comprise your security. This includes bribes, thievery, or even pressure-activated tape recorders hidden in corporate officers' chairs. However, it is often not this clear of a situation. Most threats to a company's intellectual property assets operate in an ill-defined zone.

In order to create solid intellectual property protection defensive and offensive measures, consider how these types of intelligent thieves work:

Security Breach Offenders Look for Publicly Available Information

A competitive intelligence expert might tell you that more damage is done by a company's inadequate (or lack thereof) security practices than by thieves themselves.

Consider these common examples: salespeople showing off upcoming products at trade shows; technical organizations describing their key technology activities in publicly proclaimed job listings; supplier organizations describing their sales numbers on public Web sites; public relations departments issuing press releases about new patent filings; companies in industries targeted by regulators over-reporting information about manufacturing facilities to the Environmental Protection Agency or OSHA, which can become part of the public record; or employees posting comments on Internet bulletin boards should also be carefully controlled.

All of these types of data tells a competitor what your company is doing. Combined, the right details might help a rival reduce your first-to-market advantage, improve the efficiency of their own manufacturing facility, or refocus their research in a profitable direction.

Security Breach Offenders Often Work the Phones

Some phone solicitation schemes yield amazing stories of what people will tell their uninvited or even invited callers over the phone. There are cases like the publicly acclaimed "dumpster diving" espionage case involving Procter & Gamble and Unilever.

Criminally minded people have many ways of getting people to open-up and talk. In fact, people like this are the primary reason that seemingly all companies should very closely guard innocent lists of company employee names, titles and phone extensions, or internal newsletters announcing retirements or promotions. This is because the more these criminals know about the single person who answers the telephone—the better he or she can deceive that person in malicious ways in order to gain the information he or she is seeking.

Telephone criminals will identify themselves and say something like, "I'm working on a project, and I'm told you're the guru when it comes to the newer technologies in this device. Is this a good time to talk, or should I call you back?" Oddly enough, 50% of the people called by these criminals are willing to talk about that kind of information.

The other 50%—what will they do? They might ask what the person calling on the phone does before they answer any questions. They might ask what organization the caller is a part of, and who they report to in that management chain.

Sometimes, the caller may reply (and this is true) that they are calling on behalf of a Research Corporation, working on a project for a client he or she cannot name because of a confidentiality agreement. Hopefully, everyone will hang up on that kind of a vague response. Fortunately, many of the people will simply hang up the telephone, and unfortunately, many people will just start talking.

Once a person starts talking, these criminals begin taking careful notes that will eventually make their way into one of a couple of files. The first file is information for his or her client asking for the information, and the second file (the darker file), is a database of hundreds of thousands previous information sources. These files include information about the calling respondents' expertise, how friendly they were, and personal details such as their hobbies or where they went to college or high school. The best advice here is very simple and straightforward—hang up the phone. You owe these unsolicited callers nothing (including courtesy). One favorite response is to ask for their home phone numbers or office numbers, so you can call them right back. They will never give out their home phone numbers, and also rarely agree to give out their real office numbers—but do not hesitate to bother you on your numbers. I remind them that I did not give them my phone number, so isn't it fair that they give me theirs in exchange?

Often times, business intelligence miners utilize well-practiced tactics for gathering information without directly asking for it. They accomplish this by implying that they are someone they are not as they begin their lies. This particularly deceptive practice is the tactic known as "social engineering." Such scam artists might also include "pretext" calls from someone pretending to be a student working on a research project, an employee at a conference who needs some paperwork, or a board member's secretary who needs an address list to mail Christmas cards.

Most of these calls are actually not technically illegal, at least not by themselves. Lawyers will proclaim that while it is against the law to impersonate someone else, it is not illegal to be a liar or dishonest.

These Information Miners Go into the Field of Practice Seeking Information

As another example, during the recent Internet technology boom, one early-morning flight from Austin, Texas, to San Jose, California, earned the nickname of "the nerd bird." It shuttled business people from one high-tech center to the other. That flight and others like it became excellent places for job recruiters. They also became great places for competitive intelligence professionals to overhear casual discussions between coworkers discussing sensitive information. The miners on these flights were also able to sometimes sneak a peek at a fellow passenger's business presentation or financial spreadsheets. Be careful on aircrafts and, for that matter, trains or any type of public transportation vehicles.

Any public place where employees go, competitive information gatherers can also go: for example, airports, taxis, coffee shops, restaurants, and especially bars near company offices and facilities—and, of course, professional trade shows. An operative working practice for the competition might be to corner one of your business leaders after a company presentation or to pose as a potential customer. They do this in order to try to get a demonstration of a new product or learn about pricing scenarios from your sales team. Or that information gatherer might simply take off his name badge before approaching your booth at a trade show.

Professionals must know when not to speak about sensitive business matters in public forums or places: They must be vigilant about this. These items can be associated with, or worse yet, directly related to intellectual property that the company wishes to protect. Professionals must also know how to work with the their marketing departments to ensure the risks of divulging internal information at a conference or trade show, does not outweigh the benefits of gaining new business.

Employment interviews can also turn into possible disclosures of sensitive information. Competitors may sometimes risk sending one of their own employees to a job interview. They could also hire a competitive intelligence firm to do the same. Conversely, a competitor might invite one of your employees in for a job interview, with no other purpose than gleaning information about your sensitive products, endeavors, and/or processes.

Competitive Intelligence Gatherers Are Experts at Putting the Pieces Together

In many ways, trade secrets are very easy to protect. Stealing trade secrets is illegal under the "1996 Economic Espionage Act." Employees usually know that trade secrets can be very valuable to the right parties, and nondisclosure agreements may protect your company further. What is more complicated is helping employees understand how seemingly innocuous details can be strung together into a bigger picture (as we just discussed), and think about how simply a company's phone list now can become a weapon in the hands of information gatherers.

Consider the following scenario: An unnamed competitive intelligence research executive once had a client who requested him to find out whether any competitive rivals were working on a specific technology area. During his research of the public records, he was able to discover nine or ten authors who had been publishing several white papers on this specialized technology area. These authors seemed to have been aware of each other for some time, and in some cases, were friends or acquaintances with each other. Then, all of a sudden, these authors all stopped writing about this technology area. This research executive then performed some background investigative work and discovered that each of these authors had moved to a certain part of the country and now worked for the same company. None of that constituted a trade secret or even, necessarily, strategic information. However, the competitive research executive was now clearly beginning to see a big picture forming.

What that told him was that these authors had probably stopped publishing information about this technology area, perhaps because they recognized that the technology had achieved a point where it was probably going to be profitable. Then, by calling the authors on the phone, attending public meetings where they were speaking on other topics, and later asking them after their presentations about the research they were no longer speaking publicly about, the competitive search firm was now able to figure out when the technology was planned to hit the market. This information then gave his client a two-year window into the competition's plans. This big picture the research executive was able to piece together may have in fact been based on gathering this intellectual property, which could very well affect the revenues streams of the company planning to release this technology area.

Some Competitive Research Consultants May Chose to Extend Beyond Acceptable Ethics
Some other countries around the world may have vastly different ethical and legal guidelines for information gathering. Almost everything we have talked about until this point in this chapter is legal in the United States—or, arguably, legal in the hands of a very clever lawyer of the court. However, there is yet another much darker realm of corporate intellectual property sleuthing. Less ethical tactics (at least in the U.S.) include utilizing hidden recording devices, bribery and thievery, and even extortion, which is widely practiced elsewhere in the world.

For example, an unnamed bank in South America suspected espionage and had already retained a private security consultancy for internal purposes. They also selected this private security consultancy to perform an exhaustive sweep of the facilities, searching for any hidden recording devices. Nothing was found. However, since this loss of information continued after this initial sweep, the bank then chose to retain (yet again) a different security consultancy team. This second security team found 27 different hidden recording devices. The entire executive suite was wired for both motion and sound. As it turned out, the first team engaged to look for these recording devices was suspected to have been the team installing these espionage devices.

Espionage is sometimes sanctioned in certain countries—or sometimes even carried out by foreign governments, which may view this as assisting local companies to keep competitive positions on foreign rivals. Some foreign governments might purportedly view this as an acceptable means to boost the country's economy.

This is why there is no single set of guidelines for protecting intellectual property that will work everywhere in the world. The security department's role is to evaluate the risks for every country where the company conducts business and act accordingly, even if this means briefing their professionals prior to their entry into that country. Some company procedures, such as reminding people to protect their laptops, will remain unchanged. Remember that these devices, too, can retain immense amounts of intellectual property. However, for certain countries, it is paramount that more precautions be set in-place. Executives traveling to Pakistan, for example, might need to register under pseudonyms, have their hotel rooms or workspaces swept for bugs, or even have security guards help protect information. One of the authors of this book has been assigned armed drivers in several countries visited, due to corporate kidnappings and protections of other sorts. These topics are not to be taken lightly with regards to intellectual property protection and conducting business as a professional in foreign countries.

Ensure That You Understand Sensitivities of Countries Where You, as a Professional, Must Conduct Business

During the last few years, it has been proven that some countries have developed reputations as places where industrial espionage is widely accepted, even encouraged, as a way of promoting the country's economy. Many other countries are worse.

An excellent resource for evaluating the threat of doing business in different parts of the world is the *Corruption Perceptions Index,* published each year by "Transparency International" (and made famous by *The Economist*).

In 2003, the Corruption Perceptions Index ranked 12 countries as being perceived as the most corrupt. These countries were (at that time): Bangladesh, Nigeria, Haiti, Paraguay, Myanmar, Tajikistan, Georgia, Cameroon, Azerbaijan, Angola, Kenya, and Indonesia.

Another list ranked some large countries where companies are most likely to extend and pay bribes in order to win or retain business in their emerging markets. The worst scores belonged to Russia, China, Taiwan, and South Korea, followed by Italy, Hong Kong, Malaysia, Japan, USA, and France.[16]

India is another country of increasing importance to global businesses, primarily because of the rapid rise of offshore outsourcing. The prevalence of outsourcing of IT functions now introduces some unique vulnerability to companies that may not think of themselves as having a global presence.

In legal terms, the most widely recognized global standard is the World Trade Organization's intellectual property add-on, TRIPS (Trade-Related Aspects of Intellectual Property Rights). However, TRIPS protection must be enforced locally, and none of the countries prominent in software outsourcing, including India, have local laws covering theft of trade secrets. TRIPS signatures (or not) only happen, if a country's culture does not respect property, then, the courts are unlikely to enforce any respective laws.

Here are ten best practices for protecting intellectual property, specifically where a company might be leveraging offshore software park development work:

1. Register intellectual property as appropriate, as a copyright, patent, trademark, or trade secret.

2. Inspect the physical premises where any software will be developed. Note whether buildings have basic security check-in procedures. Find out what kind of access people have to the key development/testing systems.

3. Analyze networks functions, especially if you plan to use virtual private networks (VPNs). These are excellent for cross-facility communications and make it easier for remote employees to work from home or other remote locations; unfortunately, this benefit can increase vulnerability across the network.

---

[16]   For more information, please reference this index at Transparency International http://www.transparency.org.

4. Protect important information (e.g., source code) with passwords and access codes and make sure that these information assets are not widely available, either in the United States or at any of the outsourcing locations. Resist the urge to place any of these assets on removable disk media, as this will make protection and audit of who handles this information virtually impossible.

5. Demand that the outsourcing parties practice responsible human resource screening procedures. Analyze employee retention figures, and find out if competitors do business with these same companies; if so, work to ensure that there is no contact between any of the personnel teams.

6. Understand what risks your organization can take and what risks the organization is unwilling to manage. Some types of regulated industries (e.g., health care and financial services) need to ensure closer controls over data and software development than, let's say, packaged goods companies.

7. Work to understand the legal systems and cultures of all countries involved in any respective business partnerships. Be sure to negotiate binding contracts/agreements that make the offshore company responsible for the actions of its employees. Realize that when doing business in foreign countries, it is very likely that you are at the will of that country's legal system.

8. Budget for greatly increased telecom costs, as well as for regular visits to the outsourcer. Ensure that both these acts of conducting telecom transmissions and conducting visits to these countries have all the necessary safeguards available.

9. Make sure that any test case data being utilized does not expose real information, especially types of information that might be traceable to real customers.

10. Always maintain original and secured copies of all source code.

Companies that do not have the resources to take these steps should very carefully consider exactly what (if anything) they are putting at risk by leveraging offshore capabilities or international business relations. This is important to consider whether it is software development or some other International function, such as multi-national call centers involving sensitive customer data.

Intellectual property is indeed a sensitive, complex, and rather complicated subject: Complicated, as we can see, across several dimensions. We have discussed in prior chapters acceptable methods of intellectual property protection (at least in the U.S.). In this chapter, we have also discussed the risks associated with International business engagements. The bottom line is that all intellectual property has some form of value. Protection of these types of assets will vary, depending on the nature of the asset, the country the asset was born in, and the laws surrounding business ethics for that country.

More Reading

1. *Copyright and Neighboring Rights Laws and Treaties.* (Geneva: World Intellectual Property Organization, 1987–). A multi-volume loose-leaf service containing the texts of national laws and treaties in the field of copyright. It is updated monthly. Future installments may be combined with a subscription to the monthly periodical *Copyright.*

2. *Copyright Laws and Treaties of the World.* United Nations Educational, Scientific and Cultural Organization (Washington, D.C.: BNA, 1956–). A loose-leaf compilation of laws and regulations of more than 100 countries and major multilateral treaties relating to copyright protection.

3. *Industrial Property Laws and Treaties.* (Geneva: World Intellectual Property Organization, 1976–). A multi-volume loose-leaf service containing the texts of treaties and national legislation of individual countries relating to the protection of patents, trademarks, and other forms of intellectual property. It is updated monthly. Future installments may be combined with a subscription to the monthly periodical *Industrial Property.*

4. *International Treaties on Intellectual Property.* Marshall Leafer (Washington, D.C., BNA, 1990). A single volume monograph containing texts and introductory comments on the major treaties on copyrights, patents, trademarks, and industrial property.

5. *World Patent Laws and Practice.* John Sinnott (Albany: Matthew Bender, 1974–). A loose-leaf compilation of the texts of multilateral treaties and national legislation relating to patent protection.

Case Study Patents for Further Research

This appendix contains the core patent descriptions that were referenced in Chapter 3 "Search Strategies, Techniques, and Search Tools to Validate the Uniqueness of Any Invention". There are graphic figures associated with these references that are not contained in this appendix; however, these graphics are available online from the U.S. Patents and Trademark Office. For further information regarding these "patents pending," refer to the U.S. Patent and Trademark Office Web site at http//:www.uspto.gov.

United States Patent Application	20030192045
Kind Code	A1
Fellenstein, Craig William; et al.	October 9, 2003

Apparatus and Method for Blocking Television Commercials and Displaying Alternative Programming

Abstract

A logical unit and a commercial blocking program in the logical unit allow alternative viewing options so that the user may define the alternative programming to replace the unwanted communication. The commercial blocking program breaks all incoming television signals into time, video and audio components and is able to recognize specific commercials based on those components. Upon viewing an unwanted commercial, the user indicates that he wants to block the commercial through one of a variety of input methods. The commercial blocking program then prevents the commercial from being displayed on the user's television and causes alternative programming to be displayed instead. The user may configure the alternative programming via the alternative programming logic. The user may configure the alternative programming as a universal television channel, based on the specific commercial, based on the television station, based on the time of day, or based on an elaborate viewing hierarchy. At the end of the blocked commercial, the commercial blocking program displays the television program that was originally displayed on the user's television. Alternatively, the commercial blocking program can buffer the various television programs received from the cable provider and record segments of the cable signal based on certain keywords. The commercial blocking program searches for user-defined keywords, records television programs complying with the search terms, and displays the recorded television programming stored in the memory.

Claims

What is claimed is:

1. A method for blocking television programming comprising: receiving a first television signal; recognizing said first television signal; blocking said first television signal; and displaying said second television signal.

2. The method of claim 1 wherein said first television signal is a commercial.

3. The method of claim 1 wherein said first television signal is recognized by the time, audio, and video components of said first television signal.

4. The method of claim 1 wherein said first television signal is recognized by an identifying tag.

5. The method of claim 1 further comprising receiving user input defining said second television signal.

6. The method of claim 5 wherein said second television signal is defined as universal alternative programming.

7. The method of claim 5 wherein said second television signal is defined as alternative programming based on said first television signal.

8. The method of claim 5 wherein said second television signal is defined as alternative programming based on a television channel.

9. The method of claim 5 wherein said second television signal is defined as alternative programming based on the time of day.

10. The method of claim 5 wherein said second television signal is defined as an elaborate viewing hierarchy.

11. The method of claim 1 further comprising: buffering a third television signal; searching said third television signal; and recording part of said third television signal in a memory.

12. The method of claim 11 wherein said second television signal is defined as the contents of said memory.

13. A method of determining alternative programming displayed during a blocked television commercial comprising: displaying a plurality of alternative programming options to a user; receiving input from said user; blocking a first television signal; and displaying a second television signal based on said input.

14. The method of claim 13 wherein said second television signal is defined as universal alternative programming.

15. The method of claim 13 wherein said second television signal is defined as alternative programming based on said first television signal.

16. The method of claim 13 wherein said second television signal is defined as alternative programming based on a television channel.

17. The method of claim 13 wherein said second television signal is defined as alternative programming based on the time of day.

18. The method of claim 13 wherein said second television signal is defined as an elaborate viewing hierarchy.

19. The method of claim 13 further comprising: buffering a third television signal; searching said third television signal; and recording part of said third television signal in a memory.

20. The method of claim 20 wherein said second television signal is defined as the contents of said memory.

21. A programmable apparatus for blocking television programs comprising: programmable hardware; software; said hardware being directed by said software to: receive a first television signal; recognize said first television signal; block said first television signal; and display said second television signal.

22. The apparatus of claim 21 wherein said first television signal is a commercial.

23. The apparatus of claim 21 wherein said first television signal is recognized by the time, audio, and video components of said first television signal.

24. The apparatus of claim 21 wherein said first television signal is recognized by an identifying tag.

25. The apparatus of claim 21 wherein said software further directs said hardware to receive user input defining said second television signal.

26. The apparatus of claim 25 wherein said second television signal is defined as universal alternative programming.

27. The apparatus of claim 25 wherein said second television signal is defined as alternative programming based on said first television signal.

28. The apparatus of claim 25 wherein said second television signal is defined as alternative programming based on a television channel.

29. The apparatus of claim 25 wherein said second television signal is defined as alternative programming based on the time of day.

30. The apparatus of claim 25 wherein said second television signal is defined as an elaborate viewing hierarchy.

31. The apparatus of claim 21 wherein said software further directs said hardware to: buffer a third television signal; search said third television signal; and record part of said third television signal in a memory.

32. The apparatus of claim 31 wherein said second television signal is defined as the contents of said memory.

33. A programmable apparatus for determining alternative programming displayed during a blocked television commercial comprising: programmable hardware; software; said hardware being directed by said software to: display a plurality of alternative programming options to a user; receive input from said user; block a first television signal; and display a second television signal based on said input.

34. The apparatus of claim 33 wherein said second television signal is defined as universal alternative programming.

35. The apparatus of claim 33 wherein said second television signal is defined as alternative programming based on said first television signal.

36. The apparatus of claim 33 wherein said second television signal is defined as alternative programming based on a television channel.

37. The apparatus of claim 33 wherein said second television signal is defined as alternative programming based on the time of day.

38. The apparatus of claim 33 wherein said second television signal is defined as an elaborate viewing hierarchy.

39. The apparatus of claim 33 wherein said software further directs said hardware to: buffer a third television signal; search said third television signal; and record part of said third television signal in a memory.

40. The apparatus of claim 39 wherein said second television signal is defined as the contents of said memory.

Description

FIELD OF THE INVENTION

[0001] The present invention relates to an apparatus and method for blocking undesired television commercials and displaying alternative programming instead of the blocked commercials.

BACKGROUND OF THE INVENTION

[0002] Debates today rage about both the delivery and funding of informational content in all of its forms. On the Internet, many content providers are moving away from their advertisement-based business models and moving towards subscription-based business models. Despite rapid advances in technology, the delivery mechanisms and methods of generating revenue for content delivered through television broadcasts have been relatively stagnant, when compared to the delivery mechanisms and methods of generating revenue for the Internet and web delivery systems. In television broadcasts, advertisers still attempt to reach users using the same techniques that they have used for decades which are the thirty and sixty second commercials interspaced throughout specific television programs. In addition to technology, the viewer is becoming increasingly sophisticated and is demanding that every second of their time, whether engaged in work or leisure pursuits, be well spent. For the vast majority of television viewers, time engaged in viewing undesired advertisements is not considered time well spent. Therefore, a need exists for an apparatus and method of preventing a television viewer from viewing unwanted commercials.

[0003] Additionally, television viewers generally do not prefer to have periods of interrupted programming or "dead air" when they are viewing a program. It would be preferable if the blocked commercial could be replaced with user-defined alternative programming. Therefore, a need exists for an apparatus and method for replacing a blocked commercial with alternative programming which is more acceptable to the television viewer.

[0004] Furthermore, television viewers may want to play a more active role in determining what type of programming will replace the commercials they have chosen to block. Television viewers who choose to block certain commercials may want to selectively determine alternative programming which will replace the blocked commercial. The alternative programming may differ depending on the time of day or the particular channel which is currently being viewed. Therefore, a need exists for an apparatus and method which will allow television viewers to define the alternative programming content.

[0005] Finally, television viewers may want to view a program that they may have missed instead of the commercial. In other words, it may be preferable to replace an unwanted commercial with television programming from another time on another television channel. Therefore, a need exists for an apparatus and method for buffering desired programming and displaying the desired programming in the time slot where the blocked commercial previously resided.

SUMMARY OF THE INVENTION

[0006] The present invention, which meets the needs stated above, is an apparatus and method for blocking specific television commercials from the viewer's television based upon the characteristics of the television commercial. A logical unit and a commercial blocking program in the logical unit allow alternative viewing options so that the user may define the alternative programming to replace the unwanted communication.

[0007] The commercial blocking program recognizes a unique digital identifying tag that distinguishes a particular commercial from all other commercials. Alternatively, the commercial blocking program identifies a commercial by a "component signature" or an "overall digital signature." Upon viewing an unwanted commercial, the user indicates that he wants to block the commercial through one of a variety of input methods. The commercial blocking program then prevents the commercial from being displayed on the user's television and causes alternative programming to be displayed instead. The user may configure the alternative programming via the alternative programming logic. The user may configure the alternative programming as a universal television channel, based on the specific commercial, based on the television station, based on the time of day, or based on an elaborate viewing hierarchy. At the end of the alternate programming, the commercial blocking program ends so that unblocked television programming resumes. Alternatively, the commercial blocking program can buffer the various television programs received from the cable provider and record segments of the cable signal based on certain keywords. The commercial blocking program searches for user defined keywords, records television programs complying with the search terms, and displays the recorded television programming stored in the memory.

BRIEF DESCRIPTION OF THE DRAWINGS

[0008] FIG. 1 is an illustration of the invention interacting with a cable provider and a television.

[0009] FIG. 2A is a flowchart of the commercial blocking program.

[0010] FIG. 2B is a flowchart of the alternative programming logic.

[0011] FIG. 3 is a depiction of the data processing system contained within the logical unit.

DETAILED DESCRIPTION OF THE PREFERRED EMBODIMENT

[0012] The term "multiplex" as used herein means the process of funneling several different streams of data over a common communications line. The term "cable provider" as used herein means a company which provides television service to multiple users and includes satellite television providers. The term "buffering" as used herein means a process of examining the closed captioning text or audio signal associated with television signals and configuring the examined signal such that it may be searched for specific keywords. As used herein, the term "alternate viewing" means content displayed in place of a blocked commercial and may include one or more of the following: (1) a brief message displayed to inform the viewer that alternative programming will be presented during the commercial interval; (2) an on-screen counter, showing how many seconds are left before the planned return to primary viewing and (3) directions to the tuner to go to a particular station. The directions to the tuner may be universal, by commercial, by originating station, by time of day or by definition of an elaborate viewing hierarchy. As used herein, the term "universal" means using content from a particular station to replace all blocked commercials. As used herein, the term "by commercial" means using content from a particular station to replace the specifically identified commercial. As used herein, the term "by originating station" means using the original station to determine the alternative content which will replace all blocked commercials. As used herein, the term "by time of day" means using the time of day to determine which station to use as alternative content for all blocked commercials. As used herein, the term "elaborate viewing hierarchy" means a combination of a plurality of universal, by commercial, by originating station, or by time or day alternative viewing formats As used herein, the term "unique digital identifying tag" means a number sequence before the header and after the trailer of each commercial. The number sequence is assigned according to an industry standard that allows each commercial to be identified from every other commercial. As used herein, a "component signature" is a group of variables, based on a time component, an X video component, a Y video component, and an audio component, that is used to identify a commercial from all other commercials when a "unique digital identifying tag is not available. As used herein, the term "cumulative digital signature" means the aggregation of one or more selected characteristics of a data sequence to provide a unique number for identification of the complete data sequence. FIG. 1 is an illustration of the invention 100 interacting with a cable provider and a television set. The depiction of the cable provider is by way of illustration only and is not intended to limit the scope of the invention. Persons skilled in the art will recognize that the invention may be used with either a cable or wireless data transmission system. The cable provider (not shown) provides a television signal through a coaxial cable 102 that runs through the user's wall 104 and into the logical unit 106. Logical unit 106 analyzes the cable signal as described below and displays the information on television 110 via television connection 108. Logical unit 106 can optionally be combined with television 110. Alternatively, logical unit 106 may be placed at the same location as the cable provider such that it is unnecessary to have logical unit 106 at the user's location.

[0013] FIG. 2A is a flowchart of commercial blocking program 200 which operates inside logical unit 106. Commercial blocking program 200 starts (202) whenever multiplexed cable signals are broadcast (204). In the preferred embodiment, each commercial has a unique digital identifying tag, similar to a serial number, which identifies a particular commercial. Logical unit 106 recognizes a particular commercial based on the unique identifying tag.

[0014] In an alternate embodiment, logical unit 106 identifies commercials by a "component signature." Multiplexed cable signals are defined by four components: a time component, an X video component, a Y video component, and an audio component. Every television program and/or commercial can be readily identified by these components. There is generally allowed some amount of time skew in the synchronization of the four components to identify the absolute beginning of a program or commercial. By taking the time skew into consideration, commercial blocking program 200 can identify a particular commercial. For example, a given pattern of video/audio signals occurring at a time "delta" (perhaps but not necessarily in the order of 500 microseconds) around the nominal beginning of an advertisement, may point back to a specified commercial.

[0015] Alternatively, logical unit 106 establishes an "overall digital signature" for a particular commercial. In this event, the signal need not be dissembled into its video/audio components as in the "component signature," but rather, analysis of cumulative digital characteristics may be used to identify the commercial to be blocked. One or more characteristics of a data sequence is selected and aggregated to provide a unique number for identification purposes of the complete data sequence. The advantage of using cumulative digital characteristics is that all commercials could be blocked using this technique. In the case of commercials to be identified by an "overall digital signature," the logical unit develops a library at the set-top of the "overall digital signature" of the blocked advertisements. For example, it may be assumed that some time interval,

"T.sub.sample" is great enough to ascertain with accuracies approaching one hundred percent the identity of a given advertisement. "T.sub.sample" may be a sub-second or it may be multi-second, depending on the processing power behind the logical unit and the uniqueness of the commercial. Once a commercial signal is detected to be identical to a blocked advertisement, then the logical unit takes the actions it has been programmed to implement.

[0016] As a commercial airs, the user has the option of blocking the commercial (206) by means of commercial blocking program 200 located in the local memory 209 of logical unit 106 (See FIGS. 1 and 3). If the user chooses not to block the commercial, then commercial blocking program 200 allows the commercial to air (207) and returns to step 206. If at step 206 the user chooses to block the commercial, then the logical unit will block the commercial (208). In blocking the commercial, the logical unit prevents the specific commercial from displaying on the user's television and displays alternative content instead (210). After commercial blocking program 200 has displayed the alternative programming, the original programming of the original television channel is displayed (212) and commercial blocking program 200 ends (214).

[0017] There are many different types of alternative programming that commercial blocking program 200 can display on the user's television instead of the blocked commercial. In one embodiment, commercial blocking program 200 can display a blank screen for the duration of the blocked commercial. However, in the preferred embodiment, commercial blocking program 200 displays the programming according to alternative programming logic 250 in FIG. 2B. Alternative programming logic 250 starts (252) and queries the user if he or she would like to define the alternative programming as a universal television channel that will replace all blocked television commercials (254). A universal television channel is one which will display the contents of a specific television channel on the user's television whenever the blocked commercial airs. For example, whenever a blocked commercial airs, commercial blocking program 200 will cause the The Weather Channel to be displayed. A universal television channel may include Web TV or any programming variation that may be made available to the user of the television to which the logical unit is connected. If the user determines that they would like to select a universal alternative channel, then the user specifies which channel is the universal television channel (256) and alternative programming logic 250 ends (274). If at step 254 the user determines that he or she would not like to select a universal television channel, then alternative programming logic 250 queries the user if he or she would like to define the alternative programming based on the blocked commercial (258). Alternative programming based on the blocked commercial will display a particular television channel whenever a specific blocked commercial airs. For example, whenever commercial X airs, commercial blocking program 200 will cause The Weather Channel to be displayed. If the user determines that he or she would like to define the alternative programming based on the blocked commercial, then the user selects a specific television channel that will display whenever the specific television commercial airs (260) and alternative programming logic 250 ends (274). If the user determines at step 258 that he or she do not want to define the alternative programming based on the commercial, alternative programming logic 250 queries the user whether he or she would like to define alternative programming based on the television channel (262). Alternative programming based on the television channel will display television content based on a preferred television channel and a contingent television channel when the blocked commercial airs. For example, whenever a blocked commercial airs, The Weather Channel will be displayed, and in the event The Weather Channel is already being displayed, then CNN will be displayed. If the user determines that he or she would like to define the alternative programming based on the television channel, then the user defines the preferred and contingent television channels (264) and alternative programming logic 250 ends (274). Optionally, a contingent television channel may be selected by a Content Interrogation Program (CIP) that selects a particular television channel based upon selected search criteria. For example, the CIP may be set by the user to search for news alerts, weather alerts, or some other criteria presented to the user from a CIP menu. If at step 262 the user determines that he or she does not want to define alternative programming based on the television channel, then alternative programming logic 250 queries the user whether he or she would like to define alternative programming based on the time of day (266). Alternative programming based on the time of day displays a specific television channel depending on the time of the blocked commercial. For example, if the blocked commercial airs before noon, The Weather Channel will be displayed, and if the blocked commercial airs after noon, CNN will be displayed. If the user would like to define the alternative programming based on the time of day, then the user defines the alternative television channels and the time associated with each alternate channel (268) and alternative programming logic 250 ends (274). If at step 270 the user determines that he or she does not want to define the alternative programming based on the time of day, alternative programming logic 250 queries the user whether he or she would like to define alternative programming based on an elaborate viewing hierarchy (270).

[0018] An elaborate viewing hierarchy is a combination of the alternative programming determinations in steps 254, 258, 262, and 266. There are numerous possible combinations of the programming determinations that will create elaborate viewing hierarchies. For example, one possible elaborate viewing hierarchy would be "whenever a blocked commercial airs, display The Weather Channel; however, if there is also a blocked commercial on The Weather Channel, then go to CNN before noon and CNBC after noon." The elaborate viewing hierarchy may offer the user the option to "mix and match" various combinations of blocked and unblocked signals. For example, the user may select a split screen option where the blocked commercial appears in a portion of the screen while alternate programming appears in the remaining portion of the screen. The user may select an option that will display alternative programming while also displaying the close captioned text of the blocked commercial. Further in the alternative, the user may elect to have more than one alternate programming option displayed. For example, the user may elect to have a split screen display CNN on one portion of the screen and the Weather Channel on the other portion of the screen. If the user would like to define an elaborate viewing hierarchy, then the user enters the appropriate information (i.e. time, channel, and commercial) to define the hierarchy (272) and alternative programming logic 250 ends (274). If at step 270 the user determines that he or she would not like to define an alternative viewing hierarchy, alternative programming logic 250 ends (274). In an alternative embodiment of alternative programming logic 250, a negative determination at step 270 would send the user back to step 254 so that the options may be viewed again. Additionally, there are other types of alternative programming which may be displayed at step 210. Logical unit 106 can buffer the multiplexed cable signal. Such technology is known in the art. U.S. Pat. No. 5,481,296 issued on Jan. 2, 1996 discloses an "Apparatus and Method for Selectively Viewing Video Information." The user can then enter search criteria and search program 200 will record the television signal based on the specific time, channel, and/or keywords. For example whenever "and now your local forecast" is found in the audio component of the cable signal for The Weather Channel, logical unit 106 can record the accompanying local forecast. Additionally, logical unit 106 can be set to record a specific show. For example, logical unit 106 could be set to record the 11 a.m. Sports Center on ESPN. In either case, the recorded programming can be displayed in place of the blocked commercial.

[0019] Many optional features can be displayed along with the alternative programming. For example, it may be beneficial to display a timer in the corner of the screen which shows the time remaining until the end of the blocked commercial. Additionally, the user may desire to have a brief description of which commercial is being blocked. Moreover, the user may wish to have a timer counting down the amount of time until the desired television content returns. Furthermore, the inventive concept contained herein can be utilized to block all commercials and display only desired programming. If the user desires to block all television commercials, then the logical unit develops a library of the unwanted commercials. The library of blocked commercials could be accessed by the user according to an Archive Interrogation Program (AIP) that would allow the library of blocked commercials to be searched by key words, phrases, date and time or other any other method that a person skilled in the art may use to search a library of stored data. Commercials designated as blocked by the user are added to the library and blocked in the future. Alternatively, the logical unit can buffer the entire multiplexed signal, delay the signal a predetermined time (i.e. sixty seconds) and block out all television programming that is not greater than sixty seconds. This would block all thirty and sixty second television commercials. This implementation can also be orchestrated at the cable provider rather than the user's television or the logical unit. The user may have the option to block selected commercials permanently (without the recourse to unblock the commercial at a later time) while designating other commercials as non-permanently blocked commercials (with the recourse to unblock the commercial at a later time). The user may have the option to block all previously blocked commercials (and to view new commercials) or to block all commercials. In addition, the user may be provided with the option to block, unblock and access the programming of the logical unit by means of voice commands or audible signals such as clapping.

[0020] FIG. 3 is a depiction of the data processing system 300 contained within housing of logical unit 106. Data processing system 300 comprises processor 302, boot ram 304, and LCD controller 305 coupled to system bus 306. Also connected to system bus 306 is memory controller/cache 308, which provides an interface to local memory 309. I/O bus bridge 310 is connected to system bus 306 and provides an interface to I/O bus 312. Memory controller/cache 308 and I/O bus bridge 310 may be integrated as depicted. Peripheral components are connected via I/O bus 312. Typical peripheral components include Universal Asynchronous Receiver Transmitter (UART) 318, a keypad or touch screen 320, digital-to-analog converters 328, analog-to-digital converters 330, serial interface controller 340, clocks and timers 342, cable output to the television 344, power controller 346, cable input from the cable provider 348, and infrared ports 350. Those skilled in the art will appreciate the depiction of data processing system 300 in FIG. 3 is exemplary and is not intended as an architectural limitation of the present invention. Data processing system 300 may be a separate single controller.

[0021] With respect to the above description then, it is to be realized that the optimum dimensional relationships for the parts of the invention, to include variations in size, materials, shape, form, function and manner of operation, assembly and use, are deemed readily apparent and obvious to one skilled in the art, and all equivalent relationships to those illustrated in the drawings and described in the specification are intended to be encompassed by the present invention.

United States Patent Application   20030227475
Kind Code   A1
Fellenstein, Craig William; et al.   December 11, 2003

Apparatus and Method for Blocking Television Commercials and Delivering Micro-Programming Content

Abstract

An apparatus and method is disclosed for blocking specific television commercials from the viewer's television based upon the characteristics of the television commercial and replacing the commercial with a micro-programming segment prepared by an alternate viewing provider. A logical unit and a commercial blocking program in the logical unit allow alternative viewing options so that the user may choose micro-programming options to replace the unwanted communication. The commercial blocking program recognizes a unique digital identifying tag that distinguishes a particular commercial from all other commercials. Alternatively, the commercial blocking program identifies a commercial by a "component signature" or an "overall digital signature." Upon viewing an unwanted commercial, the user indicates that he wants to block the commercial through one of a variety of input methods. The commercial blocking program then prevents the commercial from being displayed on the user's television and causes alternative programming to be displayed instead. The user may configure the alternative programming via the alternative programming logic and choose to display micro-programming segments in place of the blocked commercial. The micro-programming segments are designed to provide a complete informational exchange or entertainment package in the time segment. The alternate viewing provider may provide the micro-programming by subscription service, or by non-subscription service where the micro-programming contains non-intrusive advertising.

Claims

What is claimed is:

1. A method for displaying alternate viewing packages in place of television commercials comprising: using a logical unit, selecting a micro-programming option; receiving a first television signal; recognizing said first television signal in the logical unit; blocking said first television signal by the logical unit; and displaying a second signal wherein said signal is an alternate viewing package.

2. The method of claim 1 wherein said first television signal is a commercial.

3. The method of claim 1 wherein said first television signal is recognized by the time, audio, and video components of said first television signal.

4. The method of claim 1 wherein said first television signal is recognized by an identifying tag.

5. The method of claim 1 further comprising: buffering the alternate viewing package.

6. The method of claim 1 further comprising: selecting a staggered time option.

7. The method of claim 1 further comprising: selecting a time synchronized option.

8. The method of claim 1 further comprising: selecting a buffered package option.

9. A method of determining alternative programming displayed during a blocked television commercial comprising: displaying a micro-programming option to a user; receiving a micro-programming selection from said user; blocking a first television signal; and responsive to user selection of the micro-programming option, displaying an alternate viewing package based on the user selection.

10. The method of claim 9 further comprising: buffering the alternate viewing package.

11. The method of claim 9 further comprising: displaying the alternate viewing package in staggered time.

12. The method of claim 9 further comprising: displaying the alternate viewing package in synchronization.

13. The method of claim 9 further comprising: displaying a buffered alternative viewing package.

14. A programmable apparatus for displaying micro-programming in place of blocked television programs comprising: programmable hardware; software; said hardware being directed by said software to: receive a first television signal; recognize said first television signal; block said first television signal; and display a second television signal; wherein said second television signal is an alternate viewing package.

15. The apparatus of claim 14 wherein said first television signal is a commercial.

16. The apparatus of claim 14 wherein said software further directs said hardware to: buffer the alternate viewing package; and store the alternate viewing package in a memory.

17. The apparatus of claim 16 wherein said second television signal is defined as the contents of said memory.

18. The apparatus of claim 14 wherein the second television signal is synchronized.

19. The apparatus of claim 14 wherein the second television signal is buffered.

20. The apparatus of claim 14 wherein the second television signal is staggered.

21. A programmable apparatus for displaying micro-programming in place of a blocked television commercial comprising: programmable hardware; software; said hardware being directed by said software to: display a plurality of alternative programming options to a user; receive input from said user; block a first television signal; and responsive to a selection by the user of a micro-programming option, display a second television signal based on said selection.

22. The apparatus of claim 21 wherein said software further directs said hardware to: buffer a second television signal; record said second television signal in a memory.

23. The apparatus of claim 21 wherein said second television signal is defined as the contents of said memory.

24. The apparatus of claim 21 wherein the second television signal is synchronized.

25. The apparatus of claim 21 wherein the second television signal is buffered.

26. The apparatus of claim 21 wherein the second television signal is staggered.

Description

RELATED APPLICATIONS

[0001] This application is related to AUS920020014US1, "Apparatus and Method for *Blocking Television Commercials* and Displaying Alternative Programming."

FIELD OF THE INVENTION

[0002] The present invention relates to an apparatus and method for blocking undesired television commercials and displaying micro-programming in place of the blocked commercials.

BACKGROUND OF THE INVENTION

[0003] Debates today rage about both the delivery and funding of informational content in all of its forms. On the Internet, many content providers are moving away from their advertisement-based business models and moving towards subscription-based business models. Despite rapid advances in technology, the delivery mechanisms and methods of generating revenue for content delivered through television broadcasts have been relatively stagnant, when compared to the delivery mechanisms and methods of generating revenue for the Internet and web delivery systems. In television broadcasts, advertisers still attempt to reach users using the same techniques that they have used for decades which are the thirty and sixty second commercials interspaced throughout specific television programs. In addition to technology, the viewer is becoming increasingly sophisticated and is demanding that every second of their time, whether engaged in work or leisure pursuits, be well spent. For the vast majority of television viewers, time engaged in viewing undesired advertisements is not considered time well spent. Therefore, a need exists for an apparatus and method of preventing a television viewer from viewing unwanted commercials.

[0004] Additionally, television viewers generally do not prefer to have periods of interrupted programming or "dead air" when they are viewing a program. It would be preferable if the blocked commercial could be replaced with user-defined alternative programming. Therefore, a need exists for an apparatus and method for replacing a blocked commercial with alternative programming which is more acceptable to the television viewer.

[0005] Furthermore, television viewers may want to play a more active role in determining what type of programming will replace the commercials they have chosen to block. Television viewers who choose to block certain commercials may want to selectively determine alternative programming which will replace the blocked commercial. The alternative programming may differ depending on the time of day or the particular channel which is currently being viewed. Therefore, a need exists for an apparatus and method which will allow television viewers to define the alternative programming content.

[0006] Television viewers may want to view a program that they may have missed instead of the commercial. In other words, it may be preferable to replace an unwanted commercial with television programming from another time on another television channel. Therefore, a need exists for an apparatus and method for buffering desired programming and displaying the desired programming in the time slot where the blocked commercial previously resided.

[0007] The time slots made available by a blocked commercial are short. Therefore, a need exists for specially designed alternative television programming in lengths designed to fit into commercial time slots. A further need exists for micro-programming that can be buffered for access as desired.

SUMMARY OF THE INVENTION

[0008] The present invention, which meets the needs stated above, is an apparatus and method for blocking specific television commercials from the viewer's television based upon the characteristics of the television commercial and replacing the commercial with a micro-programming segment prepared by an alternate viewing provider. A logical unit and a commercial blocking program in the logical unit allow alternative viewing options so that the user may choose microprogramming options to replace the unwanted communication.

[0009] The commercial blocking program recognizes a unique digital identifying tag that distinguishes a particular commercial from all other commercials. Alternatively, the commercial blocking program identifies a commercial by a "component signature" or an "overall digital signature." Upon viewing an unwanted commercial, the user indicates that he wants to block the commercial through one of a variety of input methods. The commercial blocking program then prevents the commercial from being displayed on the user's television and causes alternative programming to be displayed instead. The user may configure the alternative programming via the alternative programming logic and choose to display micro-programming segments in place of the blocked commercial. The micro-programming segments are designed to provide a complete informational exchange or entertainment package in the time segment. The alternate viewing provider may provide the micro-programming by subscription service, or by non-subscription service where the micro-programming contains non-intrusive advertising.

BRIEF DESCRIPTION OF THE DRAWINGS

[0010] FIG. 1 is an illustration of the invention interacting with a cable provider and a television.

[0011] FIG. 2A is a flowchart of the commercial blocking program.

[0012] FIG. 2B is a flowchart of the alternative programming logic.

[0013] FIG. 2C is a flowchart of the micro-programming option.

[0014] FIG. 3 is a depiction of the data processing system contained within the logical unit.

DETAILED DESCRIPTION OF THE PREFERRED EMBODIMENT

[0015] As used herein, the term "alternate viewing provider" means an entity that offers micro-programming to a user for display in conjunction with a logical unit. The term micro-programming, as used herein, means one or more "alternate viewing packages" that each contain a complete information exchange or an entertainment package in a segment of time that is adapted to fit into the time available from one or more commercials blocked by a logical unit. For example, an alternate viewing package could contain news headlines, weather updates, sports updates, or very short live action or animated shorts that are designed to entertain the user in a crisp, concise segment. An alternate viewing package would normally be thirty or sixty seconds in length but could be designed for any length of time that a logical unit could make available. The term "multiplex" as used herein means the process of funneling several different streams of data over a common communications line. The term "cable provider" as used herein means a company which provides television service to multiple users and includes satellite television providers. The term "buffering" as used herein means a process of examining the closed captioning text or audio signal associated with television signals and configuring the examined signal such that it may be searched for specific keywords. As used herein, the term "alternate viewing" means content displayed in place of a blocked commercial and may include one or more of the following: (1) a brief message displayed to inform the viewer that alternative programming will be presented during the commercial interval; (2) an on-screen counter, showing how many seconds are left before the planned return to primary viewing and (3) directions to the tuner to go to a particular station. The directions to the tuner may be universal, by commercial, by originating station, by time of day, by definition of an elaborate viewing hierarchy, or to a micro-programming station or to buffered micro-programming. As used herein, the term "staggered time alternate viewing package" means an alternate viewing package broadcast on start times that are staggered for a number of seconds to coincide with the time slots of blocked commercials. For example, an alternate viewing package may start at the top and bottom of the minute on a given station, and at 15 and 45 seconds on another station. Accordingly, the station with the alternate viewing package start time closest to the start time of the blocked commercial would be chosen. As used herein, the term "time synchronized" means an alternate viewing package, delivered on demand in which the user joins the broadcast at the exact start point of the micro-program. As used herein, the term "buffered" means an alternate viewing package stored in the memory of a logical unit or at the cable service provider so that synchronization problems between the "switchover" point and the alternate programming delivery do not occur. In other words, when a request for alternative programming is made, the logical unit can draw from a buffered alternate viewing package so that the user does not risk joining the alternate viewing package in progress. As used herein, the term "universal" means using content from a particular station to replace all blocked commercials. As used herein, the term "by commercial" means using content from a particular station to replace the specifically identified commercial. As used herein, the term "by originating station" means using the original station to determine the alternative content which will replace all blocked commercials. As used herein, the term "by time of day" means using the time of day to determine which station to use as alternative content for all blocked commercials. As used herein, the term "elaborate viewing hierarchy" means a combination of a plurality of universal, by commercial, by originating station, or by time or day alternative viewing formats As used herein, the term "unique digital identifying tag" means a number sequence before the header and after the trailer of each commercial. The number sequence is assigned according to an industry standard that allows each commercial to be identified from every other commercial. As used herein, a "component signature" is a group of variables, based on a time component, an X video component, a Y video component, and an audio component, that is used to identify a commercial from all other commercials when a "unique digital identifying tag is not available. As used herein, the term "cumulative digital signature" means the aggregation of one or more selected characteristics of a data sequence to provide a unique number for identification of the complete data sequence.

[0016] FIG. 1 is an illustration of the invention 100 interacting with a cable provider and a television set. The depiction of the cable provider is by way of illustration only and is not intended to limit the scope of the invention. Persons skilled in the art will recognize that the invention may be used with either a cable or wireless data transmission system. The cable provider (not shown) provides a television signal through a coaxial cable 102 that runs through the user's wall 104 and into the logical unit 106. Logical unit 106 analyzes the cable signal as described below and displays the information on television 110 via television connection 108. Logical unit 106 can optionally be combined with television 110. Alternatively, logical unit 106 may be placed at the same location as the cable provider such that it is unnecessary to have logical unit 106 at the user's location.

[0017] FIG. 2A is a flowchart of commercial blocking program 200 which operates inside logical unit 106. Commercial blocking program 200 starts (202) whenever multiplexed cable signals are broadcast (204). In the preferred embodiment, each commercial has a unique digital identifying tag, similar to a serial number, which identifies a particular commercial. Logical unit 106 recognizes a particular commercial based on the unique identifying tag.

[0018] In an alternate embodiment, logical unit 106 identifies commercials by a "component signature." Multiplexed cable signals are defined by four components: a time component, an X video component, a Y video component, and an audio component. Every television program and/or commercial can be readily identified by these components. There is generally allowed some amount of time skew in the synchronization of the four components to identify the absolute beginning of a program or commercial. By taking the time skew into consideration, commercial blocking program 200 can identify a particular commercial. For example, a given pattern of video/audio signals occurring at a time "delta" (perhaps but not necessarily in the order of 500 microseconds) around the nominal beginning of an advertisement, may point back to a specified commercial.

[0019] Alternatively, logical unit 106 establishes an "overall digital signature" for a particular commercial. In this event, the signal need not be dissembled into its video/audio components as in the "component signature," but rather, analysis of cumulative digital characteristics may be used to identify the commercial to be blocked. One or more characteristics of a data sequence is selected and aggregated to provide a unique number for identification purposes of the complete data sequence. The advantage of using cumulative digital characteristics is that all commercials could be blocked using this technique. In the case of commercials to be identified by an "overall digital signature," the logical unit develops a library at the set-top of the "overall digital signature" of the blocked advertisements. For example, it may be assumed that some time interval, "T.sub.sample" is great enough to ascertain with accuracies approaching one hundred percent the identity of a given advertisement. "T.sub.sample" may be a sub-second or it may be multi-second, depending on the processing power behind the logical unit and the uniqueness of the commercial. Once a commercial signal is detected to be identical to a blocked advertisement, then the logical unit takes the actions it has been programmed to implement.

[0020] As a commercial airs, the user has the option of blocking the commercial (206) by means of commercial blocking program 200 located in the local memory 209 of logical unit 106 (See FIGS. 1 and 3). If the user chooses not to block the commercial, then commercial blocking program 200 allows the commercial to air (207) and returns to step 206. If at step 206 the user chooses to block the commercial, then the logical unit will block the commercial (208). In blocking the commercial, the logical unit prevents the specific commercial from displaying on the user's television and displays alternative content instead (210). After commercial blocking program 200 has displayed the alternative programming, the original programming of the original television channel is displayed (212) and commercial blocking program 200 ends (214).

[0021] There are many different types of alternative programming that commercial blocking program 200 can display on the user's television instead of the blocked commercial. In one embodiment, commercial blocking program 200 can display a blank screen for the duration of the blocked commercial. However, in the preferred embodiment, commercial blocking program 200 displays the programming according to alternative programming logic 250 in FIG. 2B. Alternative programming logic 250 starts (252) and queries the user if he or she would like to define the alternative programming as a universal television channel that will replace all blocked television commercials (254). A universal television channel is one which will display the contents of a specific television channel on the user's television whenever the blocked commercial airs. For example, whenever a blocked commercial airs, commercial blocking program 200 will cause the The Weather Channel to be displayed. A universal television channel may include Web TV or any programming variation that may be made available to the user of the television to which the logical unit is connected. If the user determines that they would like to select a universal alternative channel, then the user specifies which channel is the universal television channel (256) and alternative programming logic 250 ends (294). If at step 254 the user determines that he or she would not like to select a universal television channel, then alternative programming logic 250 queries the user if he or she would like to define the alternative programming based on the blocked commercial (258). Alternative programming based on the blocked commercial will display a particular television channel whenever a specific blocked commercial airs. For example, whenever commercial X airs, commercial blocking program 200 will cause The Weather Channel to be displayed. If the user determines that he or she would like to define the alternative programming based on the blocked commercial, then the user selects a specific television channel that will display whenever the specific television commercial airs (260) and alternative programming logic 250 ends (298). If the user determines at step 258 that he or she do not want to define the alternative programming based on the commercial, alternative programming logic 250 queries the user whether he or she would like to define alternative programming based on the television channel (262). Alternative programming based on the television channel will display television content based on a preferred television channel and a contingent television channel when the blocked commercial airs. For example, whenever a blocked commercial airs, The Weather Channel will be displayed, and in the event The Weather Channel is already being displayed, then CNN will be displayed. If the user determines that he or she would like to define the alternative programming based on the television channel, then the user defines the preferred and contingent television channels (264) and alternative programming logic 250 ends (298). Optionally, a contingent television channel may be selected by a Content Interrogation Program (CIP) that selects a particular television channel based upon selected search criteria. For example, the CIP may be set by the user to search for news alerts, weather alerts, or some other criteria presented to the user from a CIP menu. If at step 262 the user determines that he or she does not want to define alternative programming based on the television channel, then alternative programming logic 250 queries the user whether he or she would like to define alternative programming based on the time of day (266). Alternative programming based on the time of day displays a specific television channel depending on the time of the blocked commercial. For example, if the blocked commercial airs before noon, The Weather Channel will be displayed, and if the blocked commercial airs after noon, CNN will be displayed. If the user would like to define the alternative programming based on the time of day, then the user defines the alternative television channels and the time associated with each alternate channel (268) and alternative programming logic 250 ends (298). If at step 266 the user determines that he or she does not want to define the alternative programming based on the time of day, alternative programming logic 250 queries the user whether he or she would like to define alternative programming based on an elaborate viewing hierarchy (270).

[0022] An elaborate viewing hierarchy is a combination of the alternative programming determinations in steps 254, 258, 262, and 266. There are numerous possible combinations of the programming determinations that will create elaborate viewing hierarchies. For example, one possible elaborate viewing hierarchy would be "whenever a blocked commercial airs, display The Weather Channel; however, if there is also a blocked commercial on The Weather Channel, then go to CNN before noon and CNBC after noon." The elaborate viewing hierarchy may offer the user the option to "mix and match" various combinations of blocked and unblocked signals. For example, the user may select a split screen option where the blocked commercial appears in a portion of the screen while alternate programming appears in the remaining portion of the screen. The user may select an option that will display alternative programming while also displaying the close captioned text of the blocked commercial. Further in the alternative, the user may elect to have more than one alternate programming option displayed. For example, the user may elect to have a split screen display CNN on one portion of the screen and the Weather Channel on the other portion of the screen. If the user would like to define an elaborate viewing hierarchy, then the user enters the appropriate information (i.e. time, channel, and commercial) to define the hierarchy (272) and alternative programming logic 250 ends (298). If at step 270 the user determines that he or she would not like to define an alternative viewing hierarchy, alternative programming logic 250 goes to step 282 (See FIG. 2C).

[0023] Next a determination is made as to whether the user wants to select micro-programming (282). If the user does not want to select micro-programming, alternate programming logic 250 ends (298). If at step 282 the user determines that he or she wants to select micro-programming, a determination is made as to whether staggered time alternate viewing packages are desired (284). If staggered time alternate viewing packages are desired, then the selection is entered (286) and alternate programming logic 250 goes to step 296. If staggered time alternate viewing packages are not selected, then a determination is made as to whether the user wants to select time synchronized alternate viewing packages (288). If the user desires to selected time synchronized alternate viewing packages, then the selection is entered (290) and alternate programming logic 250 goes to step 296. If the user does not select time synchronized alternate viewing packages, then a determination is made as to whether a buffered alternate viewing package is desired (292). If a buffered alternate viewing package is desired, then the selection is entered (294). If a buffered alternate viewing package is not desired, then a determination is made as to whether another selection is made (296). If another selection is to be made, alternate programming logic 250 goes to step 284. If another selection is not to be made, alternate programming logic 250 ends (298). A default option may also be available if the alternate viewing service provider plays continuously broadcast alternate viewing packages. In that case the default option would be that the television would move to the alternate viewing broadcast at the time of the blocked commercial and pick up the alternate viewing package playing at that time.

[0024] In an alternative embodiment of alternative programming logic 250, a negative determination at step 296 would send the user back to step 254 so that the options may be viewed again. Additionally, there are other types of alternative programming which may be displayed at step 210. Logical unit 106 can buffer the multiplexed cable signal. Such technology is known in the art. U.S. Pat. No. 5,481,296 issued on Jan. 2, 1996 discloses an "Apparatus and Method for Selectively Viewing Video Information." The user can then enter search criteria and search program 200 will record the television signal based on the specific time, channel, and/or keywords. For example whenever "and now your local forecast" is found in the audio component of the cable signal for The Weather Channel, logical unit 106 can record the accompanying local forecast. Additionally, logical unit 106 can be set to record a specific show. For example, logical unit 106 could be set to record the 11 a.m. Sports Center on ESPN. In either case, the recorded programming can be displayed in place of the blocked commercial.

[0025] Many optional features can be displayed along with the alternative programming. For example, it may be beneficial to display a timer in the corner of the screen which shows the time remaining until the end of the blocked commercial. Additionally, the user may desire to have a brief description of which commercial is being blocked. Moreover, the user may wish to have a timer counting down the amount of time until the desired television content returns. Furthermore, the inventive concept contained herein can be utilized to block all commercials and display only desired programming. If the user desires to block all television commercials, then the logical unit develops a library of the unwanted commercials. The library of blocked commercials could be accessed by the user according to an Archive Interrogation Program (AIP) that would allow the library of blocked commercials to be searched by key words, phrases, date and time or other any other method that a person skilled in the art may use to search a library of stored data. Commercials designated as blocked by the user are added to the library and blocked in the future. Alternatively, the logical unit can buffer the entire multiplexed signal, delay the signal a pre-determined time (i.e. sixty seconds) and block out all television programming that is not greater than sixty seconds. This would block all thirty and sixty second television commercials. This implementation can also be orchestrated at the cable provider rather than the user's television or the logical unit. The user may have the option to block selected commercials permanently (without the recourse to unblock the commercial at a later time) while designating other commercials as non-permanently blocked commercials (with the recourse to unblock the commercial at a later time). The user may have the option to block all previously blocked commercials (and to view new commercials) or to block all commercials. In addition, the user may be provided with the option to block, unblock and access the programming of the logical unit by means of voice commands or audible signals such as clapping.

[0026] FIG. 3 is a depiction of the data processing system 300 contained within housing of logical unit 106. Data processing system 300 comprises processor 302, boot ram 304, and LCD controller 305 coupled to system bus 306. Also connected to system bus 306 is memory controller/cache 308, which provides an interface to local memory 309. I/O bus bridge 310 is connected to system bus 306 and provides an interface to I/O bus 312. Memory controller /cache 308 and I/O bus bridge 310 may be integrated as depicted. Peripheral components are connected via I/O bus 312. Typical peripheral components include Universal Asynchronous Receiver Transmitter (UART) 318, a keypad or touch screen 320, digital-to-analog converters 328, analog-to-digital converters 330, serial interface controller 340, clocks and timers 342, cable output to the television 344, power controller 346, cable input from the cable provider 348, and infrared ports 350. Those skilled in the art will appreciate the depiction of data processing system 300 in FIG. 3 is exemplary and is not intended as an architectural limitation of the present invention. Data processing system 300 may be a separate single controller.

[0027] With respect to the above description then, it is to be realized that the optimum dimensional relationships for the parts of the invention, to include variations in size, materials, shape, form, function and manner of operation, assembly and use, are deemed readily apparent and obvious to one skilled in the art, and all equivalent relationships to those illustrated in the drawings and described in the specification are intended to be encompassed by the present invention.

United States Patent Application   20040019904

Kind Code   A1

Fellenstein, Craig William; et al.   January 29, 2004

Apparatus and Method for *Blocking Television Commercials* with a Content Interrogation Program

Abstract

An apparatus and method is disclosed for blocking specific television commercials from the viewer's television based upon the characteristics of the television commercial and replacing the commercial with television content located by a content interrogation program. The content interrogation program seeks out television content based upon a user search term specifically for use as contingent programming to replace the blocked commercial. The content interrogation program can have multiple search terms and provide prioritized multiple searches to identify multiple segments to play in spaces created by blocked commercials.

Claims

What is claimed is:

1. A method for displaying a television segment in place of a blocked television commercial based on interrogation of a television signal comprising: receiving a first television signal; recognizing said first television signal in a logical unit; blocking said first television

signal by the logical unit; buffering a second television signal; specifying at least one search parameter; searching said second television signal for a data that matches said search parameters; responsive to finding the data that matches said search parameters, identifying a contingent television segment as a third signal; and displaying the third signal in place of the first television signal.

2. The method of claim 1 further comprising defining a length of the third signal as T before wherein T means a numerical value corresponding to a playing time of the data and T before means a length of the third signal equal to the data and extending before the data for a time equal to T.

3. The method of claim 1 further comprising defining a length of the third signal as T after wherein T means a numerical value corresponding to a playing time of the data and T before means a length of the third signal equal to the data and extending after the data for a time equal to T.

4. The method of claim 1 further comprising defining a length of the third signal as T center wherein T means a numerical value corresponding to a playing time of the data and T center means a length of the third signal equal to the data and extending before the data for a time equal to 1/2 T and extending after the data for a time equal to 1/2 T.

5. The method of claim 1 wherein said search parameter is a keyword.

6. The method of claim 1 wherein said data is a closed captioning signal.

7. The method of claim 1 wherein said buffering occurs when a television unit is not activated.

8. The method of claim 1 further comprising decoding said television signal.

9. The method of claim 1 further comprising linking said search parameters by at least one logical relationship.

10. The method of claim 1 further comprising comparing said search parameters to a dictionary.

11. The method of claim 10 further comprising obtaining lexically parsed equivalents and searching said television signal for data that matches said lexically parsed equivalents.

12. The method of claim 1 further comprising comparing said search parameters to a thesaurus.

13. The method of claim 12 further comprising obtaining synonym equivalents and searching said television signal for data that matches said synonym equivalents.

14. The method of claim 1 wherein said buffering simultaneously occurs over a plurality of television channels embedded within said television signal.

15. The method of claim 1 wherein said first television signal is a commercial.

16. The method of claim 1 wherein said first television signal is recognized by the time, audio, and video components of said first television signal.

17. The method of claim 1 wherein said first television signal is recognized by an identifying tag.

18. The method of claim 1 wherein said parameter is a user-defined parameter.

19. An apparatus for identifying an alternate viewing segment to replace a blocked television commercial comprising: a logical unit with a memory; a program stored in said memory; said memory, so configured by said program, causes said logical unit perform operations comprising: receiving a first television signal; recognizing said first television signal in the logical unit; blocking said first television signal by the logical unit; buffering a second television signal; specifying at least one search parameter; searching said second television signal for data that matches said search parameters; responsive to finding a data that matches said search parameters, identifying a contingent television segment as a third signal; displaying the third signal in place of the first television signal.

20. The apparatus of claim 19 further comprising defining a length of the third signal as T before wherein T means a numerical value corresponding to a playing time of the data and T before means a length of the third signal equal to the data and extending before the data for a time equal to T.

21. The method of claim 19 further comprising defining a length of the third signal as T after wherein T means a numerical value corresponding to a playing time of the data and T before means a length of the third signal equal to the data and extending after the data for a time equal to T.

22. The method of claim 19 further comprising defining a length of the third signal as T center wherein T means a numerical value corresponding to a playing time of the data and T center means a length of the third signal equal to the data and extending before the data for a time equal to 1/2 T and extending after the data for a time equal to 1/2 T.

23. The apparatus of claim 19 wherein said signal is a television signal.

24. The apparatus of claim 19 wherein said parameter is a user-defined parameter.

25. The apparatus of claim 19 wherein said search parameter is a keyword.

26. The apparatus of claim 19 wherein said data is a closed captioning signal.

27. The apparatus of claim 19 wherein said buffering occurs when a television unit is not activated.

28. The apparatus of claim 19 wherein said operations further comprise decoding said television signal.

29. The apparatus of claim 19 wherein said operations further comprise linking said search parameters by at least one logical relationship.

30. The apparatus of claim 19 wherein said operations further comprise comparing said search parameters to a dictionary.

31. The apparatus of claim 19 wherein said operations further comprise obtaining lexically parsed equivalents and searching said television signal for data that matches said lexically parsed equivalents.

32. The apparatus of claim 19 wherein said operations further comprise comparing said search parameters to a thesaurus.

33. The apparatus of claim 19 wherein said operations further comprise obtaining synonym equivalents and searching said television signal for data that matches said synonym equivalents.

34. The apparatus of claim 19 wherein said buffering simultaneously occurs over a plurality of television channels embedded within said television signal.

35. An apparatus for identifying an alternate viewing segment to replace a blocked television commercial comprising: means for receiving a first television signal; means for recognizing said first television signal in the logical unit; means for blocking said first television signal by the logical unit; means for buffering a second television signal; means for specifying at least one search parameter; means for searching said second television signal for data that matches said search parameters; means for responsive to finding a data that matches said search parameters, identifying a contingent television segment as a third signal; and means for displaying the third signal in place of the first television signal.

36. The apparatus of claim 35 further comprising a means for defining a length of the third signal as T before wherein T means a numerical value corresponding to a playing time of the data and T before means a length of the third signal equal to the data and extending before the data for a time equal to T.

37. The apparatus of claim 35 further comprising a means for defining a length of the third signal as T after wherein T means a numerical value corresponding to a playing time of the data and T before means a length of the third signal equal to the data and extending after the data for a time equal to T.

38. The apparatus of claim 35 further comprising defining a length of the third signal as T center wherein T means a numerical value corresponding to a playing time of the data and T center means a length of the third signal equal to the data and extending before the data for a time equal to 1/2 T and extending after the data for a time equal to 1/2 T.

Description

RELATED APPLICATIONS

[0001] This application is related to application Ser. No. 10/105,124, "Apparatus and Method of Searching for Desired Television Content," application Ser. No. 10/116,613, "Apparatus and Method for *Blocking Television Commercials* and Displaying Alternative Programming," and to Application docket number AUS920020258US1, "Apparatus and Method for *Blocking Television Commercials* and Displaying Micro-Programming Content."

FIELD OF THE INVENTION

[0002] The present invention relates to an apparatus and method for blocking undesired television commercials and interrogating the content of the programming in order to select alternate viewing to take the place of the blocked programming.

BACKGROUND OF THE INVENTION

[0003] Debates today rage about both the delivery and funding of informational content in all of its forms. On the Internet, many content providers are moving away from their advertisement-based business models and moving towards subscription-based business models. Despite rapid advances in technology, the delivery mechanisms and methods of generating revenue for content delivered through television broadcasts have been relatively stagnant, when compared to the delivery mechanisms and methods of generating revenue for the Internet and web delivery systems. In television broadcasts, advertisers still attempt to reach users using the same techniques that they have used for decades which are the thirty and sixty second commercials interspaced throughout specific television programs. In addition to technology, the viewer is becoming increasingly sophisticated and is demanding that every second of their time, whether engaged in work or leisure pursuits, be well spent. For the vast majority of television viewers, time engaged in viewing undesired advertisements is not considered time well spent. Therefore, a need exists for an apparatus and method of preventing a television viewer from viewing unwanted commercials.

[0004] Additionally, television viewers generally do not prefer to have periods of interrupted programming or "dead air" when they are viewing a program. It would be preferable if the blocked commercial could be replaced with user-defined alternative programming.

[0005] Application Ser. No. 10/116,613, "Apparatus and Method for *Blocking Television Commercials* and Displaying Alternative Programming" discloses a logical unit and a commercial blocking program in the logical unit to allow alternative viewing options so that the user may define the alternative programming to replace the unwanted commercial. The commercial blocking program breaks all incoming television signals into time, video and audio components and is able to recognize specific commercials based on those components. Upon viewing an unwanted commercial, the user indicates that he wants to block the commercial through one of a variety of input methods. The commercial blocking program then prevents the commercial from being displayed on the user's television and causes alternative programming to be displayed instead. The user may configure the alternative programming via the alternative programming logic. The user may configure the alternative programming as a universal television channel, based on the specific commercial, based on the television station, based on the time of day, or based on an elaborate viewing hierarchy. At the end of the blocked commercial, the commercial blocking program displays the television program that was originally displayed on the user's television. Alternatively, the commercial blocking program can buffer the various television programs received from the cable provider and record segments of the cable signal based on certain keywords. The commercial blocking program searches for user defined keywords, records television programs complying with the search terms, and displays the recorded television programming stored in the memory.

[0006] Application Ser. No. 10/105,124, "Apparatus and Method of Searching for Desired Television Content, disclosed an apparatus and method for allowing a user to search for specific content across many television channels in order to locate desirable television shows related to the searched content. Multiplexed cable signals flow thorough a logical unit which buffers text associated with the voice stream of each station via the pre-encoded closed-captioning signal or through the real-time voice translation within the logical unit. The user then enters search terms through one of a variety of different input devices. Upon entry of the search terms, the logical unit will compare the entered term with those available keywords stored in each buffer. Lexical parsing associates terms which may differ from plural to singular forms or in tense. Additionally, synonym comparisons may be made. The logical unit will return a list of matches for the search criteria and allows the user the option of going directly to the television program. The logical unit also evaluates each returned item for its relevancy to the keywords. When not in use, the logical unit maintains a quiescent but monitoring state permitting continuous creation of lexical buffers. This permits the user who turns the television on to immediately have such search terms available. Alternatively, the logic is implemented at the cable provider and enabled through interactive links to the home. In that case, the home logical unit is unnecessary.

[0007] What is needed is a combination of the blocked television commercials and the television content searching to provide a way to seek contingent programming to fill the space created by blocked commercials.

SUMMARY OF THE INVENTION

[0008] The present invention, which meets the needs stated above, is an apparatus and method for blocking specific television commercials from the viewer's television based upon the characteristics of the television commercial and replacing the commercial with television content located by a content interrogation program. The content interrogation program seeks out television content based upon a user search term specifically for use as contingent programming to replace the blocked commercial. The content interrogation program can have multiple search terms and provide prioritized multiple searches to identify multiple segments to play in spaces created by blocked commercials.

BRIEF DESCRIPTION OF THE DRAWINGS

[0009] FIG. 1 is an illustration of the invention interacting with a cable provider and a television.

[0010] FIG. 2A is a flowchart of the commercial blocking program.

[0011] FIG. 2B is a flowchart of the commercial blocking program.

[0012] FIG. 2C is a flowchart of the commercial blocking program.

[0013] FIG. 3 is a flowchart of the search program.

[0014] FIG. 4 is a block chart of the content interrogation program.

[0015] FIG. 5 is a flowchart of the menu program of the CIP.

[0016] FIG. 6 is a flowchart of the set program of the CIP.

[0017] FIG. 7 is flowchart of the interrogation program.

[0018] FIG. 8 is a depiction of the data processing system contained within the logical unit.

DETAILED DESCRIPTION OF THE PREFERRED EMBODIMENT

[0019] The terms below are defined for all uses herein as follows:

[0020] "Alternate viewing" means content displayed in place of a blocked commercial and may include one or more of the following: (1) a brief message displayed to inform the viewer that alternative programming will be presented during the commercial interval; (2) an on-screen counter, showing how many seconds are left before the planned return to primary viewing; and (3) directions to the tuner to go to a particular station. The directions to the tuner may be universal, by commercial, by originating station, by time of day, by definition of an elaborate viewing hierarchy, or to a micro-programming station or to buffered microprogramming.

[0021] "Alternate viewing provider" means an entity that offers micro-programming to a user for display in conjunction with a logical unit.

[0022] "Buffered" means an alternate viewing package stored in the memory of a logical unit or at the cable service provider so that synchronization problems between the "switchover" point and the alternate programming delivery do not occur. In other words, when a request for alternative programming is made, the logical unit can draw from a buffered alternate viewing package so that the user does not risk joining the alternate viewing package in progress.

[0023] "Buffering" means a process of examining the closed captioning text or audio signal associated with television signals and configuring the examined signal such that it may be searched for specific keywords.

[0024] "By commercial" means using content from a particular station to replace the specifically identified commercial.

[0025] "By originating station" means using the original station to determine the alternative content which will replace all blocked commercials.

[0026] "By time of day" means using the time of day to determine which station to use as alternative content for all blocked commercials.

[0027] "Cable provider" means a company which provides television service to multiple users and includes satellite television providers.

[0028] "Component signature" is a group of variables, based on a time component, an X video component, a Y video component, and an audio component, that is used to identify a commercial from all other commercials when a "unique digital identifying tag is not available.

[0029] "Cumulative digital signature" means the aggregation of one or more selected characteristics of a data sequence to provide a unique number for identification of the complete data sequence.

[0030] "Elaborate viewing hierarchy" means a combination of a plurality of universal, by commercial, by originating station, or by time or day alternative viewing formats.

[0031] "Lexical parsing" as used herein means a process of finding matches to a desired search term by comparing the desired search term letter-by-letter with the terms in an available database.

[0032] "Micro-programming," means one or more "alternate viewing packages" that each contain a complete information exchange or an entertainment package in a segment of time that is adapted to fit into the time available from one or more commercials blocked by a logical unit. For example, an alternate viewing package could contain news headlines, weather updates, sports updates, or very short live action or animated shorts that are designed to entertain the user in a crisp, concise segment. An alternate viewing package would normally be thirty or sixty seconds in length but could be designed for any length of time that a logical unit could make available.

[0033] "Multiplex" means the process of funneling several different streams of data over a common communications line.

[0034] "Staggered time alternate viewing package" means an alternate viewing package broadcast on start times that are staggered for a number of seconds to coincide with the time slots of blocked commercials. For example, an alternate viewing package may start at the top and bottom of the minute on a given station, and at 15 and 45 seconds on another station. Accordingly, the station with the alternate viewing package start time closest to the start time of the blocked commercial would be chosen.

[0035] "T" means a numerical value corresponding to playing time of a video segment containing a data that matches a search criterion.

[0036] T "before" means defining a video segment as the portion of a video segment containing a data that matches a search criteria plus a portion of the video segment before the data that runs for time equal to T.

[0037] T "after" means defining a video segment as the portion of a video segment containing a data that matches a search criteria plus a portion of the video segment after the data that runs for time equal to T.

[0038] T "center" means defining a video segment as the portion of a video segment containing a data that matches a search criteria plus a portion of the video segment before the data that runs for time equal to 1/2 T and a portion of the video segment after the data that runs for a time equal to 1/2 T.

[0039] "Time synchronized" means an alternate viewing package, delivered on demand in which the user joins the broadcast at the exact start point of the micro-program.

[0040] "Unique digital identifying tag" means a number sequence before the header and after the trailer of each commercial. The number sequence is assigned according to an industry standard that allows each commercial to be identified from every other commercial.

[0041] "Universal" means using content from a particular station to replace all blocked commercials.

[0042] FIG. 1 is an illustration of the invention 100 interacting with a cable provider and a television set. The depiction of the cable provider is by way of illustration only and is not intended to limit the scope of the invention. Persons skilled in the art will recognize that the invention may be used with either a cable or wireless data transmission system. The cable provider (not shown) provides a television signal through a coaxial cable 102 that runs through the user's wall 104 and into logical unit 106. Logical unit 106 analyzes the cable signal as described below and displays the information on television 110 via television connection 108. Logical unit 106 can optionally be combined with television 110. Alternatively, logical unit 106 may be placed at the same location as the cable provider such that it is unnecessary to have logical unit 106 at the user's location.

[0043] FIG. 2A is a flowchart of commercial blocking program 200 which operates inside logical unit 106. Commercial blocking program 200 starts (202) whenever multiplexed cable signals are broadcast (204). In the preferred embodiment, each commercial has a unique digital identifying tag, similar to a serial number, which identifies a particular commercial. Logical unit 106 recognizes a particular commercial based on the unique identifying tag.

[0044] In an alternate embodiment, logical unit 106 identifies commercials by a "component signature." Multiplexed cable signals are defined by four components: a time component, an X video component, a Y video component, and an audio component. Every television program and/or commercial can be readily identified by these components. There is generally allowed some amount of time skew in the synchronization of the four components to identify the absolute beginning of a program or commercial. By taking the time skew into consideration, commercial blocking program 200 can identify a particular commercial. For example, a given pattern of video/audio signals occurring at a time "delta" (perhaps but not necessarily in the order of 500 microseconds) around the nominal beginning of an advertisement, may point back to a specified commercial.

[0045] Alternatively, logical unit 106 establishes an "overall digital signature" for a particular commercial. In this event, the signal need not be dissembled into its video/audio components as in the "component signature," but rather, analysis of cumulative digital characteristics may be used to identify the commercial to be blocked. One or more characteristics of a data sequence is selected and aggregated to provide a unique number for identification purposes of the complete data sequence. The advantage of using cumulative digital characteristics is that all commercials could be blocked using this technique. In the case of commercials to be identified by an "overall digital signature," the logical unit develops a library at the set-top of the "overall digital signature" of the blocked advertisements. For example, it may be assumed that some time interval, "T.sub.sample" is great enough to ascertain with accuracies approaching one hundred percent the identity of a given advertisement. "T.sub.sample" may be a sub-second or it may be multi-second, depending on the processing power behind the logical unit and the uniqueness of the commercial. Once a commercial signal is detected to be identical to a blocked advertisement, then the logical unit takes the actions it has been programmed to implement.

[0046] As a commercial airs, the user has the option of blocking the commercial (206) by means of commercial blocking program 200 located in the local memory 209 of logical unit 106 (See FIGS. 1 and 8). If the user chooses not to block the commercial, then commercial blocking program 200 allows the commercial to air (207) and returns to step 206. If at step 206 the user chooses to block the commercial, then the logical unit will block the commercial (208). In blocking the commercial, the logical unit prevents the specific commercial from displaying on the user's television and displays alternative content instead (210). After commercial blocking program 200 has displayed the alternative programming, the original programming of the original television channel is displayed (212) and commercial blocking program 200 ends (214).

[0047] There are many different types of alternative programming that commercial blocking program 200 can display on the user's television instead of the blocked commercial. In one embodiment, commercial blocking program 200 can display a blank screen for the duration of the blocked commercial. However, in the preferred embodiment, commercial blocking program 200 displays the programming according to alternative programming logic 250 in FIGS. 2B and 2C. Alternative programming logic 250 starts (252) and queries the user if he or she would like to define the alternative programming as a universal television channel that will replace all blocked television commercials (254). A universal television channel is one which will display the contents of a specific television channel on the user's television whenever the blocked commercial airs. For example, whenever a blocked commercial airs, commercial blocking program 200 will cause the The Weather Channel to be displayed. A universal television channel may include Web TV or any programming variation that may be made available to the user of the television to which the logical unit is connected. If the user determines that they would like to select a universal alternative channel, then the user specifies which channel is the universal television channel (256) and alternative programming logic 250 ends (294). If at step 254 the user determines that he or she would not like to select a universal television channel, then alternative programming logic 250 queries the user if he or she would like to define the alternative programming based on the blocked commercial (258). Alternative programming based on the blocked commercial will display a particular television channel whenever a specific blocked commercial airs. For example, whenever commercial X airs, commercial blocking program 200 will cause The Weather Channel to be displayed. If the user determines that he or she would like to define the alternative programming based on the blocked commercial, then the user selects a specific television channel that will display whenever the specific television commercial airs (260) and alternative programming logic 250 ends (298). If the user determines at step 258 that he or she does not want to define the alternative programming based on the commercial, alternative programming logic 250 queries the user whether he or she would like to define alternative programming based on the television channel (262). Alternative programming based on the television channel will display television content based on a preferred television channel and a contingent television channel when the blocked commercial airs. For example, whenever a blocked commercial airs, The Weather Channel will be displayed, and in the event The Weather Channel is already being displayed, then CNN will be displayed. If the user determines that he or she would like to define the alternative programming based on the television channel, then the user defines the preferred and contingent television channels (264) and alternative programming logic 250 ends (298). A contingent television channel may be selected by a Content Interrogation Program (CIP) (see FIG. 4) that selects a particular television channel based upon selected search criteria. If at step 262 the user determines that he or she does not want to define alternative programming based on the television channel, then alternative programming logic 250 queries the user whether he or she would like to define alternative programming based on the time of day (266). Alternative programming based on the time of day displays a specific television channel depending on the time of the blocked commercial. For example, if the blocked commercial airs before noon, The Weather Channel will be displayed, and if the blocked commercial airs after noon, CNN will be displayed. If the user would like to define the alternative programming based on the time of day, then the user defines the alternative television channels and the time associated with each alternate channel (268) and alternative programming logic 250 ends (298). If at step 266 the user determines that he or she does not want to define the alternative programming based on the time of day, alternative programming logic 250 queries the user whether he or she would like to define alternative programming based on an elaborate viewing hierarchy (270).

[0048] An elaborate viewing hierarchy is a combination of the alternative programming determinations in steps 254, 258, 262, and 266. There are numerous possible combinations of the programming determinations that will create elaborate viewing hierarchies. For example, one possible elaborate viewing hierarchy would be "whenever a blocked commercial airs, display The Weather Channel; however, if there is also a blocked commercial on The Weather Channel, then go to CNN before noon and CNBC after noon." The elaborate viewing hierarchy may offer the user the option to "mix and match" various combinations of blocked and unblocked signals. For example, the user may select a split screen option where the blocked commercial appears in a portion of the screen while alternate programming appears in the remaining portion of the screen. The user may select an option that will display alternative programming while also displaying the close captioned text of the blocked commercial. Further in the alternative, the user may elect to have more than one alternate programming option displayed. For example, the user may elect to have a split screen display CNN on one portion of the screen and the Weather Channel on the other portion of the screen. If the user would like to define an elaborate viewing hierarchy, then the user enters the appropriate information (i.e. time, channel, and commercial) to define the hierarchy (272) and alternative programming logic 250 ends (298). If at step 270 the user determines that he or she would not like to define an alternative viewing hierarchy, alternative programming logic 250 goes to step 282 (See FIG. 2C).

[0049] Next a determination is made as to whether the user wants to select micro-programming (282). If the user does not want to select micro-programming, alternate programming logic 250 ends (298). If at step 282 the user determines that he or she wants to select microprogramming, a determination is made as to whether staggered time alternate viewing packages are desired (284). If staggered time alternate viewing packages are desired, then the selection is entered (286) and alternate programming logic 250 goes to step 296. If staggered time alternate viewing packages are not selected, then a determination is made as to whether the user wants to select time synchronized alternate viewing packages (288). If the user desires to selected time synchronized alternate viewing packages, then the selection is entered (290) and alternate programming logic 250 goes to step 296. If the user does not select time synchronized alternate viewing packages, then a determination is made as to whether a buffered alternate viewing package is desired (292). If a buffered alternate viewing package is desired, then the selection is entered (294). If a buffered alternate viewing package is not desired, then a determination is made as to whether another selection is made (296). If another selection is to be made, alternate programming logic 250 goes to step 284. If another selection is not to be made, alternate programming logic 250 ends (298). A default option may also be available if the alternate viewing service provider plays continuously broadcast alternate viewing packages. In that case the default option would be that the television would move to the alternate viewing broadcast at the time of the blocked commercial and pick up the alternate viewing package playing at that time.

[0050] In an alternative embodiment of alternative programming logic 250, a negative determination at step 296 would send the user back to step 254 so that the options may be viewed again. Additionally, there are other types of alternative programming which may be displayed at step 210. The user can then enter search criteria and search program 300 (See FIG. 3) will record the television signal based on the specific time, channel, and/or keywords. For example, whenever "and now your local forecast" is found in the audio component of the cable signal for The Weather Channel, logical unit 106 can record the accompanying local forecast. Additionally, logical unit 106 can be set to record a specific show. For example, logical unit 106 could be set to record the 11 a.m. Sports Center on ESPN. In either case, the recorded programming can be displayed in place of the blocked commercial.

[0051] FIG. 3 is a flowchart of the search program contained within logical unit 106 of the present invention. Search program 300 starts (302) and logical unit 106 receives the cable signal transmitted by the cable provider (304). The cable signal is multiplexed and comprises at least a visual signal, an audio signal, and a closed caption text signal. Moreover, the multiplexed cable signal is not limited to real-time cable programming. The multiplexed signal may also contain information regarding past and future television programs. As logical unit 106 receives the signal, search program 300 continuously buffers the transmitted multiplexed cable signal (306). In buffering the signal, search program 300 obtains the closed-caption text from the cable signal and stores the words contained in the captioning text along with the television channel number and time of the television program. Alternatively, search program 300 can buffer the television signal by analyzing the audio signal and buffering the keywords from the audio signal. The text buffering described above is known in the art. Furthermore, the buffering process is not limited to one television channel or one specific time period. If a user desires to buffer different channels at different times, then the user may do so by means of search program 300. For example, if search program 300 has ten hours of buffering time available, the user can have search program 300 buffer ten hours of a channel such as Cable Network News (CNN). Alternatively, search program 300 can buffer four hours of CBS, four hours of CNN, and two hours of the weather channel. Furthermore, the buffering times do not have to be similar. The user can define the CBS buffering time from 5 am to 9 am, the CNN buffering time from 8 am to noon, and the weather channel from 1 pm to 3 pm. Additionally, search program 300 is not limited to the English language. Search program 300 is capable of buffering television in multiple languages simultaneously. Thus, at any given time search program 300 is capable of buffering an enormous variety of television programs.

[0052] The user then enters keyword terms that represent the search criteria for search program 300 (308). The search terms can be entered via a keyboard, stylus, infrared port, or on-screen programming. In entering the search terms, search program 300 will recognize conventional Boolean search terms such as "AND", "OR", and "NOT". Search program 300 is capable of accepting wildcard search terms. For example, the wildcard search term "run*" would search for run and all possible variations such as runner, running, runners, and so on. Search program 300 also compares each of the search terms to a dictionary database. If any of the search terms are not in the dictionary database, search program 300 will determine related words using lexical parsing and query the user if the terms are relevant to the desired search. Lexical parsing solves the problem of tense variation in the search terms. Search program 300 is also capable of resolving ambiguities in entered search terms by comparing the search terms to the dictionary database. Those skilled in the art are aware of how to configure a search program to resolve ambiguities. In alternative embodiments, the query step can be removed where search program 300 automatically adds the lexically parsed words to the list of search terms. Additionally, the search criteria can comprise a date restriction (i.e. only today's programs, only programs on this week, or only programs on Tuesdays). Furthermore, the search criteria can comprise restrictions based on specific channels (i.e. only programs on ESPN, DISCOVERY, CNN, or VH1, or alternatively, only programs on channels 8, 12, 25, 45, or 54).

[0053] Search program 300 then compares the search terms to the buffered text (310). Search program 300 will compare the search terms to the terms contained within the buffer. In comparing the search terms with the buffered programs, search program 300 will also create a list of synonym search terms. By accessing a thesaurus database, search program 300 can obtain relevant synonyms and use those terms to search the buffered text as well. When the search term matches a word in the buffered text, search program 300 will mark the program and continue to search through the rest of the buffered text. When the entire buffered text has been searched, search program 300 evaluates the relevancy of each flagged item. In evaluating the relevancy of each flagged item, search program 300 looks to the original search terms, the synonyms search terms, the lexically parsed search terms, and the date, time and channel specified by the user. Search program 300 then ranks the flagged items from most relevant to least relevant.

[0054] Search program 300 then displays the list of television programs which were previously marked in step 310 (312). Search program 300 will organize the results of the search according to how well they correspond to the entered search criteria. The results of the search are displayed with the time and television channel pertaining to the television program. The user then browses the television programs returned in step 312 (314) and makes a determination whether he or she would like to conduct another search (316). If the user does want to conduct another search, search program 300 returns to step 308. If the user does not want to conduct another search, the user makes a determination whether he or she would like to select a television program (318). If the user decides to select a television program, the user selects a television program, search program 300 displays the selected television program (320), and search program 300 ends (322). If the user does not want to select a television program, then search program 300 ends (322).

[0055] FIG. 4 depicts a block diagram of Content Interrogation Program 400 which has menu program 500, set up program 600, interrogation program 700 and saved alternate viewing segments and complete alternate viewing segment programs links 440.

[0056] FIG. 5 depicts menu program 500. Menu program 500 starts (502) and a determination is made as to whether the user wants to select set up (510). If the user wants to select set up, the set up program 600 is called (512) and the user performs set up in accordance with set up program 600 (514). Menu program 500 then goes to step 520. If the user does not desire to set up then menu program 500 goes to step 520. A determination is made as to whether the user wants to perform a search (520). If the user wants to perform a search, interrogation program 700 is called (522) and the user performs an interrogation in accordance with interrogation program 700. Menu program 500 then goes to step 530 and a determination is made as to whether the user wants to have a report (530). If the user selects report, a report is displayed (532). A determination is made as to whether there is another transaction to be performed (540). If there is another transaction, menu program 500 goes to step 510. If there is not another transaction, menu program 500 stops (550).

[0057] FIG. 6 depicts a flow chart of set up program 600. Set up program 600 starts (602) and the user selects "set up" (610). A determination is made as to whether the user wants to set limits (612). If the user wants to set limits, a determination is made as to whether the user wants to set T "before" (614). If the user wants to set T "before," the user enters a value for T based upon the length of the alternate viewing segment desired to fill the blocked commercial (618). If the user does not want to set T "before" a determination is made as to whether the user wants to enter T "after" (622). If the user wants to enter T "after," the user enters a value for T based upon the length of the alternate viewing segment desired to fill the blocked material (620). If the user does not want to set T "after", a determination is made as to whether the user wants to enter T "center" (624). If the user wants to enter T "center," the user enters a value of 1/2 T "before" and "after" (626). Set up program 600 then goes to step 628. A determination is made as to whether the user wants to store the entire program of the alternate viewing segment (628). If the user wants to store the entire program of the alternate viewing segment, the user enters a selection for storing the entire program of the alternate viewing segment (630). Next, a determination is made as to whether the user wants to customize the report (632). If so, the user will enter the items he or she wants in the customized report (634). A determination is made as to whether or not the user wants to perform another transaction (636). If the user wants to perform another transaction, set up program 600 goes to step 612. If not, set up program 600 ends (638).

[0058] FIG. 7 is a depiction of the flowchart for interrogation program 700. Interrogation program 700 begins and the user selects the interrogation program option on logical unit 106 (710). Interrogation program 700 sets x=1 (712). The user enters a search term designated term (x) (714). Term (x) is saved (722) and interrogation program 700 goes to step 716. A determination is made as to whether the user wants to enter another term (716). If the user wants to enter another term, interrogation program 700 sets x=x+1 (718) and the user enters term (x) (720). Term (x) is saved (722) and interrogation program 700 returns to step 716. If at step 716, the user does not want to enter another term, interrogation program 700 invokes search program 300 (724). Interrogation program 700 sends the term with the lowest number to search program 300 (726). A determination is made as to whether or not search program 300 matched the term with content (728). If a match was made, the matched segment is identified as an alternate viewing segment (730) and interrogation program 700 goes to step 732. If a match was not made, then interrogation program 700 goes to step 732 and a determination is made as to whether there is another term to be matched (732). If there is another term to be matched, interrogation program 700 goes to step 726. If there is not another term to be matched, interrogation program 700 stops (740).

[0059] FIG. 8 is a depiction of the data processing system 800 contained within logical unit 106 (See FIG. 1). Data processing system 800 comprises processor 802, boot rom 804, and LCD controller 805 coupled to system bus 806. Also connected to system bus 806 is memory controller/cache 808, which provides an interface to local memory 809. I/O bus bridge 810 is connected to system bus 806 and provides an interface to I/O bus 812. Memory controller/cache 808 and I/O bus bridge 810 may be integrated as depicted. Peripheral components are connected via I/O bus 812. Typical peripheral components include Universal Asynchronous Receiver Transmitter (UART) 818, a keypad or touch screen 820, digital-to-analog converters 828, analog-to-digital converters 830, serial interface controller 840, clocks and timers 842, cable output to the television 844, power controller 846, cable input from the cable provider 848, and infrared ports 850. Those skilled in the art will appreciate the depiction of data processing system 800 in FIG. 8 is exemplary and is not intended as an architectural limitation of the present invention. Data processing system 800 may be a separate single controller.

[0060] Many optional features can be displayed along with the alternative programming. For example, it may be beneficial to display a timer in the corner of the screen which shows the time remaining until the end of the blocked commercial. Additionally, the user may desire to have a brief description of which commercial is being blocked. Moreover, the user may wish to have a timer counting down the amount of time until the desired television content returns. Furthermore, the inventive concept contained herein can be utilized to block all commercials and display only desired programming. If the user desires to block all television commercials, then the logical unit develops a library of the unwanted commercials. The library of blocked commercials could be accessed by the user according to an Archive Interrogation Program (AIP) that would allow the library of blocked commercials to be searched by key words, phrases, date and time or other any other method that a person skilled in the art may use to search a library of stored data. Commercials designated as blocked by the user are added to the library and blocked in the future. Alternatively, the logical unit can buffer the entire multiplexed signal, delay the signal a pre-determined time (i.e. sixty seconds) and block out all television programming that is not greater than sixty seconds. This would block all thirty and sixty second television commercials. This implementation can also be orchestrated at the cable provider rather than the user's television or the logical unit. The user may have the option to block selected commercials permanently (without the recourse to unblock the commercial at a later time) while designating other commercials as non-permanently blocked commercials (with the recourse to unblock the commercial at a later time). The user may have the option to block all previously blocked commercials (and to view new commercials) or to block all commercials. In addition, the user may be provided with the option to block, unblock and access the programming of the logical unit by means of voice commands or audible signals such as clapping.

[0061] With respect to the above description then, it is to be realized that the optimum dimensional relationships for the parts of the invention, to include variations in size, materials, shape, form, function and manner of operation, assembly and use, are deemed readily apparent and obvious to one skilled in the art, and all equivalent relationships to those illustrated in the drawings and described in the specification are intended to be encompassed by the present invention.

United States Patent Application	20040019905
Kind Code	A1
Fellenstein, Craig William; et al.	January 29, 2004

Apparatus and Method for *Blocking Television Commercials* and Providing an Archive Interrogation Program

Abstract

An apparatus and method is disclosed for blocking specific television commercials from the viewer's television based upon the characteristics of the television commercial and a program to place the blocked television commercials into an archive. An archive interrogation program then acquires the users search criteria and sends the search criteria to the content search program for a list of matches. The matches are displayed to the user and the user can select a segment for viewing.

Claims

What is claimed is:

1. A method for searching archived blocked television commercials comprising: receiving a first television signal; recognizing said first television signal in a logical unit; blocking said first television signal by the logical unit; saving the first television signal to an archive; buffering the first television signal; specifying at least one search parameter; searching said archive for a data that matches said search parameters; responsive to finding the data that matches said search parameters, identifying the first television signal as a second signal; saving the second displaying the second signal.

2. The method of claim 1 wherein said search parameter is a keyword.

3. The method of claim 1 wherein said data is a closed captioning signal.

4. The method of claim 1 wherein said buffering occurs when a television unit is not activated.

5. The method of claim 1 further comprising decoding said television signal.

6. The method of claim 1 further comprising linking said search parameters by at least one logical relationship.

7. The method of claim 1 further comprising comparing said search parameters to a dictionary.

8. The method of claim 7 further comprising obtaining lexically parsed equivalents and searching said television signal for data that matches said lexically parsed equivalents.

9. The method of claim 1 further comprising comparing said search parameters to a thesaurus

10. The method of claim 9 further comprising obtaining synonym equivalents and searching said television signal for data that matches said synonym equivalents.

11. The method of claim 1 wherein said buffering simultaneously occurs over a plurality of television channels embedded within said television signal.

12. The method of claim 1 wherein said first television signal is a commercial.

13. The method of claim 1 wherein said first television signal is recognized by the time, audio and video components of said first television signal.

14. The method of claim 1 wherein said first television signal is recognized by an identifying tag.

15. The method of claim 1 wherein said parameter is a user-defined parameter.

16. An apparatus for searching archived blocked television commercials comprising: a logical unit with a memory; a program stored in said memory; said memory, so configured by said program, causes said logical unit perform operations comprising: receiving a first television signal; recognizing said first television signal in the logical unit; blocking

said first television signal by the logical unit; saving the first television signal to an archive; buffering the first television signal; specifying at least one search parameter; searching said archive for data that matches said search parameters; responsive to finding a data that matches said search parameters, identifying a first television signal as a second signal; displaying the second signal.

17. The apparatus of claim 16 wherein said signal is a television signal.

18. The apparatus of claim 16 wherein said parameter is a user-defined parameter.

19. The apparatus of claim 16 wherein said search parameter is a keyword.

20. The apparatus of claim 16 wherein said data is a closed captioning signal.

21. The apparatus of claim 16 wherein said buffering occurs when a television unit is not activated.

22. The apparatus of claim 16 wherein said operations further comprise decoding said television signal.

23. The apparatus of claim 16 wherein said operations further comprise linking said search parameters by at least one logical relationship.

24. The apparatus of claim 16 wherein said operations further comprise comparing said search parameters to a dictionary.

25. The apparatus of claim 16 wherein said operations further comprise obtaining lexically parsed equivalents and searching said television signal for data that matches said lexically parsed equivalents.

26. The apparatus of claim 16 wherein said operations further comprise comparing said search parameters to a thesaurus.

27. The apparatus of claim 16 wherein said operations further comprise obtaining synonym equivalents and searching said television signal for data that matches said synonym equivalents.

28. The apparatus of claim 16 wherein said buffering simultaneously occurs over a plurality of television channels embedded within said television signal.

29. An apparatus for searching archived blocked television commercials comprising: means for receiving a first television signal; means for recognizing said first television signal in the logical unit; means for blocking said first television signal by the logical unit; means for saving the first television signal to an archive; means for buffering the first television signal; means for specifying at least one search parameter; means for searching said archive for data that matches said search parameters; responsive to finding a data that matches said search parameters, means for identifying a first television signal as a second signal; means for displaying the second signal.

Description

RELATED APPLICATIONS

[0001] This application is related to application Ser. No. 10/105,124, "Apparatus and Method of Searching for Desired Television Content," application Ser. No. 10/116,613, "Apparatus and Method for *Blocking Television Commercials* and Displaying Alternative Programming," and to Application docket number AUS920020258US1, "Apparatus and Method for *Blocking Television Commercials* and Displaying Micro-Programming Content."

FIELD OF THE INVENTION

[0002] The present invention relates to an apparatus and method for blocking undesired television commercials and providing a program for creating an archive of the blocked television commercials and for interrogating the content of the blocked television commercials for later access.

BACKGROUND OF THE INVENTION

[0003] Debates today rage about both the delivery and funding of informational content in all of its forms. On the Internet, many content providers are moving away from their advertisement-based business models and moving towards subscription-based business models. Despite rapid advances in technology, the delivery mechanisms and methods of generating revenue for content delivered through television broadcasts have been relatively stagnant, when compared to the delivery mechanisms and methods of generating revenue for the Internet and web delivery systems. In television broadcasts, advertisers still attempt to reach users using the same techniques that they have used for decades which are the thirty and sixty second commercials interspaced throughout specific television programs. In addition to technology, the viewer is becoming increasingly sophisticated and is demanding that every second of their time, whether engaged in work or leisure pursuits, be well spent. For the vast majority of television viewers, time engaged in viewing undesired advertisements is not considered time well spent. Therefore, a need exists for an apparatus and method of preventing a television viewer from viewing unwanted commercials.

[0004] Additionally, television viewers generally do not prefer to have periods of interrupted programming or "dead air" when they are viewing a program. It would be preferable if the blocked commercial could be replaced with user-defined alternative programming.

[0005] Application Ser. No. 10/116,613, "Apparatus and Method for *Blocking Television Commercials* and Displaying Alternative Programming" disclosed a logical unit and a commercial blocking program in the logical unit to allow alternative viewing options so that the user may define the alternative programming to replace the unwanted communication. The commercial blocking program breaks all incoming television signals into time, video and audio components and is able to recognize specific commercials based on those components. Upon viewing an unwanted commercial, the user indicates that he wants to block the commercial through one of a variety of input methods. The commercial blocking program then prevents the commercial from being displayed on the user's television and causes alternative programming to be displayed instead. The user may configure the alternative programming via the alternative programming logic. The user may configure the alternative programming as a universal television channel, based on the specific commercial, based on the television station, based on the time of day, or based on an elaborate viewing hierarchy. At the end of the blocked commercial, the commercial blocking program displays the television program that was originally displayed on the user's television. Alternatively, the commercial blocking program can buffer the various television programs received from the cable provider and record segments of the cable signal based on certain keywords. The commercial blocking program searches for user defined keywords, records television programs complying with the search terms, and displays the recorded television programming stored in the memory.

[0006] Application Ser. No. 10/105,124, "Apparatus and Method of Searching for Desired Television Content," disclosed an apparatus and method for allowing a user to search for specific content across many television channels in order to locate desirable television shows related to the searched content. Multiplexed cable signals flow thorough a logical unit which buffers text associated with the voice stream of each station via the pre-encoded closed-captioning signal or through the real-time voice translation within the logical unit. The user then enters search terms through one of a variety of different input devices. Upon entry of the search terms, the logical unit will compare the entered term with those available keywords stored in each buffer. Lexical parsing associates terms which may differ from plural to singular forms or in tense. Additionally, synonym comparisons may be made. The logical unit will return a list of matches for the search criteria and allows the user the option of going directly to the television program. The logical unit also evaluates each returned item for its relevancy to the keywords. When not in use, the logical unit maintains a quiescent but monitoring state permitting continuous creation of lexical buffers. This permits the user who turns the television on to immediately have such search terms available. Alternatively, the logic is implemented at the cable provider and enabled through interactive links to the home. In that case, the home logical unit is unnecessary.

[0007] What is needed is an archive of blocked television commercials and an application of the television content searching engine to the archive of blocked television commercials so that a user may access an archive of blocked commercials based upon a user search criteria.

SUMMARY OF THE INVENTION

[0008] The present invention, which meets the needs stated above, is an apparatus and method for blocking specific television commercials from the viewer's television based upon the characteristics of the television commercial and a program to place the blocked television commercials into an archive. An archive interrogation program then acquires the users search criteria and sends the search criteria to the content search program for a list of matches. The matches are displayed to the user and the user can select a segment for viewing.

BRIEF DESCRIPTION OF THE DRAWINGS

[0009] FIG. 1 is an illustration of the invention interacting with a cable provider and a television.

[0010] FIG. 2A is a flowchart of the commercial blocking program.

[0011] FIG. 2B is a flowchart of the commercial blocking program.

[0012] FIG. 2C is a flowchart of the commercial blocking program.

[0013] FIG. 3 is a flowchart of the search program.

[0014] FIG. 4 is a flowchart of the archive program.

[0015] FIG. 5 is a flowchart of the archive interrogation program.

[0016] FIG. 6 is a depiction of the data processing system contained within the logical unit.

DETAILED DESCRIPTION OF THE PREFERRED EMBODIMENT

[0017] The terms below are defined for all uses herein as follows:

[0018] "Alternate viewing" means content displayed in place of a blocked commercial and may include one or more of the following: (1) a brief message displayed to inform the viewer that alternative programming will be presented during the commercial interval; (2) an on-screen counter, showing how many seconds are left before the planned return to primary viewing; and (3) directions to the tuner to go to a particular station. The directions to the tuner may be universal, by commercial, by originating station, by time of day, by definition of an elaborate viewing hierarchy, or to a micro-programming station or to buffered microprogramming.

[0019] "Alternate viewing provider" means an entity that offers micro-programming to a user for display in conjunction with a logical unit.

[0020] "Archive" means a copy of one or blocked commercials that are saved for future reference or research.

[0021] "Buffered" means an alternate viewing package stored in the memory of a logical unit or at the cable service provider so that synchronization problems between the "switchover" point and the alternate programming delivery do not occur. In other words, when a request for alternative programming is made, the logical unit can draw from a buffered alternate viewing package so that the user does not risk joining the alternate viewing package in progress.

[0022] "Buffering" means a process of examining the closed captioning text or audio signal associated with television signals and configuring the examined signal such that it may be searched for specific keywords.

[0023] "By commercial" means using content from a particular station to replace the specifically identified commercial.

[0024] "By originating station" means using the original station to determine the alternative content which will replace all blocked commercials.

[0025] "By time of day" means using the time of day to determine which station to use as alternative content for all blocked commercials.

[0026] "Cable provider" means a company which provides television service to multiple users and includes satellite television providers.

[0027] "Component signature" is a group of variables, based on a time component, an X video component, a Y video component, and an audio component, that is used to identify a commercial from all other commercials when a "unique digital identifying tag is not available.

[0028] "Cumulative digital signature" means the aggregation of one or more selected characteristics of a data sequence to provide a unique number for identification of the complete data sequence.

[0029] "Elaborate viewing hierarchy" means a combination of a plurality of universal, by commercial, by originating station, or by time or day alternative viewing formats.

[0030] "Lexical parsing" as used herein means a process of finding matches to a desired search term by comparing the desired search term letter-by-letter with the terms in an available database.

[0031] "Micro-programming," means one or more "alternate viewing packages" that each contain a complete information exchange or an entertainment package in a segment of time that is adapted to fit into the time available from one or more commercials blocked by a logical unit. For example, an alternate viewing package could contain news headlines, weather updates, sports updates, or very short live action or animated shorts that are designed to entertain the user in a crisp, concise segment. An alternate viewing package would normally be thirty or sixty seconds in length but could be designed for any length of time that a logical unit could make available.

[0032] "Multiplex" means the process of funneling several different streams of data over a common communications line.

[0033] "Staggered time alternate viewing package" means an alternate viewing package broadcast on start times that are staggered for a number of seconds to coincide with the time slots of blocked commercials. For example, an alternate viewing package may start at the top and bottom of the minute on a given station, and at 15 and 45 seconds on another station. Accordingly, the station with the alternate viewing package start time closest to the start time of the blocked commercial would be chosen.

[0034] "Time synchronized" means an alternate viewing package, delivered on demand in which the user joins the broadcast at the exact start point of the micro-program.

[0035] "Unique digital identifying tag" means a number sequence before the header and after the trailer of each commercial. The number sequence is assigned according to an industry standard that allows each commercial to be identified from every other commercial.

[0036] "Universal" means using content from a particular station to replace all blocked commercials.

[0037] FIG. 1 is an illustration of the invention 100 interacting with a cable provider and a television set. The depiction of the cable provider is by way of illustration only and is not intended to limit the scope of the invention. Persons skilled in the art will recognize that the invention may be used with either a cable or wireless data transmission system. The cable provider (not shown) provides a television signal through a coaxial cable 102 that runs through the user's wall 104 and into logical unit 106. Logical unit 106 analyzes the cable signal as described below and displays the information on television 110 via television connection 108. Logical unit 106 can optionally be combined with television 110. Alternatively, logical unit 106 may be placed at the same location as the cable provider such that it is unnecessary to have logical unit 106 at the user's location.

[0038] FIG. 2A is a flowchart of commercial blocking program 200 which operates inside logical unit 106. Commercial blocking program 200 starts (202) whenever multiplexed cable signals are broadcast (204). In the preferred embodiment, each commercial has a unique digital identifying tag, similar to a serial number, which identifies a particular commercial. Logical unit 106 recognizes a particular commercial based on the unique identifying tag.

[0039] In an alternate embodiment, logical unit 106 identifies commercials by a "component signature." Multiplexed cable signals are defined by four components: a time component, an X video component, a Y video component, and an audio component. Every television program and/or commercial can be readily identified by these components. There is generally allowed some amount of time skew in the synchronization of the four components to identify the absolute beginning of a program or commercial. By taking the time skew into consideration, commercial blocking program 200 can identify a particular commercial. For example, a given pattern of video/audio signals occurring at a time "delta" (perhaps but not necessarily in the order of 500 microseconds) around the nominal beginning of an advertisement, may point back to a specified commercial.

[0040] Alternatively, logical unit 106 establishes an "overall digital signature" for a particular commercial. In this event, the signal need not be dissembled into its video/audio components as in the "component signature," but rather, analysis of cumulative digital characteristics may be used to identify the commercial to be blocked. One or more characteristics of a data sequence is selected and aggregated to provide a unique number for identification purposes of the complete data sequence. The advantage of using cumulative digital characteristics is that all commercials could be blocked using this technique. In the case of commercials to be identified by an "overall digital signature," the logical unit develops a library at the set-top of the "overall digital signature" of the blocked advertisements. For example, it may be assumed that some time interval, "T.sub.sample" is great enough to ascertain with accuracies approaching one hundred percent the identity of a given advertisement. "T.sub.sample" may be a sub-second or it may be multi-second, depending on the processing power behind the logical unit and the uniqueness of the commercial. Once a commercial signal is detected to be identical to a blocked advertisement, then the logical unit takes the actions it has been programmed to implement.

[0041] As a commercial airs, the user has the option of blocking the commercial (206) by means of commercial blocking program 200 located in the local memory 209 of logical unit 106 (See FIGS. 1 and 6). If the user chooses not to block the commercial, then commercial blocking program 200 allows the commercial to air (207) and returns to step 206. If at step 206 the user chooses to block the commercial, then the logical unit will block the commercial (208). In blocking the commercial, the logical unit prevents the specific commercial from displaying on the user's television and displays alternative content instead (210). After commercial blocking program 200 has displayed the alternative programming, the original programming of the original television channel is displayed (212) and commercial blocking program 200 ends (214).

[0042] There are many different types of alternative programming that commercial blocking program 200 can display on the user's television instead of the blocked commercial. In one embodiment, commercial blocking program 200 can display a blank screen for the duration of the blocked commercial. However, in the preferred embodiment, commercial blocking program 200 displays the programming according to alternative programming logic 250 in FIGS. 2B and 2C. Alternative programming logic 250 starts (252) and queries the user if he or she would like to define the alternative programming as a universal television channel that will replace all blocked television commercials (254). A universal television channel is one which will display the contents of a specific television channel on the user's television whenever the blocked commercial airs. For example, whenever a blocked commercial airs, commercial blocking program 200 will cause the The Weather Channel to be displayed. A universal television channel may include Web TV or any programming variation that may be made available to the user of the television to which the logical unit is connected. If the user determines that they would like to select a universal alternative channel, then the user specifies which channel is the universal television channel (256) and alternative programming logic 250 ends (294). If at step 254 the user determines that he or she would not like to select a universal television channel, then alternative programming logic 250 queries the user if he or she would like to define the alternative programming based on the blocked commercial (258). Alternative programming based on the blocked commercial will display a particular television channel whenever a specific blocked commercial airs. For example, whenever commercial X airs, commercial blocking program 200 will cause The Weather Channel to be displayed. If the user determines that he or she would like to define the alternative programming based on the blocked commercial, then the user selects a specific television channel that will display whenever the specific television commercial airs (260) and alternative programming logic 250 ends (298). If the user determines at step 258 that he or she do not want to define the alternative programming based on the commercial, alternative programming logic 250 queries the user whether he or she would like to define alternative programming based on the television channel (262). Alternative programming based on the television channel will display television content based on a preferred television channel and a contingent television channel when the blocked commercial airs. For example, whenever a blocked commercial airs, The Weather Channel will be displayed, and in the event The Weather Channel is already being displayed, then CNN will be displayed. If the user determines that he or she would like to define the alternative programming based on the television channel, then the user defines the preferred and contingent television channels (264) and alternative programming logic 250 ends (298). If at step 262 the user determines that he or she does not want to define alternative programming based on the television channel, then alternative programming logic 250 queries the user whether he or she would like to define alternative programming based on the time of day (266). Alternative programming based on the time of day displays a specific television channel depending on the time of the blocked commercial. For example, if the blocked commercial airs before noon, The Weather Channel will be displayed, and if the blocked commercial airs after noon, CNN will be displayed. If the user would like to define the alternative programming based on the time of day, then the user defines the alternative television channels and the time associated with each alternate channel (268) and alternative programming logic 250 ends (298). If at step 266 the user determines that he or she does not want to define the alternative programming based on the time of day, alternative programming logic 250 queries the user whether he or she would like to define alternative programming based on an elaborate viewing hierarchy (270).

[0043] An elaborate viewing hierarchy is a combination of the alternative programming determinations in steps 254, 258, 262, and 266. There are numerous possible combinations of the programming determinations that will create elaborate viewing hierarchies. For example, one possible elaborate viewing hierarchy would be "whenever a blocked commercial airs, display The Weather Channel; however, if there is also a blocked commercial on The Weather Channel, then go to CNN before noon and CNBC after noon." The elaborate viewing hierarchy may offer the user the option to "mix and match" various combinations of blocked and unblocked signals. For example, the user may select a split screen option where the blocked commercial appears in a portion of the screen while alternate programming appears in the remaining portion of the screen. The user may select an option that will display alternative programming while also displaying the close captioned text of the blocked commercial. Further in the alternative, the user may elect to have more than one alternate programming option displayed. For example, the user may elect to have a split screen display CNN on one portion of the screen and the Weather Channel on the other portion of the screen. If the user would like to define an elaborate viewing hierarchy, then the user enters the appropriate information (i.e. time, channel, and commercial) to define the hierarchy (272) and alternative programming logic 250 ends (298). If at step 270 the user determines that he or she would not like to define an alternative viewing hierarchy, alternative programming logic 250 goes to step 282 (See FIG. 2C).

[0044] Next a determination is made as to whether the user wants to select micro-programming (282). If the user does not want to select micro-programming, alternate programming logic 250 ends (298). If at step 282 the user determines that he or she wants to select microprogramming, a determination is made as to whether staggered time alternate viewing packages are desired (284). If staggered time alternate viewing packages are desired, then the selection is entered (286) and alternate programming logic 250 goes to step 296. If staggered time alternate viewing packages are not selected, then a determination is made as to whether the user wants to select time synchronized alternate viewing packages (288). If the user desires to selected time synchronized alternate viewing packages, then the selection is entered (290) and alternate programming logic 250 goes to step 296. If the user does not select time synchronized alternate viewing packages, then a determination is made as to whether a buffered alternate viewing package is desired (292). If a buffered alternate viewing package is desired, then the selection is entered (294). If a buffered alternate viewing package is not desired, then a determination is made as to whether another selection is made (296). If another selection is to be made, alternate programming logic 250 goes to step 284. If another selection is not to be made, alternate programming logic 250 ends (298). A default option may also be available if the alternate viewing service provider plays continuously broadcast alternate viewing packages. In that case the default option would be that the television would move to the alternate viewing broadcast at the time of the blocked commercial and pick up the alternate viewing package playing at that time.

[0045] In an alternative embodiment of alternative programming logic 250, a negative determination at step 296 would send the user back to step 254 so that the options may be viewed again. Additionally, there are other types of alternative programming which may be displayed at step 210. The user can then enter search criteria and search program 200 will record the television signal based on the specific time, channel, and/or keywords. For example, whenever "and now your local forecast" is found in the audio component of the cable signal for The Weather Channel, logical unit 106 can record the accompanying local forecast. Additionally, logical unit 106 can be set to record a specific show. For example, logical unit 106 could be set to record the 11 a.m. Sports Center on ESPN. In either case, the recorded programming can be displayed in place of the blocked commercial.

[0046] FIG. 3 is a flowchart of the search program contained within logical unit 106 of the present invention. Search program 300 starts (302) and logical unit 106 receives the cable signal transmitted by the cable provider (304). The cable signal is multiplexed and comprises at least a visual signal, an audio signal, and a closed caption text signal. Moreover, the multiplexed cable signal is not limited to real-time cable programming. The multiplexed signal may also contain information regarding past and future television programs. As logical unit 106 receives the signal, search program 300 continuously buffers the transmitted multiplexed cable signal (306). In buffering the signal, search program 300 obtains the closed-caption text from the cable signal and store the words contained in the captioning text along with the television channel number and time of the television program. Alternatively, search program 300 can buffer the television signal by analyzing the audio signal and buffering the keywords from the audio signal. The text buffering described above is known in the art. Furthermore, the buffering process is not limited to one television channel or one specific time period. If a user desires to buffer different channels at different times, then the user may do so by means of search program 300. For example, if search program 300 has ten hours of buffering time available, the user can have search program 300 buffer ten hours of a channel such as Cable Network News (CNN). Alternatively, search program 300 can buffer four hours of CBS, four hours of CNN, and two hours of The Weather Channel. Furthermore, the buffering times do not have to be similar. The user can define the CBS buffering time from 5 am to 9 am, the CNN buffering time from 8 am to noon, and the weather channel from 1 pm to 3 pm. Additionally, search program 300 is not limited to the English language. Search program 300 is capable of buffering television in multiple languages simultaneously. Thus, at any given time search program 300 is capable of buffering an enormous variety of television programs.

[0047] The user then enters keyword terms that represent the search criteria for search program 300 (308). The search terms can be entered via a keyboard, stylus, infrared port, or on-screen programming. In entering the search terms, search program 300 will recognize conventional Boolean search terms such as "AND", "OR", and "NOT". Search program 300 is capable of accepting wildcard search terms. For example, the wildcard search term "run*" would search for run and all possible variations such as runner, running, runners, and so on. Search program 300 also compares each of the search terms to a dictionary database. If any of the search terms are not in the dictionary database, search program 300 will determine related words using lexical parsing and query the user if the terms are relevant to the desired search. Lexical parsing solves the problem of tense variation in the search terms. Search program 300 is also capable of resolving ambiguities in entered search terms by comparing the search terms to the dictionary database. Those skilled in the art are aware of how to configure a search program to resolve ambiguities. In alternative embodiments, the query step can be removed where search program 300 automatically adds the lexically parsed words to the list of search terms. Additionally, the search criteria can comprise a date restriction (i.e. only today's programs, only programs on this week, or only programs on Tuesdays). Furthermore, the search criteria can comprise restrictions based on specific channels (i.e. only programs on ESPN, Discovery, CNN, or VH1, or alternatively, only programs on channels 8, 12, 25, 45, or 54).

[0048] Search program 300 then compares the search terms to the buffered text (310). Search program 300 will compare the search terms to the terms contained within the buffer. In comparing the search terms with the buffered programs, search program 300 will also create a list of synonym search terms. By accessing a thesaurus database, search program 300 can obtain relevant synonyms and use those terms to search the buffered text as well. When the search term matches a word in the buffered text, search program 300 will mark the program and continue to search through the rest of the buffered text. When the entire buffered text has been searched, search program 300 evaluates the relevancy of each flagged item. In evaluating the relevancy of each flagged item, search program 300 looks to the original search terms, the synonyms search terms, the lexically parsed search terms, and the date, time and channel specified by the user. Search program 300 then ranks the flagged items from most relevant to least relevant.

[0049] Search program 300 then displays the list of television programs which were previously marked in step 310 (312). Search program 300 will organize the results of the search according to how well they correspond to the entered search criteria. The results of the search are displayed with the time and television channel pertaining to the television program. The user then browses the television programs returned in step 312 (314) and makes a determination whether they would like to conduct another search (316). If the user does want to conduct another search, search program 300 returns to step 308. If the user does not want to conduct another search, the user makes a determination whether they would like to select a television program (318). If the user decides to select a television program, the user selects a television program, search program 300 displays the selected television program (320), and search program 300 ends (322). If the user does not want to select a television program, then search program 300 ends (322).

[0050] FIG. 4 is a depiction of the flowchart for archive program 400. Archive program 400 begins (402) and the user selects an archive option from the logical unit (410). A television signal is received by the logical unit (420) and the logical unit identifies a segment of the signal to block (430). The logical unit blocks the identified segment (440) and sends the blocked segment to the archive (450). A determination is made as to whether or not there is another signal to be analyzed (460). If there is another signal to be analyzed archive program 400 goes to step 410. If there is not another signal to be analyzed, archive program 400 ends (470).

[0051] FIG. 5 is a depiction of the flowchart for the archive interrogation program (AIP) 500. AIP 502 begins and the user selects the AIP option from the logical unit (510). The user enters the search terms desired to locate commercials in a particular area of interest (512). The logical unit compares the search terms to text in the archived segments (514). The logical unit returns a list of matches (516). The user browses the list of matches (516). A determination is made as to whether the user wants to select a segment (522). If the user wants to select a segment, the user selects a segment from the list of matches (524). AIP 500 sends the selected segment to an open channel for viewing (526). A determination is made as to whether the user wants to conduct another search (528). If the user wants to conduct another search, the AIP 500 goes to step 512. If the user does not want to conduct another search, AIP 500 ends (530).

[0052] FIG. 6 is a depiction of the data processing system 600 contained within logical unit 106 (See FIG. 1). Data processing system 600 comprises processor 602, boot rom 604, and LCD controller 605 coupled to system bus 606. Also connected to system bus 606 is memory controller/cache 608, which provides an interface to local memory 609. I/O bus bridge 610 is connected to system bus 606 and provides an interface to I/O bus 612. Memory controller/cache 608 and I/O bus bridge 610 may be integrated as depicted. Peripheral components are connected via I/O bus 612. Typical peripheral components include Universal Asynchronous Receiver Transmitter (UART) 618, a keypad or touch screen 620, digital-to-analog converters 628, analog-to-digital converters 630, serial interface controller 640, clocks and timers 642, cable output to the television 644, power controller 646, cable input from the cable provider 648, and infrared ports 650. Those skilled in the art will appreciate the depiction of data processing system 600 in FIG. 3 is exemplary and is not intended as an architectural limitation of the present invention. Data processing system 600 may be a separate single controller.

[0053] Many optional features can be displayed along with the alternative programming. For example, it may be beneficial to display a timer in the corner of the screen which shows the time remaining until the end of the blocked commercial. Additionally, the user may desire to have a brief description of which commercial is being blocked. Moreover, the user may wish to have a timer counting down the amount of time until the desired television content returns. Furthermore, the inventive concept contained herein can be utilized to block all commercials and display only desired programming. Alternatively, the logical unit can buffer the entire multiplexed signal, delay the signal a pre-determined time (i.e. sixty seconds) and block out all television programming that is not greater than sixty seconds. This would block all thirty and sixty second television commercials. This implementation can also be orchestrated at the cable provider rather than the user's television or the logical unit. The user may have the option to block selected commercials permanently (without the recourse to unblock the commercial at a later time) while designating other commercials as non-permanently blocked commercials (with the recourse to unblock the commercial at a later time). The user may have the option to block all previously blocked commercials (and to view new commercials) or to block all commercials. In addition, the user may be provided with the option to block, unblock and access the programming of the logical unit by means of voice commands or audible signals such as clapping.

[0054] With respect to the above description then, it is to be realized that the optimum dimensional relationships for the parts of the invention, to include variations in size, materials, shape, form, function and manner of operation, assembly and use, are deemed readily apparent and obvious to one skilled in the art, and all equivalent relationships to those illustrated in the drawings and described in the specification are intended to be encompassed by the present invention.

Trade Secrets

This appendix describes the trade secrets in terms of legal perspectives.[1]

Uniform Trade Secrets Act

Drafted by the National Conference of Commissioners on Uniform State Laws, as amended 1985.

§1. Definitions

As used in this Act, unless the context requires otherwise:

(1) *"Improper means"* includes theft, bribery, misrepresentation, breach or inducement of a breach of duty to maintain secrecy, or espionage through electronic or other means.

(2) *"Misappropriation "* means: (i) acquisition of a trade secret of another by a person who knows or has reason to know that the trade secret was acquired by improper means; or (ii) disclosure or use of a trade secret of another without express or implied consent by a person who (A) used improper means to acquire knowledge of the trade secret; or (B) at the time of disclosure or use knew or had reason to know that his knowledge of the trade secret was (I) derived from or through a person who has utilized improper means to acquire it; (II) acquired under circumstances giving rise to a duty to maintain its secrecy or limit its use; or (III) derived from or through a person who owed a duty to the person seeking relief to maintain its secrecy or limit its use; or (C) before a material change of his position, knew or had reason to know that it was a trade secret ad that knowledge of it had been acquired by accident or mistake.

[1] For more information, please reference http://nsi.org/Library/Espionage/usta.htm.

(3) "*Person*" means a natural person, corporation, business trust, estate, trust, partnership, association, joint venture, government, governmental subdivision or agency, or any other legal or commercial entity.

(4) "*Trade secret*" means information, including a formula, pattern, compilation, program device, method, technique, or process, that: (i) derives independent economic value, actual or potential, from no being generally known to, and not being readily ascertainable by proper means by, other persons who can obtain economic value from its disclosure or use, and (ii) is the subject of efforts that are reasonable under the circumstances to maintain its secrecy.

§2. Injunctive Relief

(a) Actual or threatened misappropriation may be enjoined. Upon application to the court an injunction shall be terminated when the trade secret has ceased to exist, but the injunction may be continued for an additional reasonable period of time in order to eliminate commercial advantage that otherwise would be derived from the misappropriation.

(b) In exceptional circumstances, an injunction may condition future use upon payment of a reasonable royalty for no longer than the period of time for which use could have been prohibited. Exceptional circumstances include, but are not limited to, a material and prejudicial change of position prior to acquiring knowledge or reason to know of misappropriation that renders a prohibitive injunction inequitable.

(c) In appropriate circumstances, affirmative acts to protect a trade secret may be compelled by court order.

§3. Damages

(a) Except to the extent that a material and prejudicial change of position prior to acquiring knowledge or reason to know of misappropriation renders a monetary recovery inequitable, a complainant is entitled to recover damages for misappropriation. Damages can include both the actual loss caused by misappropriation and the unjust enrichment caused by misappropriation that is not taken into account in computing actual loss. In lieu of damages measured by any other methods, the damages caused by misappropriation may be measured by imposition of liability for a reasonable royalty for a misappropriator's unauthorized disclosure or use of a trade secret.

(b) If willful and malicious misappropriation exists, the court may award exemplary damages in the amount not exceeding twice any award made under subsection (a).

§4. Attorney's Fees

If (i) a claim of misappropriation is made in bad faith, (ii) a motion to terminate an injunction is made or resisted in bad faith, or (iii) willful and malicious misappropriation exists, the court may award reasonable attorney's fees to the prevailing party.

§5. Preservation of Secrecy

In action under this Act, a court shall preserve the secrecy of an alleged trade secret by reasonable means, which may include granting protective orders in connection with discovery proceedings, holding in-camera hearings, sealing the records of the action, and ordering any person involved in the litigation not to disclose an alleged trade secret without prior court approval.

§6. Statute of Limitations

An action for misappropriation must be brought within 3 years after the misappropriation is discovered or by the exercise of reasonable diligence should have been discovered. For the purposes of this section, a continuing misappropriation constitutes a single claim.

§7. Effect on Other Law

(a) Except as provided in subsection (b), this [Act] displaces conflicting tort, restitutionary, and other law of this State providing civil remedies for misappropriation of a trade secret.
(b) This [Act] does not affect: (1) contractual remedies, whether or not based upon misappropriation of a trade secret; or (2) other civil remedies that are not based upon misappropriation of a trade secret; or (3) criminal remedies, whether or not based upon misappropriation of a trade secret.

§8. Uniformity of Application and Construction

This act shall be applied and construed to effectuate its general purpose to make uniform the law with respect to the subject of this Act among states enacting it.

§9. Short Title

This Act may be cited as the Uniform Trade Secrets Act.

§10. Severability

If any provision of this Act or its application to any person or circumstances is held invalid, the invalidity does not affect other provisions or applications of the Act which can be given effect without the invalid provision or application, and to this end the provisions of this Act are severable.

§11. Time of Taking Effect

This [Act] takes effect on {date} and does not apply to misappropriation occurring prior to the effective date. With respect to a continuing misappropriation that began prior to the effective date, the [Act] also does not apply to the continuing misappropriation that occurs after the effective date.

Inventor Resources

This appendix describes many interesting resources that both inventors and evaluators can utilize.

Legal Advice Is Always Recommended

Books, references, and periodicals are great ways to learn more about the inventing process, but always consult a qualified patent attorney or patent agent for the latest information on patents and patent law.

For more information on this, please refer to http://www.uspto.gov.

Resources for Inventors

How to Avoid Scams Targeting Inventors

1. The National Inventor Fraud Center (http://www.inventorfraud.com/)
2. The U.S. Patent & Trademark Office (USPTO) (http://www.uspto.gov)
3. The USPTO's Independent Inventors Web site
   (http://www.uspto.gov/web/offices/com/iip/index.htm)
4. http://www.ftc.gov/bcp/conline/pubs/services/invent.htm
5. http://www.inventnet.com/scam.html
6. http://www.patent.gov.uk/patent/howtoapply/ipromoters.htm

Invention Magazines

1. *Patent Café's Online Magazine* (http://www.cafezine.com)
2. *Inventors' Digest* (http://www.inventorsdigest.com)
3. *Invention & Technology* (http://www.americanheritage.com/it/index.shtml)

Inventor Organizations

1. The Inventors Network of the Capital Area, Bethesda, MD, USA
   (http://www.dcinventors.org)
2. United Inventors Association, Rochester, NY, USA (http://www.uiausa.com/)
3. International Federation of Inventors' Associations, Geneva, Switzerland
   (http://www.invention-ifia.ch/)
4. Invent Now, National Inventors Hall of Fame, Akron, OH, USA
   (http://www.invent.org/index.asp)
5. The American Society of Inventors, Philadelphia, PA, USA (http://www.asoi.org)

Inventor Group Listings

1. Inventors' Digest List of Inventor Groups
   (http://www.inventorsdigest.com/ME2/dirsect.asp?sid=
   C09EA28E7C3B42F6AC87F0ABECEB3F93&nm=Inventor+Organizations)
2. http://www.patentcafe.com/inventor_orgs/assoc.html
3. http://www.patentcafe.com/inventor_orgs/clubs.html

Invention Expos and Trade Shows

1. Yankee Invention Expo (http://www.yankeeinventionexpo.org/)
2. Trade Show Week Online (http://www.tradeshowweek.com)

Patent Application Software

1. PatentEase (http://www.inventorprise.com/)
2. Patent Wizard (http://www.patentwizard.com/)
3. PatentPro (http://www.4patpro.com/)

Entrepreneur Resources

1. CEO Express (http://www.ceoexpress.com/default.asp)

2. MIT Enterprise Forum of Washington DC (http://www.mitef.org/)

3. Entrepreneur Magazine (http://www.entrepreneur.com/)

Engineering and Design Resources

1. Society of Manufacturing Engineers (http://www.sme.org)

2. Industrial Designers Society of America (http://www.idsa.org/)

3. Rapid Prototyping Information (http://www.cc.utah.edu/~asn8200/rapid.html)

4. Engineering Resources (http://www.er-online.co.uk/) (includes a good link page to many patent offices)

5. Global Spec Technical Resources (http://www.globalspec.com)

Research and Development, Technology Transfer, Product Development

1. Community of Science for the Research & Development Community (http://www.cos.com/)

2. National Technology Transfer Center (http://www.nttc.edu/)

3. Intellectual property licensing and technology transfer (http://www.2xfr.com/group.asp)

4. Licensing Executives Society (http://www.usa-canada.les.org/)

Copyright Resources

1. Library of Congress Copyright Office (http://www.loc.gov/copyright/)

2. Library of Congress (http://www.loc.gov/)

3. Literature search service (http://www.dialog.com/)

Trade Information

1. The U.S. National Trade Database (http://www.stat-usa.gov/)

2. The World Trade Center Institute, Maryland, USA (http://www.wtci.org)

Technology and Science Magazines

1. *MIT's Technology Review* (http://www.technologyreview.com/)

2. *Wired* (http://www.wired.com/wired/current.html)

3. *The Journal Nature* (http://www.nature.com/)

4. *Science Magazine* (http://www.sciencemag.org/)

5. *Popular Science* (http://www.popsci.com/popsci/)

6. *Popular Mechanics* (http://popularmechanics.com/)

7. *Discover* (http://www.discover.com/)

8. *Scientific American* (http://www.sciam.com/)

9. *Reason* (http://reason.com/)

10. *The Skeptical Inquirer* (http://www.csicop.org/si/)

Search Engines

1. http://www.google.com

2. http://searchenginewatch.com/

3. http://www.dogpile.com/info.dogpl/

4. http://www.metacrawler.com/info.metac/dog/index.htm

5. http://www.ask.com/

6. http://www.altavista.com/

7. http://www.hotbot.com/

8. http://www.about.com/

9. http://www.yahoo.com

Venture Captial

Vision Venture Capital, a "seed stage venture capital firm," in conjunction with the Newcastle Stock Exchange. Global Wealth Education and Ingage Communications have $600,000 for a great business idea (http://www.vvcinternational.com).

MISCELLANEOUS

Famous Inventors and Their Companies

1. Dean Kamen (http://www.dekaresearch.com/)

2. Ray Kurzweil (http://www.kurzweilai.net/)

Invention and Technology Museums

1. Invent Now, National Inventors Hall of Fame (http://www.invent.org/index.asp)
2. Rothschild Petersen Patent Model Museum (http://www.patentmodel.org/index.html)
3. The Baltimore Museum of Industry (http://www.thebmi.org/)

MIT Lemelson Highlights

1. Smithsonian Innovative Lives
   (http://www.si.edu/lemelson/centerpieces/ilives/index.html)
2. Jerome and Dorothy Lemelson Center (http://www.si.edu/lemelson/)
3. Invention Dimension (http://web.mit.edu/invent/)

Science Resources

The Smithsonian Institution (http://www.si.edu/)

Resources for Intellectual Property Professionals

Patent Law Resources

1. The United States Patent and Trademark Office (http://www.uspto.gov)
2. Nolo law publishers (http://www.nolo.com)
3. Franklin Pierce Law Center's IP Mall (http://www.ipmall.fplc.edu/)
4. Patent law resources (http://www.patentlawnet.com/)
5. Intellectual property news and resources (http://www.intelproplaw.com/)
6. Boston College IP law page (http://www.bc.edu/bc_org/avp/law/st_org/iptf/)

Intellectual Property Publications

1. *Intellectual Property Today* (http://www.iptoday.com/)
2. *IP Law & Business* (http://www.ipww.com/)
3. *IP Worldwide* (http://www.ipww.com/ipabout.html)

Intellectual Property Organizations

1. The Intellectual Property Owners Association (http://www.ipo.org)

2. American Intellectual Property Law Association (http://www.aipla.org)

3. National Intellectual Property Researchers Association (http://www.nipra.org)

4. National Association of Patent Practitioners (http://www.napp.org/)

5. The Chartered Institute of Patent Agents (http://www.cipa.org.uk/home.html)

6. Patent Information User's Group, Inc. (http://www.piug.org/)

7. Patent Office Professional Association (http://www.popa.org/)

8. Institute of Patent and Trade Mark Attorneys of Australia (http://www.ipta.com.au/)

9. Product Development and Management Association (www.pdma.org)

10. Patent Bar exam resources (http://www.patentbarreview.com/)

Patent Offices

1. United States Patent and Trademark Office (http://www.uspto.gov)

2. European Patent Office (http://www.european-patent-office.org/)

3. The UK Patent Office (http://www.patent.gov.uk/)

4. Japan Patent Office (http://www.jpo.go.jp/)

5. Australia Intellectual Property Office (http://www.ipaustralia.gov.au/)

6. PCT home page (http://www.wipo.org/pct/en/)

7. Canadian Patents Database (http://patents1.ic.gc.ca/intro-e.html)

8. The British Library's Patent and Trademark page)
   (http://www.bl.uk/services/information/patents.html)

9. Intellectual Property Digital Library (http://pctgazette.wipo.int/)

10. Domain Name Dispute Resolution (http://arbiter.wipo.int/domains/)

Interesting Patent Resources

1. Information about bad patents that have been issued (http://www.bustpatents.com)

2. DNA Patent Database (http://dnapatents.georgetown.edu/)

3. Good links to patent databases, both free and commercial
   (http://www.indiana.edu/~cheminfo/ca_cps.html#free)

4. Information about plant variety protection (http://www.plantpatent.com/)

5. Software Patent Institute and its Database of Software Technologies
   (http://www.spi.org/)

6. Red Hat Inc.'s software related patent information
(http://www.redhat.com/legal/patent_policy.html)

7. Wacky patent of the month (http://www.colitz.com/site/wacky.htm)

8. Wacky patent of the week (http://www.patentoftheweek.com/)

Intellectual Property and Patent Databases

1. http://www.uspto.gov/patft/index.html

2. http://patentsearch.patentcafe.com

3. http://www.univentio.com/

4. http://www.derwent.co.uk/

5. http://www.delphion.com

6. http://www.micropat.com/

7. http://www.questel-orbit.com

8. http://www.dialog.com/

Patent Related Services

1. Reduced cost patent image service (http://www.getthepatent.com)

2. Patent translation services (http://www.patenttranslations.com/)

3. Patent pdf ordering service (http://www.patentgopher.com/)

International Organizations

1. Australian Patent Office (http://www.ipaustralia.gov.au/)

2. Austrian Patent Office (http://www.patent.bmwa.gv.at/)

3. Belgian Patent Office (http://www.european-patent-office.org/patlib/ country/belgium/)

4. Benelux Trademark Office (http://www.bmb-bbm.org/)

5. Brazilian Patent Office (http://www.inpi.gov.br/)

6. Canadian Intellectual Property Office (http://cipo.gc.ca/)

7. Czech Patent Office (http://www.upv.cz/)

8. Chinese Patent Office (http://www.cpo.cn.net/)

9. Croatian Patent Office (http://pubwww.srce.hr/patent/)

10. Cuban Patent Office (http://www.ceniai.inf.cu/OCPI)

11. Danish Patent Office (http://www.dkpto.dk/)

12. European Patent Office (http://www.epo.co.at/epo/)

13. Finnish Patent Office (http://www.prh.fi/engl.html)

14. French Patent Office (http://www.inpi.fr/)

15. Georgian Patent Office (http://www.global-erty.net/saqpatenti)

16. German Patent Office (http://www.deutsches-patentamt.de/)

17. Greek Industrial Property Organization
    (http://www.european-patent-office.org/patlib/country/greece/index.htm)

18. Hong Kong Patent Office (http://www.houston.com.hk/hkgipd/)

19. Hungarian Patent Office (http://www.hpo.hu/)

20. Iceland Patent Office (http://www.els.stjr.is/)

21. Indonesian Patent Office (http://www.dgip.go.id/Patent Directorat.htm)

22. Italian Patent Office (http://www.european-patent-office.org/it)

23. Japanese Patent Office (http://www.jpo.go.jp)

24. Korean Patent Office (http://www.kipo.go.kr)

25. Lithuanian Patent Office (http://www.is.lt/vpb/engl)

26. Luxembourg Patent Office (http://www.etat.lu/EC/spi/index.htm)

27. Macedonian Patent Office (http://www.ippo.gov.mk)

28. Malaysian Intellectual Property Division (http://kpdnhq.gov.my/ip)

29. Mexican Patent Office (http://www.impi.gob.mx)

30. Monaco Patent Office (http://www.european-patent-office.org/patlib/country/monaco)

31. Netherlands Patent Office (http://www.bie.minez.nl)

32. New Zealand Patent Office (http://www.iponz.govt.nz)

33. Norwegian Patent Office (http://www.patentstyret.no/english/index.html)

34. Peruvian Intellectual Property Office (http://www.indecopi.gob.pe)

35. Philippines Patent Office (http://www.dti.gov.ph/ipoo)

36. Polish Patent Office (http://saturn.ci.uw.edu.pl/up)

37. Portuguese Patent Office (http://www.inpi.pt)

38. Romanian Patent Office (http://www.osim.ro)

39. Russian Patent Office (http://www.rupto.ru)

40. Singaporean Patent Office (http://www.ipos.gov.sg)

41. Slovak Republic Patent Office (http://www.indprop.gov.sk)

42. Slovenian Patent Office (http://www.sipo.mzt.si/GLAVAGB.htm)

43. Spanish Patent Office (http://www.oepm.es)

44. Swedish Patent Office (http://www.prv.se)

45. Swiss Institute of Intellectual Property (http://www.ige.ch)

46. Thai Patent Office (http://www.dbe.moc.go.th/DIP/eng/index.html)

47. United Kingdom Patent Office (http://www.ukpats.org.uk)

48. United States Patent Office (http://www.uspto.gov)

49. World Intellectual Property Organisation (WIPO) (http://www.wipo.org)

50. World Trade Organization (WTO) (http://www.wipo.org)

Index

C

Q

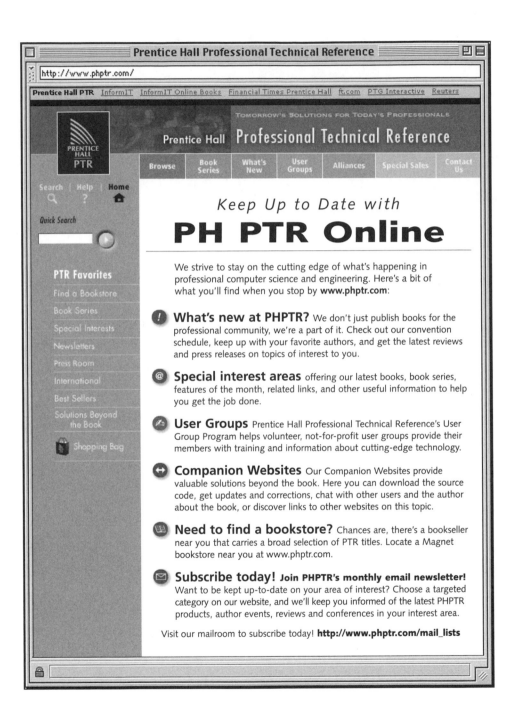